CW01511754

The Bonfire of the Insanities

THE
BONFIRE
OF THE INSANITIES

How Does This Government
Thing Work Again?

JOHN CRACE

First published by Guardian Faber in 2025
Guardian Faber is an imprint of Faber & Faber Ltd
The Bindery, 51 Hatton Garden
London EC1N 8HN

Guardian is a registered trademark of
Guardian News & Media Ltd,
Kings Place, 90 York Way, London N1 9GU

Typeset by Ian Bahrami
Printed in the UK by CPI Group (UK) Ltd, Croydon CR0 4YY

Cover illustration by Morten Morland
© *The Times*/News Licensing

A CIP record for this book
is available from the British Library

ISBN 978–1–78335–315–6

MIX
Paper | Supporting
responsible forestry
FSC
www.fsc.org
FSC® C013604

Printed and bound in the UK on FSC® certified paper in line with our continuing
commitment to ethical business practices, sustainability and the environment.
For further information see faber.co.uk/environmental-policy

Our authorised representative in the EU for product safety is
Easy Access System Europe, Mustamäe tee 50, 10621 Tallinn, Estonia
gpsr.requests@easproject.com

2 4 6 8 10 9 7 5 3 1

In memory of Herbert Hound

2011–2025

Introduction

Rishi Sunak had always been very much the Tories'
second choice as party leader and prime minister, but
after Liz Truss had self-combusted within 49 days – 10
of which had been a period of national mourning for
the late Queen – the Conservatives were left with few
options. Rishi was the last credible Tory standing, and
even he never seemed convinced that he was the man to
turn his party's fortunes around. He could read the writ-
ing on the wall: the country was fed up with the Tories.
Everyone was worse off in real terms than they had been
when the Tories first assumed power in coalition with the
Lib Dems in 2010. Austerity, Partygate and the Truss–
Kwarteng mini-budget had taken their toll. But someone
had to run the country, and Sunak thought it might as
well be him. It would all end in tears, but better to have
been a dead-duck prime minister than not to have been
prime minister at all.

At the beginning of 2023, Rishi had given a speech
in which he had outlined his five promises/pledges/
vague aspirations on which he wanted to be judged:
to halve inflation, grow the economy, reduce debt, cut

hospital waiting lists and stop the boats. By the middle of the year, it was clear that he was only ever going to meet one of those targets. Inflation would be halved, but that would not be thanks to anything Sunak had done. That was due entirely to global inflation – in particular, energy costs – falling. Every time Sunak appeared on TV and was asked about his promises, he looked more and more despondent. It would all happen soon. One day. (It really wouldn't.)

Almost everything that could go wrong for Rishi did go wrong. The Court of Appeal ruled that the Tories' plan to deport migrants who had arrived in the country via small-boat crossings from France was illegal. Not that this was ever a convincing deterrent, but it was the best the Tories had been able to come up with. One plane was stopped just as it was about to take off for Rwanda, prompting the right wing of the Conservative Party to renew its calls for the country to leave the European Convention on Human Rights.

Nadine Dorries resigned, leaving behind a letter condemning Sunak's time in office and the Tories' lack of accountability in choosing a new leader. She had never got over the fact that Boris Johnson had been forced out of office by his own party and blamed Rishi for being one of the coup's ringleaders. She didn't seem to think it mattered that Boris had repeatedly lied to the entire country and degraded the office of prime minister. It was almost touching – if it hadn't been so deluded.

Meanwhile, collective ministerial responsibility appeared to have gone missing in action. Home Secretary Suella Braverman said whatever she wanted in TV and radio interviews, going as far as to say that rough sleeping was a 'lifestyle choice'. No opportunity to undermine Sunak's authority was passed up. The impression was of an out-of-control party lurching towards disaster. Unable to prevent the inevitable. The Covid Inquiry exposed major flaws in how the government had operated during the pandemic. School buildings were found to be in danger of falling down. The HS2 railway was now going to run to somewhere only vaguely near Birmingham and might even not make it to Euston in London. You couldn't have asked for better metaphors for a country and a government that were floundering from crisis to crisis.

Even the Tory party conference in October 2023 had been an occasion Sunak would have preferred to forget. Numbers were down because MPs and party members had chosen to stay away. They, too, could see the writing on the wall. Even the main auditorium for the speeches ended up being moved to a smaller hall in the Manchester venue. Sunak's speech was a low-key disaster. He even made the schoolboy political error of getting his wife, Akshata Murty, to introduce him on stage, in a vain attempt to make him look more interesting. Murty had looked embarrassed as she rambled for five minutes about what a lovely guy her husband was. They then hugged awkwardly, before Rishi said: 'Marrying you was the best decision I ever made.' Everyone in the audience had the same thought: 'If only I had married the daughter of a billionaire . . .'

It all felt very much like the Last Days of Rome, Sunak going through the motions in a desperate attempt to delay the inevitable. Everyone in Westminster had long since known there was only one way this particular story was going to end.

Unloved by party or country, Rishi longs for his old hedge fund life in California

25 OCTOBER 2023

It's been almost exactly a year since a handful of Tory MPs shuffled Rishi Sunak into Downing Street. The good news for Sunak? He's still there. Just about. The bad news? He's still there. Just about.

The amnesty is over. After a 12-month *omertà*, Tory backbenchers are once more free to fire off letters of no confidence to the chairman of the 1922 Committee. And there are rumours that up to 25 MPs have already done so.

There is no great love for Rish! either in the country at large or within the Conservative Party. He was brought in with low expectations – the competent technocrat who wouldn't screw things up even more – and he hasn't even met them. Almost everyone feels worse off than they did a year ago. Britain feels like it's broken. Nothing really works.

Labour's lead in the opinion polls has widened to 20 points and shows no sign of shrinking. We're all just waiting for a merciful release. The general election that will put us all out of our misery. Sunak included. Being that shit at role-playing prime minister can't be any fun. Especially when you realise the only reason you're still in the job is that your party knows its reputation is so trashed there's no point in seeking a more able replacement. So Dr Death – the Tories' very own Inaction Man – just hangs on in suspended animation.

But Sunak is still obliged to go through the motions. To give the illusion the UK has a functioning prime minister and government. So what we now have for the foreseeable future is just performative politics. A meta state, where Sunak and his colleagues pop up in our consciousness to try to prove that they exist. That what they say and do has meaning. That they are not inert flotsam driven by the tidal forces of the parliamentary calendar.

If it's Wednesday, it must be prime minister's questions. So either Rish! or an avatar closely resembling him duly appeared on the government frontbench shortly before 12 p.m. His colleagues barely acknowledged his arrival. This was just another half-hour endurance test for all concerned.

Unlike last week, Keir Starmer chose not to focus his six questions on the conflict in Israel and Gaza. Mindful of not reopening any wounds within his own party over his insistence on remaining in lockstep with Sunak and not calling for a humanitarian ceasefire, he instead played to the home gallery by merely calling out Tory failures and reminding Rish! of his existential futility. At times like this, Sunak must wonder whatever possessed him to give up the hedge fund life in California. There's always next year, I guess.

The Labour leader started by welcoming the winners of last week's two by-elections to their places in the Commons. What happened next stunned everyone. Sunak actually made a joke. A good one. Probably the only time in his entire life RishGPT has made an entire room laugh. He observed that the new MP for Mid Beds would offer him more support than the last one: Nadine Dorries.

Funny. But also painfully tragicomic, because it was almost certainly true. What's more, it would also have been true for at least 150 other Tory constituencies. Because now all that's left for Sunak is to lurch ever further to the right and fight culture wars. All of which lead to a political dead end. There is no way back from this. And, tragically, he doesn't even look as if he really believes half of what he's saying.

Starmer carried on punching the bruise. The Tory candidate in Tamworth had told voters they could fuck off if they were hard up. Was this official government policy? And could the prime minister call a general election so the rest of us could have a chance to tell the Conservatives to fuck off?

'Everything is going brilliantly,' Sunak mumbled. As usual, we were lucky to have him. He couldn't understand why the country wasn't more grateful for everything he had done. Everyone had never had it so good. He had a plan – though he couldn't tell us what it was – and it was working. And we couldn't have an election. Because calling an election would be the easy thing to do. Spoilsport. Just do it. Don't put yourself out on our behalf.

It was left to the SNP and several Labour MPs – including the frontbencher Yasmin Qureshi – to ask for a ceasefire in Israel and Gaza. Not that the Israelis or Hamas are exactly waiting on us to give them a sense of direction. But it would make MPs feel better if everyone was doing the right thing. This was too much for Sunak. The principle that Israel had a right to defend itself was inviolable, no matter how many innocent Palestinians got killed in the process. The only people who would benefit from a ceasefire were Hamas, he claimed. Hmm. Apart from all those who otherwise would have been killed.

He did reluctantly agree to the possibility of a 'humanitarian pause'. Though he didn't sound entirely convinced. Couldn't the aid convoys just somehow avoid the bombs and rocket fire? Perhaps not. Maybe a 15-minute break to allow aid into Gaza. Assuming anyone agreed to open the crossing points. This logic is unsustainable. You can't have any kind of peace in the Middle East without a ceasefire. So if you're serious about a two-state solution, you have to be serious about a ceasefire.

Labour's Lilian Greenwood raised the awkward question of Sunak's missing WhatsApp messages. Surely a tech bro could access the messages on his phone.

Especially as we now knew it wasn't lost and was working just fine. Er . . . no, said RishGPT. He had handed over hundreds of messages to the Covid Inquiry. Just none of the ones it had actually wanted. Hopefully.

Most Tory MPs just looked on in despair. Those who did speak were generally unhelpful. They've long since stopped pretending to support the government in public and are now focused on trying to hold on to their seats. So we got questions about the Environment Agency, housing, renewables and flooding. Thérèse Coffey made a point of looking particularly bored during the flooding one. Nothing to do with her. Why couldn't everyone leave her alone?

The weirdest intervention came from the Conservative Peter Bottomley. He didn't have a question. He just wanted it on record that Sunak was a kind man who had always done his best. It sounded like an epitaph. A eulogy even. The chronicle of a death foretold.

If the King sounds bored by the King's Speech, what hope have the rest of us?

7 NOVEMBER 2023

The lords and ladies started filing into the upper chamber two hours before proceedings were due to start. A riot of scarlet and ermine. No dressing-up box left unturned.

Old costume tiaras from Claire's Accessories dusted down. Apart from one woman sitting near the throne who appeared to have a vegetable garden growing out of her head. They do things differently in the upper chamber.

Most of all, there was the sense of entitlement. There wasn't a man or woman in the Lords who had a moment's doubt that they deserved to be there. The great and the good. The chosen ones. Some are born great, some achieve greatness, others have greatness thrust upon them. All forms of greatness were found here. Even the youngest peer, Charlotte Owen. No one knows still why she was made a baroness. But ours is not to question the righteous order of things. Merely to bow low. We are not the chosen ones. Silence is all that is required from us.

To while away the time, many peers riffled through the programme for the first King's Speech in 70 years. It would be an unforgivable faux pas to confuse the Rouge Dragon Pursuivant with the Maltravers Herald Extraordinary. According to the running order, they would begin with 'Preliminary Movements'. Hmm. That could have been better phrased.

Just before 11.30 a.m., the King and Queen entered the chamber, attended by any number of eight-year-old pages. One of whom had been awarded a medal. I guess it must have been his 10-metre swimming badge. Then there was the sexy equerry, the breakout star from the coronation. Still wearing his favourite kilt. I guess it's in his contract.

Charles and Camilla sat down on their thrones, the King's slightly higher than the Queen's (heaven forbid that anyone may ever appear taller than the monarch), and Alex Chalk, a hopeless justice secretary but a fantastic Disney cartoon lord chancellor, handed over a copy of the King's Speech. The longest in terms of words since 2005, but with the fewest bills. The new reign was to be marked by waffle and filler. The Golden Sunak Age.

'My government,' Chas droned. He had been practising this. How to get just the right level of boredom. The top notes of dissent. The total disengagement. Anything to make it clear that he was distancing himself from almost everything in the speech. That the Tory government did not speak for him. It was just his luck that his second prime minister – remember Liz Truss? – should be a populist deadbeat. Out of touch with the country. His mother had warned him to be careful what he wished for.

Then we got down to the nitty-gritty. Rishi was going to take the difficult but necessary decisions. That's one of Sunak's easiest tells. He always says that when he means the exact opposite. Growth was really kicking off. The only problem was that it was kicking off in all the other G7 countries. In the UK, not so much. The government would be taking advantage of Brexit. Once it had discovered any advantages.

Energy security. Chazza spat out the words. For the green King, this really hurt. Having to talk a load of bollocks about British fossil fuels for British homes while pretending he still gave a toss about the environment. Charles may not be the brightest royal, but this was an insult to his intelligence.

On we moved to education. This was a joke. There was no chance of any of this happening because the Tories were going to lose the next election. Smoke-free world. Nice try. But he was looking forward to 40-year-olds getting arrested for selling snouts to 39-year-olds. Then some nonsense about housing. Anything to allow Tories with second and third homes to kick out their tenants. The usual nonsense about being tough on crime. Reheated stuff, all of it. Shame the Conservatives don't seem that keen to deal with the sex offenders in their own party.

There was no mental health bill. Of course there wasn't. Rish! has always thought that mental illness is a personal defect. People should just pull themselves together. There was also no room for a law banning seven bins. It was almost as though there never was a seven-bin policy. And nothing on Suella's brainwave to treat rough sleeping as a lifestyle choice. Though there might be later. Come the next election, dozens of Tory MPs might be at risk of becoming homeless.

A few hours later, the Commons was full as parliament began its debate on the King's Speech. As is customary, proceedings began with two light-hearted speeches from government backbenchers proposing the motion thanking the King. This is one ritual parliament could usefully dispense with as the speeches are invariably not that funny and more self-conscious than self-deprecating.

The two unfortunates chosen this year were Robert Goodwill and Siobhan Baillie. Neither exactly set the Commons alight with their brilliance. Goodwill happily heralded his imminent retirement by running through his limitations, while Baillie seemed to devote most of her time to lamenting what had been left out of the King's Speech. There again, she is odds-on to lose her Stroud seat at the next election. So call that hello and goodbye from her.

Keir Starmer began in a similar vein. Mostly by mocking Sunak. The prime minister hates this more than anything. He demands to be taken seriously. The man who is always right. You could see him getting twitchy. The Labour leader reiterated his support for Ukraine and Israel, before moving on to the general economic miserabilism of the Tories. The King's Speech had given no one any hope. All that Rish! could guarantee was that everything would get worse.

Not that Sunak saw it that way. He thought we had never had it so good. Couldn't understand why people weren't more grateful to him. He also praised the brilliance of Goodwill. An MP so talented Rishi had removed him from government and chucked him on the backbenches. Time and again, the prime minister proves himself to be a politician who is crap at politics.

Halfway through, Chris Bryant stood up to intervene. Did Sunak agree with the home secretary that homelessness was a lifestyle choice? Bizarrely, Suella shook her head at this. A Pavlovian denial. Rish! ummed and ahhed. Too weak to slap his home secretary down. Too weak to back her. A man with no real authority. Over his party or the country. His MPs looked miserable. Well they might. We, and they, have another year of this.

Sunak searches the gene puddle of Tory talent ... and finds David Cameron

13 NOVEMBER 2023

Lifestyle choices can come at you fast these days. Only on Sunday, Suella Braverman was still home secretary, free to demonstrate her self-absolution during the two-minute silence for Remembrance Sunday. A day later, and she was sacked by a prime minister too weak to have done so when it might have made a difference. After she had had time to cheer on the division that she had done so much to provoke in others on the pro-Palestine march.

Now the time was Suella's own. First to concentrate on the two-minute hate. Though it's doubtful George Orwell's time slot would be quite long enough for Suella to vent her fury at the world. She'd need at least a quarter of an hour. Even then she'd have to concentrate harder than she ever had before. Then to pack her tent and make herself homeless. There was nothing she enjoyed more than being abused or ignored. Though only for a while. Next there was the leadership bid to prepare. She would prove just how good a hater she was with her resignation letter. And if all else failed, there was always *I'm a Celebrity*. Being homeless with a £1 million pay cheque was her kind of lifestyle choice.

James Cleverly was gutted. No more flying around the world on private jets. Or, if he really must, then slumming it in first class. He had lived for travel. For people telling him he was marvellous. Hanging out in embassies. Never paying for anything. Now he had been asked to take over as home secretary. That was a thankless fucking job. Just being driven in cars to detention centres. Nothing the government did was going to stop the small boats. This was merely Sunak's endgame. Spinning out the futility till the next election. And Jimmy Dimly had no choice but to go along with it. He didn't have the self-worth to resign. Still, home sec would look good on the CV.

Just then a vaguely familiar middle-aged man was spotted walking up Downing Street. Was it . . .? Could it be . . .? It could! It was Big Dave Cameron. But what was he doing? He'd last been seen there in 2016, when he'd whistled his way back into No. 10 after single-handedly wrecking the country. Hmm. Perhaps he was on his way to do some more dodgy lobbying for Greensill. Things hadn't panned out well for Big Dave in the intervening years. He'd just drifted aimlessly from non-job to non-job. 'I used to be prime minister,' he would say sadly to anyone who would listen. We've tried to forget.

'Here's the thing, Big Dave,' said Rishi. 'I've rather scraped the bottom of the barrel. I've hunted around the gene puddle of talent that is the Tory party and concluded that not one of them is fit to be foreign secretary. So I'd like you to give it a go. It's not that hard a job. Hell, how could it be if Jimmy D's done it for a year without starting a war? And obvs, you'd get a peerage thrown in. Though, to tell you the truth, I thought you'd already have one by now. So what do you say? You wouldn't even have to answer departmental questions or appear in the House. So there would be no accountability at all!'

Big Dave stroked both his chins. This was a tricky one. A job that might actually require some work. Not his usual bag at all. 'You do know that I have been critical of almost everything you have done as prime minister,' he said. 'At almost every opportunity, you have made the wrong call. Come to think of it, you might even be slightly worse than I was.'

'That's why I want you back,' Rish! enthused. 'Because I am the "change" prime minister. I am the Conservative who will clean up the country after the Conservatives. Nothing shouts "change" more than bringing back the prime minister who started the decline to help manage the decline. So what do you say? Obviously, we'll try and keep you away from Europe. The EU hasn't forgiven you for Brexit. So do try and not be so careless this time. Concentrate for more than five minutes, if you can. OK? Now what's your plan for the rest of the world?'

'Easy,' replied Big Dave, the old confidence flooding back. 'I'd go to Moscow and tell Russia and Ukraine to have a referendum on peace. Then I'd fly to Israel and get Netanyahu and Hamas to agree to a referendum on a ceasefire. After that, I'd go to Beijing . . .'

'Why?'

'I'm not sure why, actually. Just for old times' sake. I've done a lot of defending the Chinese. That's got to be a plus, hasn't it? Now what about a job for my old mucker George? Ozzy is at a bit of a loose end now. He's even doing a dreadful podcast with Ed Balls. He couldn't be a worse chancellor than Jeremy Hunt. It will be like bringing back the old team. The austerity years are here again. People will be thrilled to be reminded of why public services don't work any more. So let's do it. It's only for a year after all. Let's face it, we're bound to lose the next election.'

As Big Dave bounced out of Downing Street, Rish! returned to his spreadsheet. Still far too many gaps. What he wouldn't give for at least one vaguely competent minister. Some hope. Obviously, Thérèse Coffey would have to go. She had been the anti-environment secretary. Her proudest legacy to the planet would be her resignation. Let the rivers rejoice! Maybe Steve Barclay could replace her. At least he was quite nice. If equally useless. But then Rish! would need a new health secretary. Who better than the entitled Victoria Atkins to take over? Someone with no experience of anything. It wasn't as if the doctors were on strike, waiting lists were at a record high and hospitals crumbling. Yup, Vicky would be perfect. What could possibly go wrong? While he was about it, he could also sack the hopeless Greg Hands as party chairman. A man who literally did nothing except tweet the same unfunny Liam Byrne letter five times a day.

Just then, there was a knock on the door. It was Oliver Dowden. Junior ministers were resigning in droves. Even the ones who were OK at their jobs. Getting out while they were still young. Had their lives ahead of them. Ready for a last-chance power drive. Their best hope of re-election was to wipe their fingerprints from government. Or just get out completely. The ultimate detox. So that just left the dregs. The desperate who would take any job. Anything. What a shit show. Imagine Grant Shapps as defence secretary. Or Esther McVey as minister for common sense. Has Sunak ever met her? Or watched her show on GB News? She's senseless. This is the end, beautiful friend . . . the end.

'Now, where was I?' Lord Big Dave dusts off old contacts book to return to top table

14 NOVEMBER 2023

The alarm went off at 7.45 a.m. Big Dave eased himself out of bed. For the first time in months, he caught himself smiling. Today was going to be a good day. For the last seven years he had felt somewhat aimless. Drifting towards futility. Sure, he had money. What former prime minister didn't? Though he was only a jobbing millionaire. Shame Greensill had gone bust before he could cash in his share options. But all he tended to do these days was potter out to the shepherd's hut and browse the John Lewis website.

Now everything had changed. He was back in the game. He still had to pinch himself. Even he had been completely blindsided by the prime minister's call, asking him to step in as foreign secretary. Not that he had really kept up with international affairs. His global contacts book had rather closed back in 2016, when he had screwed things up by accidentally taking the UK out of the EU.

Still, no harm done. And he had told – what was his name? It would come to him in a minute. That was it: Rishi Sanauk – that he'd muddle through somehow. Winging it was his USP. Best of all, he'd get to be a lord. No having to pretend to care about the great unwashed.

Sam would be thrilled. The next best thing to being born a lord: being made one. She rather looked down on him. Now he had finally come good for her.

And the House of Lords appointments committee had rushed through its approval. Had turned a blind eye to his dealings with Greensill. What was a bit of lobbying for dodgy contracts? It was a done deal. A weight off his mind. Government wouldn't be government without a bit of recreational corruption.

Lord Big Dave took his place at the cabinet table next to Oliver Dowden – 'Get me a coffee, there's a love' – almost directly opposite the prime minister. It was as if he had never left. He caught the eye of Jeremy Hunt. The face was familiar. Hadn't he been his rather ineffectual culture secretary in 2010? Those were the days. Before everything went hideously wrong.

'Why are you sitting in George Osborne's seat, Jezza?' he asked.

'I'm the chancellor.' Hunt blushed, his eyes revolving nervously.

'No. You're kidding me. You know nothing about the economy.'

'But nor does anyone else around here. I was the last person remaining who looked vaguely plausible.'

'Hmm. That bad, then. Needs must, I suppose. Right. Let's get started.'

'Excuse me . . .' said Sunak.

'What do you want?'

'Er . . . it's customary for me to start cabinet meetings.'

'Of course it is. Silly me. Keep forgetting. Euphoric recall at being back in the room. Now you run along and start the meeting.'

Rishi balanced himself precariously on a couple of cushions and tapped the table. He'd like to welcome friends old and new. He was sure they were going to make a great team. Just like he had been sure the last team would make a great team. He was nothing if not the 'change' prime minister. The Tory leader who had cleared out all the rubbish of the last 13 years and then brought the rubbish back into government. Nothing got past him.

'You go first, my lord. Talk us through the international scene, now you've had a day inside the Foreign Office.'

Lord Big Dave fiddled with his folder. To tell the truth, he hadn't actually spent any time the day before doing any work. Rather, he'd been organising the office furniture. Never mind. No one could bullshit better than him. The details were for the little people. The situation in Libya was very grave, he said. But he was sure Brexit would be a tremendous success.

'I was thinking more about Israel/Gaza and the war in Ukraine?' said Sunak, hesitantly.

'Yes. Terrible. Serious. Very serious,' Lord Big Dave barked, sounding more confident than he felt. He would be sure to send one of his juniors to investigate. In the meantime, he would be calling for an immediate referendum. That would be bound to make things better in the

Middle East and Ukraine. But no one should get too hung up, because no one there would be listening to a word the British foreign secretary had to say. So it was all just PR for the domestic punters. In any case, in a year's time we'll all be out of here . . .

'Sorry?' said Sunak.

'It's obvious,' replied Lord Big Dave. 'We all know we're going to lose the election. We're just here to try to minimise the loss. And I'm certainly not going to hang around for any longer. Far too much like real work. I'm just getting background for a podcast I've got planned. Everyone's got one these days.'

'I miss being foreign secretary,' sighed James Cleverly. 'All those flights in private jets. Now I'm holed up in the Home Office bunker trying to care about small boats.'

Lord Big Dave looked to his right. Not a clue. Didn't recognise the woman. Apparently, she was Victoria Atkins, the anti-health secretary whose husband was dedicated to fattening up the population in his job as chief exec of British Sugar. That was a good fit. Finally, he saw a face he recognised. The half-witted Esther McVey. The minister for common senselessness. Let's hear from her.

'I'm just the token GB News . . .'

'Yes, thanks, Esther,' said Sunak. 'That's all we've got time for. A brilliant meeting with some excellent contributions.'

Lord Big Dave walked out with his valet, aka Andrew Mitchell, one of his junior Foreign Office ministers.

'You run along to the Commons to give a statement on Gaza,' he said. 'I'm off to lunch.' Mitchell droned his way through the statement. Everything was really terrible, he really didn't know what to do, and it was a huge shock to find that no one in the Middle East was listening to anyone in the UK.

Labour's David Lammy responded by saying it was a shame he could talk only to the monkey. The organ grinder was off in the Lords. But he thought that what was needed was a really long humanitarian pause. But not so long as to be a ceasefire. All clear?

Not everyone on the Tory backbenches was happy with Mitchell either. There are plenty, including Julian Lewis, Liam Fox and Michael Ellis, who think they could have made a decent fist of being foreign secretary. Sunak has somehow managed to piss off all his backbenchers. They are now in a less than dignified huff. Also having a major hissy fit was Suella Braverman. Having been relatively quiet since being sacked as home secretary, she took to Twitter late on Tuesday afternoon to publish her departure letter to Sunak. The prime minister had not kept any of his promises to her. He had owed his leadership success to her and he had betrayed her. There were documents to prove it. He had betrayed the nation. He was a disgrace. The Rwanda plan was doomed to failure regardless. He was weak, weak, weak. Putting himself before the party. Putting himself before the country.

Not for the first time, the Tory party was engaged in a civil war. There will be blood. It's all about to get very nasty. Send for the popcorn.

* * *

Just when Rishi Sunak imagined that things couldn't get any worse, the Supreme Court returned its verdict on the government's Rwanda plan, backing up the Court of Appeal's ruling earlier in the year. It was even more damning than anyone had expected. Not even a chink of light suggesting that a flight to Kigali might take off at some point in the future. Rwanda was deemed an unsafe country; it would be illegal to deport refugees there. Rishi's flagship policy was in tatters.

Desperate, delusional, defeated: the Tory right are coming for Rishi! after Rwanda

15 NOVEMBER 2023

Call it the massacre of the not-so-innocents. A drive-by shooting that left almost everyone in government a casualty. Many had thought the Supreme Court would uphold Rishi Sunak's appeal over his flagship Rwanda policy, the one thing he thought he might be able to boast about. Or, at the very least, that the court might deliver a nuanced verdict, one that left the government some room for manoeuvre.

Lord Reed, the top judge on the five-strong panel, had other ideas. He just about contained a smile. It's such a perfect day. He was glad he spent it with you. There were no ifs, no buts. The Rwanda plan was a non-starter. Rwanda having a track record of killing refugees had made the court think there was something iffy about the UK deporting its refugees to the country. Funny, that. Nor should the UK think it could get round the judgement by leaving the European Convention on Human Rights. The UK was already bound by other legal obligations.

This was about as bad as it could have got. No wriggle room. No nothing. Just a stark verdict on the judgement of the government and the Home Office. Sunak and his then home secretary, Suella Braverman, had bet the bank on a divisive culture war. You never upset a right-wing gobshite by being unpleasant to foreigners.

Now, though, they were high and dry. All vestiges of competence and credibility shredded. Just aimless husks orbiting around their depleted egos. Of no relevance to the country. Or even to their friends. Not that David Pannick, the main government lawyer, would have been that bothered one way or the other. It was all just a game to him. He had just trousered the best part of £1,000 an hour for spinning Sunak's bullshit. You win some, you lose some.

Two hours later, Rish! was to be found in the Commons for prime minister's questions. The cheers that greeted his arrival were almost audible. His backbenchers are now openly plotting against him. Making no effort to keep their assignations secret.

The ironically named Common Sense brigade, led by Esther McVey, Andrea Jenkyns and Desperate Danny Kruger, were coming up with ever more idiotic suggestions. Burn the statute books! Send the planes to Kigali regardless! Not a synapse capable of electrical connection to be found anywhere. They've all basically given up, like maggots stranded at the bottom of a rubbish bin. One of seven, presumably. If Sunak really cared about the country, or indeed his party, he'd call an election. To put everyone out of their misery.

Rish! began by boasting of having cut inflation by half. But no one was listening. No one cared. It's no big deal. It wasn't hard. And it had nothing to do with government action. What matters is that inflation is still more than twice as high as the Bank of England's target. And prices are still rocketing.

He also tried to explain away the Rwanda verdict. Basically, everything was going completely to plan. The court had approved the idea of deporting refugees to a third country. Shame France wasn't interested in a deal. All that was required to get the plan up and running was for Rwanda to overhaul its courts and judiciary and hold free and fair elections. And to stop shooting refugees. And possibly to stop sending death squads into the Democratic Republic of the Congo. Apart from that, everything was good to go.

This was going to be one of Keir Starmer's easier sessions. Like shooting fish in a barrel. He started with Lord Big Dave. Why not? The man's a buffoon. An insult to the country. We're meant to think Cameron's a safe, experienced pair of hands. Instead of being the man who imposed austerity and accidentally took the UK out of the EU to settle a civil war in the Tory party. Thanks for that, Lord Big Dave. The man who then walked away, unwilling to clear up his own mess. The man who would become Lord Big Dodgy Dave through his lobbying for Greensill. The man who, despite all this, was thought better suited to the job of foreign secretary than any Tory MP.

Could Sunak list Lord Big Dave's finest achievement on the international stage? He couldn't. There was an awkward silence. Then something about holding a G8 summit. One that was already in the diary. Literally anyone could have done that. The reality is that Lord Big Dave's legacy is largely fantasy. The belief is that he must somehow be an improvement on the current bunch of halfwits. Despite the evidence.

We then moved on to Rwanda. What was the plan now there was no plan? The plan was to double down on having no plan. The Rwanda plan was already working, even though no refugees had been deported. Wasting a year and £140 million on a ruse to lure refugees into a false sense of security. We would both break any international laws we wanted – people got so squeamish about torture – and not break any. Schrödinger goes to Rwanda. Complete nonsense. A prime minister and a government in a death vortex.

The ministerial statement from the new home secretary, James Cleverly, was altogether more sedate. Mainly because most MPs think he is fundamentally decent and doesn't have his fingerprints over all this hate (Yvette Cooper shared that she knew he thought the Rwanda plan was batshit crazy). Also, because he is, reassuringly, not very bright. A bit harmless.

'It's all going swimmingly,' said Jimmy Dimly. To reassure himself, if no one else. We wouldn't be breaking any laws. Just hanging on in quiet desperation. Hoping something turned up. He had no idea what. Would that do? Most of the real headbangers left him alone to talk to himself. They were too busy plotting to turn the UK into a pariah state – the law is so overrated – sink the boats and start a third world war to notice.

Later that afternoon, a panic-stricken Sunak resurfaced to give a press conference in Downing Street. It was desperate, delusional stuff. He was going to agree a treaty with Rwanda. A special treaty in which Rwanda would agree to stop giving the appearance of being a dictatorship with an unfortunate reputation for killing people who disagreed with it. Then he would pass emergency legislation – Boris Johnson had come up with a similar plan, so the right-wingers would love it – in which Lee Anderson and Jonathan Gullis would agree that Rwanda was a top, top place. Though you wouldn't catch any MPs going there. What could go wrong?

After all this, he – the Diminutive Rish! – would just ignore any foreign courts. And the planes would take off in the spring. Except they won't. As if the courts will back off because Sunak has said so. It was the work of an entitled child. A tale told by an idiot, full of sound and fury, signifying nothing.

Jeremy Hunt delivers a budget designed to destroy a future chancellor

22 NOVEMBER 2023

It's a looking-glass world. Up is down. Black is white. War is peace. Just a few months ago, we were told the UK economy was in a desperate state. No room for tax cuts. Just more of the same. Suck it up. But in the last few weeks we've been getting noises off. Anonymous briefings from Treasury ministers. All is well. Things have never been better. Thanks to the diligence of the Tories, we can all expect some more pocket money in the autumn statement.

If you're confused by this, then spare a thought for Jeremy Hunt. The chancellor who was never meant to be chancellor. The chancellor who knows next to nothing about macroeconomics. Just think: a man of almost limitless ambition – he twice thought he would make a good prime minister – but who never once aspired to be chancellor. Because even he knew he would be hopeless at it. A glimpse of self-awareness. The entrepreneur who knows how to create a small business: start with a big one.

But greatness was thrust upon him. Or, at least, necessity was thrust upon him. This time last year, the Tories were in shit street. Kwasi Kwarteng had crashed the economy with his mini-budget and the Tory brand was on its knees. A new chancellor was needed. Someone who could be the grown-up.

And that person was Jezza. Not because of any ability, but because of his plausibility. He looked like the sort of Tory chancellor to which the country had grown accustomed. And now we're rather lumbered with him. At least for another year. An eighth chancellor in 13 years would begin to look a lot worse than carelessness. More like catatonia. A death wish.

Long before Hunt stood up to give his autumn statement, his wife and children had filed into the back seats of the visitors' gallery. You got the feeling they all knew this would be his last-but-one big set-piece event in the Commons. Jezza certainly did. This wasn't the kind of budget you would give if you had any intention of being around for the next five years to oversee its delivery. This was a budget designed to destroy a future chancellor. So

Hunt was just there to soak up the vibes. To enjoy it while he still could.

The kindest interpretation is that Jezza was just too dim to know what he was doing. That he was merely the useful idiot for Rishi Sunak. You certainly can't blame his ministerial colleagues in the Treasury. They are even more half-witted than Hunt. That's why they were chosen. Not that there is anyone better lurking on the backbenches.

Hunt began by insisting that he was putting the economy back on track. An odd admission. It rather acknowledged that the Tories had done untold damage over the last 13 years and were only now getting round to trying to fix the problem. Thanks for that. 'We've got inflation cracked,' he boasted. 'Just as the prime minister promised.' It was now only two and a half times the Bank of England's target – and its fall was nothing to do with government intervention – so could we please have a two-minute love-in for Rish!?

This was going to be an autumn statement for growth, he continued. Yup. Talk us through this one, Jezza. He did, slowly, and with few signs of understanding what someone else had written for him. His eyes started to revolve anticlockwise in terror. As if every sentence were dynamite. Sweat formed on his brow. He could sense the danger. But he didn't know what direction it was coming from. No choice but to press ahead. The Office for Budget Responsibility had revised its forecasts. Down was up. It was fantastic news. Growth would more or less stagnate for the next five years. He was a man who was going places. Perdition.

'We are taking decisions for the long term,' he announced. 'Long term' as in sheer desperation. Every government reset had failed – now there are at least two a week – and this was more or less the last throw of the dice. Thanks to his brilliance, he had managed to create extra fiscal headroom. Largely thanks to inflation and capped departmental budgets – hooray for inflation! – he had extra money to spend. So he was going to squander almost all of it on tax cuts and let public services die. Austerity 2.0.

Here the speech rather meandered. Jezza isn't the best of readers, and even the faithful Tory backbenchers could see this budget was a pig's ear. Many began to doze off. It would get a few half-hearted cheers in the Tory press for a day or so, but the electorate would soon see through it. There was nothing there to make you want to live. Though there was some gratuitous sadism, or 'compassionate' cuts aimed at the disabled. Work, you losers. Stop scrounging. Always scrounging. Most of you have deliberately chosen to have mental health problems.

Finally, after some business-tax cuts that even Hunt had to admit were well above his pay grade, we got to the 2p cut in national insurance. A cut to a tax that Rishi Sunak had raised. Go, Tories! And just in case everyone hadn't realised how screwed the government was, he was going to introduce the cut from January rather than March. Just so that everyone would feel better off before the election. Only, because of fiscal drag, the tax burden would be reaching its highest-ever level in five years' time. The tax cut that wasn't a tax cut. The chancellor who isn't a chancellor. The sweat stain of sheer panic.

In her reply, Rachel Reeves could barely contain her contempt. Where to start? She was all for tax cuts – what aspiring chancellor wouldn't be? – but this was just economic vandalism. And she would be the one left to pick up the pieces. She wasn't going to say no, obviously. But really? Did they have any more giveaways for the spring budget? There was a few billion left unspent. How about something for the most well-off? Like inheritance tax?

Over on the government benches, Sunak and Jezza giggled and bounced up and down like children. A sure tell. They knew they were busted. If they had honour – a sense of grace – they might have given up there and then. But they mean to take us all down with them. They're so pretty, oh so pretty. They're vacant.

Tories are too busy locked in a narcissistic death spiral to spare a thought for us

13 DECEMBER 2023

A thought experiment: if Tory MPs could return to year zero, who out of the misfits currently available would they choose as prime minister?

Boris Johnson? Do they really want the has-been Convict who can scarcely be bothered to take an interest in his own life? Nigel Farage? Are they really so mad that they think half the country is seriously bigoted? Suella Braverman? Ditto.

One thing we can be fairly clear about: given the chance again, the Tories definitely wouldn't choose Rishi Sunak. The safe-pair-of-hands tech bro who can't even back up his WhatsApp messages. So sad, that. The prime minister who keeps getting everything wrong. A man without friends. Most prime ministers have a core group of allies. Rish! has no one to watch his back. Apart from possibly Jeremy Hunt. Who quite likes him. A bit. And who cares what Jezza thinks? Least of all about the economy.

But it's the Tory MPs' misfortune to be lumbered with Sunak. And ours, of course. Not that the Conservatives give a second thought to our concerns. Especially not now, when they are locked in a narcissistic death spiral. This is all about them. What they want. The country doesn't get a look-in. For Tory backbenchers, it's all about making do. Even they can see that imposing yet another prime minister on the country is a non-starter. So it's all about minimising the potential losses.

Look the part. Fake it to make it. So there were huge cheers as Rish! entered the chamber for the last prime minister's questions of the year. It was all most confusing. What was all the noise for? For having not been the first prime minister since Margaret Thatcher in 1986 to lose a bill at second reading? For having come up with a Rwanda plan that was so vicious, so deranged, that only a psychopathic idiot could have come up with it? Imagine being able to choose your own reality.

Weirdly, Rish! seemed to find it all perfectly normal. His arrogance and blinkered life experience have encouraged him to confuse irony for sincerity. The cheers were no more than he expected. At last, MPs were beginning to express their gratitude for all he had done. So he bounced up and down excitedly. He was a winner! He would still be PM by the end of the year! 2024 might never happen! The polls showing him to be less popular than Johnson? He was right on track.

The sense of disconnect was to pervade the entire session. The sense of the surreal. You couldn't quite believe politicians could be so half-witted. Deliberately so. It started with Tory Greg Smith declaring that the Office for Budget Responsibility was hopeless and that the real forecasts showed the Tories were introducing the biggest-ever tax cuts, while the marginal tax rate was at its highest. Rish! had no problem with this. He was a fiscal magician.

Keir Starmer tried to insert a modicum of reality into the proceedings. Though he did start off with a couple of festive gags about the Tories being a tribal 'five families' of good cheer and Sunak being a Rishi-no-mates. Sunak looked hurt. The government was united behind him. Yup. United to stab him in the back. He had Something

Inside So Strong. Which was why he would be building the barriers around Rwanda. Or something.

By now Rish! was beginning to get tetchy again. The all-too-familiar Snippy Rishi, the PM who can't tolerate even the most gentle questioning. Whose reasonable facade soon turns to dust. He couldn't even manage a word of sympathy for the man on the *Bibby Stockholm* who was believed to have killed himself the day before.

There was an equal lack of sympathy for those who would be homeless at Christmas. Especially the kids. Why did everyone expect presents these days? Or even a roof over their head or a warm meal? The British people had gone soft. If children couldn't be arsed to work for a living, why should they be indulged? Young people were all take, take, take. How about a little more appreciation for what he had done? Rish! was sick to death of being mistaken for someone who gave a shit about the least well-off. What had they ever done for him? Hell, he had gone out of his way to try to send the economy into recession, to make it impossible to get a hospital appointment and to make sure inflation raced along at an unsustainable level. Where were the thanks? The country was living the dream under the Conservatives. Apart from the lack of pool cleaners. That was intolerable.

Things didn't improve when Sunak moved on to backbenchers' questions. The same sense of total disconnect. The feeling that whatever world the prime minister lives in, it isn't the same one as the rest of us. An altered reality where we are human guinea pigs in a macabre game show. So, no, there was no need for the DUP to ever return to a power-sharing assembly. Why change the habit of a lifetime?

The fact that the government was booking up hotel accommodation for asylum seekers till 2030? That should in no way be taken as an indication that the government thought the small-boats crossings would still be an issue in 2030. It was typically shoddy thinking on the part of the Labour Party to assume this. Talking down Britain.

Rish! ended with a note of Christmas cheer for Gaza. There could be no respite from the bombardment for the Palestinian kiddies until the Hamas terrorists who raped and murdered the Israelis were brought to justice. Though, oddly, he was happy to turn a blind eye to the Rwanda-backed insurgents who raped and murdered in the Democratic Republic of Congo. Because we had declared Rwanda to be a safe country. So these murders had been safe murders.

Welcome to Sunak's moral microverse.

* * *

Prime ministers tend to use the new year as an opportunity to wipe the slate clean. A chance to make a speech or give an interview in which they try to get the country to forget everything that has gone wrong in the past 12 months. To imagine a world in which everything is

going swimmingly. All the things that had been prom-
ised and never materialised were now up and running in
the Brave New World.

Only, this January, Rishi Sunak could barely even
summon the energy to get out of bed and lie about his
achievements. Instead, he left it to his trusted lieutenant,
Home Secretary James Cleverly – aka Jimmy Dimly –
to take to the airwaves. It was a disaster. Jimmy had
insisted on the Today *programme that the government*
had cleared the backlog of asylum seekers. He seemed
to think that saying something somehow made it true.
Luckily for him, he isn't the sharpest mind, and so had no
idea that he had crashed and burned as presenter Mishal
Husain introduced him to reality. There was nothing else
for it. Sunak would have to come out of hiding.

Rishi's five pledges became five vague aspirations, and now . . . nada

4 JANUARY 2024

The Curious Incident of the Dog That Didn't Bark in the Night-Time. Exactly a year ago today, Rishi Sunak began the first of his many relaunches with a speech in which he announced his five pledges. Pledges that were downgraded over the course of the next few months, first to promises and then to vague aspirations. Pledges that had been chosen not because they were hard, but because they weren't. Come 2024, he would be able to boast that he wasn't a complete failure.

Now election year is upon us, and . . . nada. Normally, a prime minister would choose to mark the occasion with a big set-piece speech. A few Tory donors and supporters to make up the numbers and loads of hacks to report every word. A live TV feed to every news network. This month, not so much. It's almost as if Sunak is ashamed of his record and is trying to slip under the radar, his latest relaunch – the softest of soft relaunches – shrouded in secrecy. A private performance for his own benefit.

But then it's not as if Rish! has any good news to impart. The only one of the five pledges he has delivered on is to halve inflation. And that was nothing to do with him. Just a fall in global energy prices. So he's left with four crosses on the scorecard. Even the diehard Tory media, conditioned to see the best in everything Sunak does, aren't trying to pretend that he has succeeded.

So, on Thursday morning, Sunak snuck out of Downing Street, with no media in tow, and headed off to meet a group of bewildered people in a Nottinghamshire youth centre. Rish! tried to inject some positivity into the occasion. Look on the bright side, he said. 2024 was going to be marginally better than 2023. Hooray! Though that wasn't what many economists were saying. They all thought the economy was going to bump along the bottom, with 0% growth. But hey! At least we weren't heading for another recession. Happy days. We'd all continue to become more broke, albeit at a slower rate. Things would still be unaffordable. It would just take us a wee bit longer to notice that prices were still rising way too fast.

The best bit of news was that there would definitely be a general election in 2024. Though this wasn't quite such good news for Rish!, as the Tories are currently 17 points behind in the opinion polls. So, by this time next year, he would be out of a job, sitting on the beach in Malibu and polishing his CV before his interview with Elon Musk. Still, at least he wouldn't have to get by on a prime ministerial pittance any more. He could barely afford his Peloton subscription on that.

'My working assumption,' he said, 'is we'll have an election in the second half of the year.' No shit. He made it sound as if he had no idea that the timing of an election was entirely within his gift. Maybe he's stupider than we thought. But then no one had ever seriously thought he would call an election in May. That idea had only been touted around by Labour so that Sunak would look weak when he delayed it. Come on, lads. Why would Rish! knowingly give up being prime minister in May, when he could hang on for another six months? Why relinquish more freebies and baubles? Not to mention the chance to wreck the country a wee bit more in order to make life trickier for an incoming Labour government.

Instead, it was left to Keir Starmer to do the big set-piece event in front of the TV cameras. To take countless questions from all shades of the media. Not just the True Blue reporters, as Sunak does. You can almost see the axis of power shifting in front of your eyes. The world turning. The country gravitating towards its new, once and future king. The real prime minister.

The speech at the National Composites Centre in Bristol had been billed by many as another chance for the Labour leader to redefine himself for an apathetic public. To throw off the shackles of the boring facade and reveal the real persona within. This, though, rather missed the point. Because the thing is, Starmer is a wee bit dull. A wee bit worthy. But that's precisely his strength. Obviously, him being boring isn't necessarily a good thing for me. Sketch writers like their politicians to be larger than life, their personality flaws all too obvious. But the country could do with a prime minister upon whom we can depend to do the right thing, so we don't have to tune in to the news five times a day to discover what new clusterfuck has been visited upon us.

So how was the speech? It covered all the bases of public service, of doing the right thing, of restoring trust in politics. It was light on policy detail. No unfunded tax cuts, just a promise to switch on the growth 'lever'. Now why hasn't any previous prime minister thought of doing that? But that's a quibble. The point is that it was all easy on the ear. A few reporters insisted they still didn't know what Labour was for. What it would do. That was either a category error or they just hadn't been listening. Because

Starmer has told us often enough. His five missions. You may not like them. They may not be very exciting. But they are hiding in plain sight.

Starmer isn't promising a revolution. He's not that kind of guy. Much of what he is promising is more of the same, only done properly. Done decently. He isn't a voice of protest. He is a voice of government. And after 14 years of the Tories, that's a relief.

* * *

Election years probably don't get off to a worse start than this. An ITV drama, Mr Bates vs the Post Office, *had reminded everyone that the government had done almost nothing to redress the injustice done to hundreds of sub-postmasters and sub-postmistresses over the Horizon scandal. Next, the government had only just managed to pass one of its more absurd pieces of legislation: the Rwanda Bill, which sought to circumvent the Supreme Court's ruling. A bill to declare Rwanda a safe country to which asylum seekers could be deported. Even if it wasn't. A law that was tantamount to declaring that up was down.*

Then there was the latest opinion poll. Sunak's Tories were now 27 points behind Labour. That's the same gap that Liz Truss engineered after dynamiting the economy. Imagine being that bad. That mistrusted. And Rishi was meant to be a safe pair of hands. The tech bro who could manage the party's decline. Now he was officially less popular and effective than a lettuce. That was some achievement. Borderline heroic.

You don't need to be a ship-jumping polls guru to work out that Rish!'s numbers are dire

25 JANUARY 2024

Drip, drip, drip. The first rule of any political rebellion is to learn how to count. Something the none too bright Simon Clarke has yet to master. Though, to be fair, it is more than possible that several MPs who promised to support his call for Rishi Sunak to be replaced faded back into the shadows when the time came. Disloyalty can be contagious. If you can betray Rish!, then it's all too easy to betray Simple Simon. And the Tory right are not noted for keeping their promises.

So Clarke had been left to go it alone. A one-man rebellion shouted down by Tories from both the left and right of the party. It was the closest to unity the Conservatives had come in months. And all because Simple Simon had committed the cardinal sin of telling the truth. That kind of error just can't be tolerated. Every Tory knows that the polling is desperate, that Sunak is hugely unpopular and that the government faces annihilation at the election. It's just that this information has to be borne with a stoicism bordering on denial. Not least because to suggest doing something about it by replacing Rishi risks a more immediate disaster of yet another unelected prime minister. It's lose–lose.

Having originally stomped off in a sulk after finding himself on his own, Simple Simon came out of hiding for a few minutes to give a short interview to the BBC. Mainly, it seemed to troll Liz Truss with a few gags about iceberg lettuces – presumably, he had imagined she would be putting herself forward as the nation's saviour – rather than add anything new. His basic argument was that the Tories were fucked if they stuck with Rishi and fucked if they didn't. But the latter option might be more exciting. And it wasn't as if the government was doing anything.

But it turned out Simple Simon wasn't entirely alone. Because also jumping ship was Will Dry, a previously unknown special adviser in No. 10. Dry, it turned out, was 26 going on 14. A photo of him revealed a teen who had been rejected at an audition for *The Inbetweeners* on the grounds that he looked far too young. And yet Will had somehow come to be a Downing Street essential. Sunak couldn't function without him. The man-boy, who knew little and had done less, was more or less running the country. No wonder everything was going so well.

But, in his short working life, Dry has been on quite the journey. As a second-year undergraduate, he was part of a campaign to rejoin the EU. That seems to be the last sensible thing anyone can remember him doing. Because even as it became clearer to everyone that all of the so-called Brexit bonuses had turned out to be imaginary, Will became a Brexit believer and a signed-up member of the Sunak fan club.

Will couldn't leave it there, though. For now Sunak is too mainstream, too centrist for him. The Rwanda plan is for wimps. So Dry has jumped ship and hooked up with the Conservative Britain Alliance (CBA), a largely anonymous group of right-wing misfits headed up by that serial failure, David Frost. Give Dry a few more minutes and he'll be in bed with Richard Tice and Nigel Farage. And, by the end of the year, he will be working with Vladimir Putin. You get the feeling Dry likes strong government.

It seems that Will's specialism is polling. Some call him a 'guru'. That would be his imaginary friends. After all, you don't need to be a genius to work out that the polling data for Sunak is dire. And his main contribution to his new – temporary – soulmates at the CBA has been to compile one of the most idiotic set of questions in polling history. 'If there was a really brilliant Tory leader, one who everybody in the country really liked and could cut taxes while not crashing the economy, who could find a cure for dementia and bring world peace, would you then vote for him, rather than Keir Starmer?' Clearly, the boy will go far.

On second thoughts, maybe you can see why Tories aren't rushing to rally behind Simple Simon. From one loser to another. But, in the meantime, the government has to maintain the fiction that they are actually doing something other than fighting among themselves. So it was the turn of the junior policing minister, Chris Philp, to look busy.

Philp is something of a collector's item. Widely considered – even by fellow ministers – to be less than competent, but adored by himself. Seemingly undeterred by his slide down the pecking order – he was once a cabinet minister under Liz Truss, a sure sign that he isn't actually very good – Chris is quite happy to repeat any nonsense that anyone in power wants him to. It's doubtful he actually believes in anything much at all, because to believe requires some thought and some integrity. Albeit, in this case, misguided. Rather, he is the brown-noser's brown-noser.

Still, the Philpster loves himself. Even though he lacks self-awareness. His Twitter biography describes him as a 'serial entrepreneur'. Maybe one day he will get round to repaying those who lost thousands when businesses he founded went bankrupt. Just a thought. But, on Thursday morning, Chris was out and about on the airwaves bigging up the government's latest ideas to reduce knife crime.

It didn't go altogether to plan. Not least because every interviewer could spot the very obvious flaws. First, the government had come up with 16 previous proposals that hadn't worked. Why should this one? Especially when it wasn't due to be implemented until the autumn. Philp was all bristle and bustle. No one could possibly have foreseen that manufacturers would get around legislation by making zombie knives without markings, he said. That had really blindsided him. And, no, he hadn't thought to include swords because . . . because . . . why would he? 'Look,' he continued. 'I know the legislation will need tightening up, but we can tighten it up later.'

Run that past us again. You know it's bad legislation, but you can't be bothered to get it right now? Yup, that was exactly it, Chris nodded enthusiastically. So why had the government cut youth services by 75%? That was because Labour had crashed the economy. Not only was this untrue, but it was a measure of his government's failure. The Tories have been in power for 14 years and are still disowning any responsibility.

And that was that. Philp went back to the Home Office, genuinely believing he had nailed it. This can't go on. The next rebellion can't be far away.

Weak, weak, weak: needy Rish! makes a spectacle of himself at PMQs

7 FEBRUARY 2024

It's not hard to count the things that are out of Rishi Sunak's control. He can't really help being less popular than everyone in the Tory party except for Liz Truss.

It's not really his fault that the economy is barely out of recession. Covid, Brexit and Radon Liz (her again) have seen to that. Nor is he wholly to blame for the NHS being on its knees. Though blocking attempts to end the doctors' strike haven't helped. And it's not on him that, almost to a man and a woman, his Tory MPs are inadequate. It's a wretched time for the Conservative gene pool.

But these days Sunak can't even control the things within his agency. He is a man almost entirely without political instincts, a piece of unwanted flotsam being tossed carelessly from side to side. Time and again his character is exposed and he is found wanting. Decades of inhabiting a gilded cage have turned him into an *ingénu*. Someone unable to deal with the real world. Unable to respond as a human to other people's lives – or, indeed, their tragedies. He is all at sea. His wiring is all wrong, unusable even in a faulty 1980s computer. What he is doing in No. 10 is something that is exercising the minds of almost every Tory MP, many of whom are actively trying to remove him. The rest have merely decided it would look worse to get rid of him.

So Rishi gets to stay. The interim prime minister. Loved and admired by no one. Not even his cabinet colleagues. Especially his cabinet colleagues. They are the ones who get to see his shortcomings close up. The ones whose ambitions and careers are sacrificed on his altar. Whether this can last till the next election is touch and go, because the more we get to see of Sunak's character, the less there is to like. And at Wednesday's PMQs, we may just have scraped the barrel.

Keir Starmer began the session by welcoming Esther Ghey, the mother of the murdered teenager Brianna, to the public gallery. Esther wasn't actually in her seat just yet, but she soon would be, as a guest of her local Warrington MP, Charlotte Nichols. The Labour leader spoke of his admiration for Ghey. The dignity with which she had conducted herself throughout her suffering. The generosity of her compassion for the families of her daughter's killers.

All of this just bypassed Sunak. He wasn't bothered. Not even enough to go through the motions of offering his own condolences. There was nothing in Brianna's murder for him. No political advantage to be gained. So why should he be bothered? That was last week's story. Esther Ghey should just get on with her life and leave him to get on with running the country. Watch and learn, Esther. You might even pick up a few tips.

So Sunak merely indulged in an unedifying game of political banter, one he was always going to lose anyway, as his hand is so rubbish. Name us one thing that's going well, Rishi? Oh, you can't. But that didn't stop Rish!. Bizarrely, he actually thinks he is good at this game. That he is a natural born winner. That he can bluff his way out of any situation. The Man with the Golden Voice.

'The Labour leader has broken every promise,' he sneered, the insistent, entitled nasal whine getting ever more high-pitched and needy. Sunak, though, was to show himself as a man of no promise. No integrity. He said Starmer couldn't even define a woman. It was as if he was expecting a roar of approval from his own side. Which he got from his own frontbench. The health secretary, Victoria Atkins, roared with laughter, slapping her thigh. It seems there's nothing she likes more than an anti-trans joke. If she had any self-respect, she wouldn't show her face in public for weeks.

Starmer was understandably outraged. On this, of all days, was it really the time to be making transphobic gags? When the mother of a murdered trans teenager was in the chamber? He offered Sunak the chance to apologise. But Rish! knew no shame. Saw no reason to say sorry. People like him don't go round apologising to working-class women from Warrington. She wasn't even a millionaire. Hell, Ghey should be the one showing gratitude to him. After all he had done. Seldom, if ever, can a prime minister have made quite such a spectacle of themselves during PMQs.

Weirdly, it's not even as if Sunak personally is much of a transphobe. He's almost certainly never given the issue much thought. It's just that he's pathetically needy for the approval of all the culture-war Tories on the far right. Craven even. He will do and say anything to get their attention. To win a few cheap laughs. Join the attacks on minorities. Blame the elites. I guess Goldman Sachs doesn't count. Because, at heart, Rish! has no convictions beyond his own short-term survival. Nothing in which he believes. He is, as Tony Blair said of John Major, 'Weak, weak, weak.'

The Labour MP Liz Twist later gave Sunak another chance to apologise. To even acknowledge Ghey's presence. Starmer pointed up to the gallery. But Sunak still couldn't bring himself to do it. Couldn't admit that he had made a mistake. At heart, he has the mind of a child, unable to do the right thing. He thinks he's being tough when everyone else sees frailty. A Man of No Quality. Finally, after one of his advisers got a message to him that even his own team thought he looked shit, Sunak mumbled a quick non-apology right at the end of the session. Too little, too late.

This wasn't the first time that Sunak's character defects were shown up this week. There was also the £1,000 bet with Piers Morgan over the deportation of refugees. Because having a punt over other people's suffering is what you would expect of any prime minister. Why not make a £1,000 bet on when Brianna's killers will get out?

Rish! has tried to laugh off the bet. To make out that he had been bullied into it by Morgan. That he couldn't wriggle out of it. Except he could have done. No one has to do whatever a narcissist tells you to do in the course of an interview. You don't have to kneel before a fool with a massive ego and little else. Try it. Morgan is surprisingly thin-skinned. He can't take criticism. Sunak could try calling him out. And also Morgan's boss, Rupert Murdoch.

Except Sunak couldn't. He was bound to make the bet. Because that's who he is. So, naturally enough, Starmer also played on that weakness at PMQs. Rish! had no reply. He had been shown up. The Emperor with No Clothes. This is who he is. Time for a darkened room. How much longer can this go on?

Tory Top Team send the Mighty Philpster to tackle PMQs trans joke fallout

8 FEBRUARY 2024

There was a deep despair hanging over No. 10. A slough of despond. Staff tiptoed from room to room, anxious not to create a disturbance or catch one another's eyes. Few words were spoken, and then only in whispers.

'Where's Rishi?' asked Isaac Levido.

'He's locked in his study,' replied James Forsyth. 'He won't come out. He's been sobbing for hours. All he can do to distract himself from his PMQs disaster is watch his new two-and-a-half-minute flipchart party political broadcast on repeat.'

Levido: 'Hmm. That bad. Well, let's just hope he doesn't notice that he made three spelling mistakes. The halfwit can't even get "furlough", "priorities" and "mortgage" right . . .'

Forsyth: 'I'm sure no one will notice. And it's not as bad as Jezza. He can't count. My main worry is he will realise he forgot to list "Brexit", "Liz Truss" and "14 years of Tory fuck-ups" in the list of reasons why the economy is tanking.'

But this was all comparatively minor stuff under the circumstances. They could live with yet another video clip that made them look as if they didn't know what they were doing. The Tory Top Team were more worried about getting through the next 24 hours without looking as if they were insulting the parents of a murdered child.

Levido took Forsyth to one side. 'We need a plan. Urgently,' he said. So far nothing had worked. They had tried Kemi Badenoch. She had merely started yet another culture war, claiming it had been Keir Starmer's fault that Sunak had made a joke about trans issues while Brianna Ghey's mother had been in parliament. It had been Labour who had politicised the parents' grief. It was just that the parents were too dumb to realise this.

Then they had sent out Jeremy Hunt. He had merely insisted that nothing was true and none of this had ever happened. Jezza is finding reality increasingly hard to bear. For a last hurrah, the terminally dim Laura Trott had tried to convince herself that Rishi hadn't been making a joke. Which made you wonder why he, Victoria Atkins and dozens of Tory MPs had been laughing hysterically. Perhaps they were all just having a collective breakdown.

'We'll need a useful idiot for the morning media round,' said Levido. 'Someone too stupid to realise he's been set up. Someone completely expendable. Someone we can rely on to say the unsayable.' Isaac and James looked at each other and spontaneously shouted, in unison, 'Send for Chris Philp.' Provided they could extract his nose from someone's arse in time, he would be ideal.

So, shortly after 7 a.m., Philp appeared on *BBC Breakfast*. The presenter, Naga Munchetty, was unimpressed. Six times she asked whether the minister felt that Sunak's joke had been appropriate and respectful, and six times Philp just shrugged and avoided giving an answer. He really wasn't that bothered. Hell, it wasn't his child who had been murdered, so just relax. Maybe Brianna's parents should learn to take a joke.

You could sense the disbelief in Munchetty. Regardless of the rights and the wrongs of the trans debates, how about some sensitivity and decency? Brianna's father had said he found the prime minister's comments dehumanising and had asked for an apology. Was Philp saying that Peter Spooner was wrong?

Well . . . yes, that's precisely what he was saying, come to think of it. Maybe Brianna's parents were a bit thick and had missed the point. They needed to chill out and listen a bit more carefully before they rushed to take offence. Because he, Chris, the Mighty Philpster, had gone back to listen to what Sunak had said. And what he had heard was an outpouring of tenderness from Rishi and vile, transphobic hate from Keir Starmer. So maybe everyone should shut up a bit and listen to the Philp remix.

There would be no apologies. No nothing. This was a battle the Tory right were prepared to fight to the death.

Sure, it would have been better if Esther Ghey had not been there, but there was a principle at stake. Which was that it's fine to make trans gags in parliament.

A short while later, a red-eyed Rishi sneaked into the Downing Street kitchen. Levido was there, waiting for him. 'Cheer up,' he said. 'I've got a fun day planned for you. We're going to forget your inability to read the room and depart from a script when required. You're going to go for a nice, pointless ride in your favourite helicopter to Cornwall. You'll like that. And here you're just going to double down and say it's Brianna's parents who ought to be apologising for having misunderstood you. Where's their gratitude? In any case, it's not as if we're going to win the election, so it will make no difference. So we might as well be true to our Inner Bastard.'

It wasn't just the Tories who were thinking about the election. Over at Labour HQ, Starmer and Rachel Reeves were deep in conversation over the fate of their £28-billion-a-year green commitment. 'Maybe it would be best if we didn't have any plans at all,' said Starmer. 'That way, the Tories can never accuse us of making unfunded spending promises.'

'Look,' replied Reeves, talking extra slowly because she knew Keir had difficulty with large numbers, 'all I've said is that the economic climate has changed since we came up with the plan two years ago. Interest rates have rocketed, and the Tories have spunked all the money on tax cuts. So we don't have to abandon the whole policy. Just say we will do as much of it as we can under the fiscal rules.'

This sounded far too sensible to Starmer. Secretly, he had always been more impressed by Jezza, who couldn't operate a pocket calculator, than his own shadow chancellor, who had worked at the Bank of England. 'The Tories keep saying we flip-flop,' he squeaked, the panic evident in his voice. 'So maybe the best thing we can do is to flip-flop. At least that shows we're being consistent.'

What people wanted was nothing in which to believe. After 14 years of big ideas from the Tories, they wanted really small ones from a Labour government. Ones that really wouldn't make a difference. Quantum policies. Ones that could be both there and not there.

'I'll tell you what I'm going to do,' said Starmer. 'I'm going to summon the press to a secret Q&A where no cameras are allowed. Because if it's not filmed, no one can say for certain if it ever happened. And then I'm going to cancel the £28 billion.'

'But we've already cancelled it several times before,' observed Reeves, drily.

'That's the beauty of it. We'll say it's been cancelled, but no one can really be sure. So we could always bring it back next week if we feel like it. Brilliant, isn't it?'

This was shaping up into the election no one wanted to win.

* * *

For much of the year it felt as if we were just filling in time before Rishi Sunak chose to call an election. Sunak even turned up at the National Farmers' Union conference in a desperate attempt to show that he was on their side. Things were so bleak for the Tories that they couldn't even take the rural vote for granted.

But, from time to time, global events rightly took centre stage. None more so than the crisis in the Middle East. In late February, the SNP were granted an opposition day debate on the conflict in Gaza. It turned out to be a low point for almost everyone involved.

While people die in Gaza, the UK parliament goes to war over the ceasefire

21 FEBRUARY 2024

Just when you hoped you'd reached rock bottom, parliament finds a way of going still lower. Westminster bows to no one in its efforts to let you and the country down. Luckily, it can't let itself down. That would imply it had some primitive, protozoan conscience. Politicians who strive for dignity – who demand respect – have proved themselves to be made of straw. Little men and women driven entirely by their own worst instincts.

Take the conflict in Israel and Gaza. The murder of about 1,200 Israelis by Hamas terrorists on 7 October.

More than 100 hostages still held. The killing of 30,000 Palestinians, most of them women and children. Much of Gaza reduced to rubble. Food, water and medical supplies all critical. This should have been the time for MPs to come together. They are always talking sanctimoniously about doing this. As if they had a monopoly on enlightenment. As if they alone can channel the nation's higher power.

What we got was the exact opposite. An SNP opposition day debate designed to highlight splits in the Labour Party. A Labour amendment created to prevent a split in the party's own ranks, one that bridged the gap between the SNP's position and the Labour leadership's. A Tory amendment whose only function was to knock out Labour's, as there was hardly a cigarette paper between them, under the parliamentary precedent that government amendments kick out opposition ones on such occasions.

So there we had it. While more men, women and children were dying in Gaza, all of the UK parties were using the conflict for marginal, parochial gains. Just lip service to a higher calling. All claiming they cared only about bringing the war to an end. All so detached from reality they couldn't even see they were lying to themselves. Just indulging in performative politics, knowing there was no chance an IDF or Hamas commander was listening in. Nothing they said would make a difference. So they could say what they liked.

There were rumours early on Wednesday that Labour was leaning on the Speaker, Lindsay Hoyle, to break with convention and allow both the Labour and Tory amendments to be debated. To save face for Keir Starmer. To head off a mass rebellion. There had certainly been no sign of Hoyle during the science and technology questions that had preceded PMQs. Ample time for him to be got at. Though it could be that he had simply chosen to avoid listening to minister Michelle Donelan. She is the equivalent of a liquid cosh. One sentence and you're out cold.

Hoyle had reappeared for prime minister's questions, but the moment it ended he was out the door. Hotly pursued by Starmer's team once more. Clearly, the Speaker had yet to make up his mind over how to proceed: to go with convention and drop the Labour amendment, or plead special circumstances and let the house vote on both amendments as well as the SNP motion.

The first sign of shithousery came when Labour MPs interrupted proceedings with a series of largely irrelevant points of order. First from Lucy Powell. Could the Deputy Speaker – Rosie Winterton was now in the chair – think of a way to get Rishi Sunak to answer the questions he had ignored during PMQs about whether Kemi Badenoch's power of recall was sound or not? Rosie shrugged. If Labour was going to ask about Sunak not providing answers and Kemi being a liability, then we'd be here all day.

Next up was Liam Byrne. He, too, was concerned about Kemi. Were the Canada trade talks actually happening or going on only in her mind? Kemi? Deluded? Who would have imagined that? John McDonnell wondered if Winterton could help with visitor access to Westminster Hall. Rosie closed her eyes. Talk to the hand. On we went. Diana Johnson demanded help in accessing the 15 Home Office reports that James Cleverly was sitting on. Christ, Jimmy Dimly can't get a refugee on a plane, let alone construct a coherent sentence. Then there was concern over a £2.3 billion fine owed to the EU – 'Cheap at the price,' yelled the Tories – followed by worries about yet more government trouble over the Post Office Horizon scandal. Above my pay grade, sobbed Rosie.

Finally, Hoyle returned to the chamber. He had made a decision. He would allow both the Labour and the government amendments. The Tory and SNP benches went wild with outrage. And there we were, all thinking that what they really wanted was for the hostages to be returned and an end to the fighting in Gaza. Silly us. There were shouts and jeers. The always pointless Desmond Swayne snarled: 'Bring back Bercow.' Parliament was about to start its own civil war. So much more exciting than the conflict in the Middle East.

Someone else shouted: 'You ought to be ashamed, Lindsay.' Hoyle didn't look entirely comfortable. He couldn't front this one out. There was a reasonable case for breaking with convention, and he should have remained defiant. But he wants to be loved too much. Maybe he couldn't bear the thought of not getting that peerage. It takes all sorts. He looked as though he would rather be anywhere but in the Speaker's chair.

The speeches themselves were unremarkable, except for the unusual hybrid of piety and bitterness. Everyone holier than thou. Sanctimony on their side. Everyone wanted a ceasefire. Only they wanted their own ceasefire, not anyone else's. Unbelievably, it all got worse. Much worse. Just before the vote was about to be taken on the Labour amendment, Penny Mordaunt made a point of order. Having failed to get one over on Labour, the Tories were going to throw their toys out of the pram and not vote on anything. Not even their own amendment. Astonishingly, Mordaunt thought she was grabbing the moral high ground. Pass the sick bag. Cue total chaos. A vote to chuck everyone out of the public gallery and sit in private. The SNP not even getting to vote on their own motion. An emotional speaker apologising to the house.

None of this was good enough. Not nearly. And over a war. If MPs were capable of self-reflection, they would be in a downward shame spiral.

This was their finest hour.

Mordaunt receives Labour's olive twig with theatrical fury after Gaza omnishambles

22 FEBRUARY 2024

A rule of thumb: when you're in a hole, it's generally best to stop digging. So, after a spectacular display of pompous self-indulgence and partisan politics from MPs of all parties during an opposition day debate on Gaza the night before, the least you might have expected was a little contrition on Thursday morning. A walk of shame into the Commons. MPs trying not to catch one another's eyes. We've all had a drink . . .

And it all started off quite well during culture department questions. Everyone was determined not to mention the war. No, not that one in the Middle East. The one that had been fought across the dispatch box. The one that MPs were really bothered about. The Speaker was also in his chair. Everyone wanted to pretend that everything was normal. 'Yes, Mr Speaker. No, Mr Speaker.' The only hint that anything was amiss was the excessive politeness.

The tiptoeing continued through two urgent questions, the junior business minister, Kevin Hollinrake, bowing and scraping so low as he suggested that Labour's Kevan Jones knew far more about the Post Office Horizon scandal than he did. After the second UQ, on the government's decision to cut funding to an inter-faith group – no one dared to point out the irony in the timing of this – Lindsay Hoyle made his excuses and left. It had been a long two hours for him. Exhausting.

So it was left to the shadow leader of the house, Lucy Powell, to mention the elephant in the room during business questions. Lucy was never a prize student at charm school. She finds it easier to make enemies than friends. There is a brusqueness to her. An awkwardness she can't quite shake off. But she wanted to try to make amends for Wednesday's fiasco. An olive twig, if not a branch.

It was like this, she said. She accepted that Labour hadn't exactly covered itself in glory. The party had been in a hole over the Gaza vote and had talked the Speaker into changing the parliamentary procedures to get around it. The sort of thing any party would do in a similar situation. They could hardly be blamed for trying it on.

But then no one was totally guilt-free. The Scottish National Party had chosen the Gaza motion as much to embarrass Labour as anything else. It wasn't as if the result of the vote would make a blind bit of difference to Israel or Hamas. And the Tories were in it up to their necks. They had tabled their own amendment, which was almost identical to Labour's, purely as a wrecking motion and had been furious to be outmanoeuvred. They had then panicked about losing the vote and had thrown their toys out of the pram and walked out. Cue chaos.

Powell paused, looked up from her script and made this offer: how about everyone owned up to their part in this humiliation of the vanities? No need to make a big deal about it. Don't worry about the embarrassing details. Just mumble something vaguely apologetic. Miss Otis Regrets. Enough to give the public the impression that MPs had a few basic signs of emotional intelligence. Then we could all move on. Pretend it had never happened.

This sounded like a decent offer. Only not to the Commons leader, Penny Mordaunt. A walking disaster of emotional stupidity. Not to mention brazen dishonesty. A woman incapable of recognising the most basic truths. Who thinks that her brief cameo at the coronation has given her iconic status. A Britannia for the 21st century.

Planet Earth to Penny. Planet Earth to Penny. Is there anyone there? Apparently not. All you did was carry a sword for a while. OK, you did it well. But it wasn't that hard. You can't go on expecting the rest of us to thank you for ever. Yet Penny is in Penny World. Seldom has any woman taken herself quite so seriously. Apart from Liz Truss, possibly. And Penny is just as deranged. Of all the days on which to launch your latest leadership bid, this was not the one. Not least because she'll be lucky to keep her seat at the next election.

Penny was all ice. The theatrical fury of the intellectually compromised. Unable to see that putting all the blame onto Labour and exonerating Hoyle was an untenable position. The Speaker is not without agency. Worse, she had the nerve to pretend that all she cared about was the little people. The rights of the SNP. Mordaunt has never cared about the SNP. Walking out before the vote was all about creating a diversion away from a possible defeat for the government. Nothing more, nothing less. To pretend otherwise was an insult to the country. At a time when people were hoping for something better from their MPs, Penny chose to kick them in the teeth again. As for parliamentary conventions, she has never cared for them either. Anyone remember the prorogation? Mordaunt would rather you didn't. Though she was a fan at the time.

To their credit, Penny's preening display of sanctimony was too much for many of her fellow Tory MPs. It's hard to imagine there ever being a time and a place for such self-indulgent denial, but this certainly wasn't it. Most chose to ignore her. To distance themselves from her by refusing to pander to her hauteur. Some took her on. None better than Mark Francois – not a line I would ever have imagined writing.

Francois is often a purple ball of inchoate anger, seething at a world he doesn't understand, that refuses to bend to his will. On Thursday, the storm clouds had temporarily parted. No one came out well from the Gaza omnishambles. No one. That was directed pointedly at Penny. Nor was everyone perfect. Hoyle had admitted his mistake. Now was the time for forgiveness. Magnanimity. A time of grace.

Not for the SNP's Westminster leader, Stephen Flynn. He was going to pursue this one to the ends of the earth.

Lindsay was guilty of the greatest possible sin: crimes against the SNP. Flynn would be happy to take part in the firing squad. Though you might have thought he could have granted a royal pardon. The SNP was coming out of this one smelling of roses. With another opposition day debate in the bag.

Then Hoyle himself intervened. Again he fessed up. He had made a mistake. He was sorry. He wished it had turned out otherwise. He hadn't been nobbled by the Labour heavies. It had been the threat of violence to MPs. He couldn't live with another phone call saying a friend had been murdered.

Penny grunted. She wasn't happy. Not ready to think through the implications of parliamentary democracy being undermined by terror groups. She tried to sound understanding, but she spat out the words as if she had swallowed a wasp. Lindsay had been weak. Weak, I tell you. She would never have given in. Some things were worth dying for. And *Erskine May* was one of them.

* * *

You might have thought the Tories would have wanted to capitalise on a rare moment when the focus was off them for a while, with the behaviour of the Speaker and the Labour Party under scrutiny instead. Yet, for the Conservatives, there was to be no let-up from their own psychodrama. Step forward Lee Anderson. Aka 30p Lee.

Nothing to see here, say Tories of their hero, 30p Lee

26 FEBRUARY 2024

How do you solve a problem like Lee? If you're Rishi Sunak, then the answer is: with the greatest reluctance. And extremely carefully. Lee Anderson is a man to be treated with kid gloves. To be loved back into a state of grace.

It would be a push to call Lee a 'national treasure'. But he is certainly the closest the Conservative Party has to a local hero. An MP far more popular among fellow Tories than with Rishi or any of his cabinet colleagues. Viewers tune in to his GB News programme to be drip-fed divine truths. For the unsayable to be made flesh. Lee is their beating heart.

How this came about is more of a mystery. Lee has been on quite the journey. He started life as a Labour councillor, making prejudiced remarks about Travellers before jumping ship to the Tories. A party that would be more indulgent to his racism. And to the fact that he had campaigned on behalf of Jeremy Corbyn in the 2017 general election.

Since then, Lee has made a career out of hypocrisy and stupidity. First, he lashed out at fellow MPs who took second jobs. MPs should be content to serve their constituents on their parliamentary salary, he insisted, moments before signing a £100,000-a-year deal to present his own show on GB News. He then turned out for the launch of Popular Conservatism, as their voice on climate change. Burning coal was just fine, he told us. Because coal came from trees, and trees were green. Some people even applauded this nonsense.

But Lee doesn't care if people think he's stupid or racist. In fact, the more that people call him out, the more he likes it. It makes him feel good. Feeds his dysfunctionality. His overwhelming narcissism. More to the point, he binds all those supporters whom the Tories like to pretend don't exist but on whom they increasingly rely. So much so that the Conservative Party chose to bung him an extra £10,000 a year. The only Brexit bonus anyone is likely to see.

And it was all going so well, until Lee went openly racist on GB news on Friday night and declared that Sadiq Khan had been taken over by Islamists and London was now being run by terrorists. Take a trip on the Northern line, and your train will be driven by a suicide bomber. Every bus was on its own personal jihad.

Now you could say that Lee was unlucky. That he happened to deliver his rant at a time when someone was actually watching. Who knows how many other hate crimes he has committed that have gone unremarked. If a tree falls in the forest and no one is there to hear it, does it make a sound? But what had been heard could not now be unheard. And while there were plenty of Tories willing to attest that they had personally seen the London mayor take part in the 7 October terrorist attack, there were still a few who thought that maybe – just maybe – Anderson had gone too far this time.

Then up stepped brave Rish!. Or not. The prime minister was notably silent for 24 hours. Hoping that Lee would retract his statement. Say he had got it wrong this time. And that everyone could go back to being only a little bit racist. After all, racism-lite is the new acceptable face of Conservatism. But no. Still nothing. So Sunak was finally persuaded to withdraw the whip. With the clear understanding that Lee was still a figure of the divine. A human love pump. And was welcome back whenever he wanted.

Rish! was no more coherent when he gave a series of interviews to local radio stations in Yorkshire on Monday morning. What Lee had said was wrong, he said. But it definitely wasn't racist or Islamophobic. Er . . . run that past us again. Lee had done something wrong, but the wrong thing wasn't racist or Islamophobic. So what was wrong about it? That he was actually far too nice? Sunak couldn't explain. Other than that it was a category error. The Tory party had no problem with Islamophobia or racism, so therefore Lee couldn't have said anything wrong. Apart from the wrong thing he had said. We were rapidly going round in ever-decreasing circles. Sunak's party is having the same problem with Islamophobia as Jeremy Corbyn's Labour had with anti-Semitism.

That provided the cue for almost everyone to go slightly mad. Paul Scully, a Tory junior minister who is normally considered one of the saner members of the government, gave an interview in which he insisted that words mattered. Lee should apologise. Only for him then to say that there were no-go areas in Birmingham. The terrorists were in control there, too. It's a wonder any of us secular types get through the day without being beheaded.

Meanwhile, Lee himself was loving it. Thrilled to still be the centre of attention. So he gave a statement to GB News, which he insisted another presenter read out for him and which doubled down on his racism. Even as Lee didn't speak, Sadiq was in talks to turn the M25 into a mosque. Any motorist who wasn't radicalised would not be allowed into the centre of London. The ULEZ charge was funding Hamas.

Not to be outdone, the always idiotic Jonathan Gullis accused the Speaker, Lindsay Hoyle, of radicalising most of his Stoke constituents. Suella Braverman went further. The whole of the establishment were now terrorists. When she looked around the cabinet table, she couldn't be sure that one of her colleagues wasn't about to blow up the room.

Then there was the brown-noser par excellence, Chris Philp. He, too, had counted hundreds of terrorists on his way to work. You could always spot a terrorist, he said. They were the ones who had nothing but contempt for the planning laws. The holy writ of the green belt. It's possible that the Philpster is actually more stupid than 30p Lee. At least Lee doesn't pretend to be anything but dim.

Even Tom Tugendhat, who wouldn't look out of place in a Keir Starmer cabinet, couldn't bring himself to call out Lee. What he had said was wrong, but he couldn't squeeze out the word 'Islamophobia'. Come the early-evening news, Rish! was at it again. The Tory party definitely, definitely didn't have a problem with Islamophobia. It was just a total coincidence that everywhere he looked there were men with swords yelling 'Allahu Akbar'. And that was just the leadership team of the Bank of England.

Rish! cowers in No. 10 as mob demands peace in lawless London

29 FEBRUARY 2024

The United Kingdom, February 2024. A cold wind blew down Whitehall. The streets were nearly empty. The shops boarded up. Just a few veiled women, keeping their heads bowed as they hurried home. Inside 10 Downing Street, the prime minister cowered under his desk. 'No more,' he sobbed.

Over in City Hall, Sadiq Khan signed the death warrants of another 50 motorists who had failed to pay the ULEZ charge. His original order had been that first offenders should only have both hands cut off, but he had been overruled by the ayatollahs. Sharia law should never be that lenient.

In Threadneedle Street, Andrew Bailey, the governor of the Bank of England, was pacing the vast boardroom. The woman he was expecting, the editor of the *Financial Times*, was late. On the table were laid out two bandanas and two suicide vests. In under an hour they – and Jeremy Hunt – would both be dead. Well, what would you do? After all that Jezza has done to the economy. The fight-back of the deep state starts here.

Still, the caliphate was expanding its reach. Down in the Cotswolds, Boris Johnson was being dragged through the centre of Chipping Norton. In an hour's time he would be stoned to death. The punishment for adultery. Let him be an example to other politicians. Up in the balcony of the town hall, David Cameron – aka Lord Big Dave – allowed himself a wry smile. He would be throwing the first stone.

Er . . . actually, scrub that intro. That was the Lee Anderson and Liz Truss vision of Britain on Monday. It's now Thursday.

The United Kingdom, February 2024. A cold wind still blew down Whitehall. The streets were also still empty and the shops boarded up. And Rishi Sunak hadn't moved since Monday. Nobody had managed to talk him out from under his desk.

Out on Oxford Street, a group of murderous terrorists had formed an orderly queue outside Selfridges. They claimed to be waiting for the shop to open so that they could buy the new *Call of Duty* video game. But Rish! knew better. He alone had attended the COBRA briefing led by Suella Braverman. Before long, some of the terrorists would be waving flags and walking somewhere else. Some might even be smiling and demanding 'peace'. Imagine that.

It was the same throughout the rest of this once prosperous land. In the countryside, sheep were lying with donkeys and crops were rotting in the fields. The roads were unpassable, blocked by overturned cars and looted lorries. The sun no longer shone and beggars howled to the skies, their cries unanswered. Bodies lay unburied in the street. And still the mob demanded peace.

James Cleverly was just the latest cabinet member to tiptoe into No. 10 via the secret tunnel. It was far too dangerous for him to use the front door. He kept his head down in the corridors in case his movements attracted the attention of a sniper. He needed to coax the prime minister out. He hadn't been to the toilet for days.

'What do you want?' Rish! sobbed. 'Leave me alone! Leave me alone!'

'It's OK,' said Jimmy Dimly tenderly.

'Is it safe? Is it safe?'

'Is what safe?'

'Is it safe? Is it safe? The country has descended into mob rule. We no longer have a functioning government. By the way, who is the prime minister? And which party has been in power for the last 14 years?'

'You don't want to know,' said Jimmy D. 'But I have a cunning plan. We're going to let everyone have three protests and then say: "You've made your point. Enough is enough. Time to go home now and everything will be fine."'

'You say all the sweetest things, Jimmy,' said Rish!. 'I don't know where I'd be without you.'

Weirdly, this wasn't a line of reasoning that the security minister, Tom Tugendhat, chose to employ in his statement to the Commons on MPs' safety. In fact, he got through the whole hour without mentioning the words 'mob rule'. Almost as if he was a bit ashamed by his leader. Embarrassed by him. You get the feeling that the end of this parliament can't come too soon for Tories like Tugendhat.

Instead, Tugendhat just stuck to basics. MPs are increasingly under threat and need protection. No one was going to argue with that. Though he was understandably unwilling to think what might have prompted the surge in death threats. That it might have all kicked off with the coarsening of the debate during the Brexit years. Right-wing newspapers branding MPs and judges as traitors and enemies of the people. And the government just standing by in passive acceptance. Nodding it through.

Back in Downing Street, Jimmy D was still trying to lure Sunak out.

'It's the big annual Tory fundraiser tonight. The Black and White Ball,' Dimly explained. 'We need to extract as much dosh as possible with the election coming.'

'What have others given so far?' squeaked Rish!. 'Let me see . . . Suella has offered a lifelong break in Rwanda. Stay in a two-star hotel. The advance bidding on that has been slow. And Honest Bob Jenrick is offering to help with controversial planning applications. Pornographers especially welcome . . .'

'And what are you giving?'

'A luxury five-night stay on the *Bibby Stockholm*, with a banquet dinner cooked by 30p Lee.'

'That's amazing.'

'To cap it all, I will offer an honorary knighthood. Preferably to someone linked to my father-in-law's business interests.'

'You're all heart,' said Jimmy Dimly. 'All this giving is very tiring.'

* * *

It felt as though the country was stuck in a loop. Nothing was really happening, and Rishi looked increasingly desperate. He was hoping against hope that he could find something – anything – that would reverse the Tories' fortunes. Even an upcoming budget didn't offer much excitement.

The end is nigh! Kill me now! The Sunaks have done the *Grazia* video

5 MARCH 2024

Forget about Wednesday's budget. That 2p reduction on national insurance that worked so well last year. That surprise decision to maintain the freeze on fuel duty for the 437th year in a row. Those cuts to public services that Jeremy Hunt is trying to pretend he hasn't been briefing the newspapers about. None of this matters. Nothing is going to switch the dial. There is nothing more Rishi Sunak can do. If you don't love him now, you never will.

We are now in the Tunnel. That parallel political universe in which everything and nothing happens. You can take your pick. The news schedules are busier than ever but the news itself is forgotten within hours. Because nothing really matters. We are now on a rinse, spin and repeat cycle that will only end with a general election. Where the debate gets ever more extreme yet somehow less substantial. Most people have long since switched off. You can almost hear their screams of 'Make it stop'.

Just count the days. Breathe deeply. Squeeze in an extra Pilates session. Anything to distract yourself. Be of good comfort. The end is getting ever closer. How can we be sure? Because Rish! has just done a video for *Grazia*.

The inevitable kiss of death. You know there is no way out now. This is the fate of every party leader with an election imminent. But there is no comeback. Once sold, your soul can never be redeemed.

This is the Sunaks relaxing at home together. Or rather Rish! and Akshata staring miserably into a camera while sitting on a sofa. A more excruciating five and a half minutes would be hard to find. You can see the look of death behind Rish!'s eyes. Even he – someone notoriously unself-aware – knows this is a video too far. But then he's come too far to back down now. The wheels are spinning far too fast for him to get off now. All he can do is wait till they stop. Only then will he discover where he's been spat out.

So he smiles and smiles and smiles. And still he doesn't come close to warmth or sincerity. It is the icy smile of a man praying that his wife doesn't land him in it. Because Akshata, at least, still seems up for it. No one has told her there are no winners in this latest PR stunt. The best you can hope for is to come out unscathed. Either she is terminally bored with her life and finds mind-numbingly dumb questions a merciful release or she is a stunningly good actor. Put it like this: this is the level of interview you would even trust Chris Philp not to screw up. On second thoughts, perhaps not.

Let's start with the chores. Who makes the bed? Definitely not me, said Akshata. Full of energy, totes engaging with this. 'I'm not a morning person. At college,

77

Rish!' – she's even adopted my nickname for him – 'would come round, and I'd still be in bed eating.'

'Er, yes,' Sunak interrupted. This was too much information. Time to take control of the narrative. He really, really cared about bed-making. So much so that he would sometimes interrupt a meeting of the cabinet to go upstairs to the Downing Street flat to make sure it was done properly.

SCOOP.

How about loading the dishwasher? Rish! dived in. This was also very much his territory. He happened to also really, really care about this. If it wasn't done properly, he would empty it and start again.

KILL ME NOW. Literally, who cares? I mean, here we have a prime minister who has guided the economy into a recession. Who is prepared to break international law to fly a plane-load of refugees to Rwanda. Who has done nothing to stop the NHS from falling apart. Who is now trying to fight a culture war that he has started. Who takes no responsibility for the extremism in his own party. And now we're all supposed to think, 'You know what, I can overlook all this because he loads the dishwasher. That's my kind of guy. He gets my vote. What a human! What a hero!' Er . . . if it's all the same, I'd be perfectly happy if Rish! never went anywhere near the kitchen, provided he made a decent job of running the country.

But that wasn't the agenda. So on we went. How about the children? Akshata was quite strict with them about their schoolwork, but otherwise wasn't that bothered. Rish! liked to give them snacks. Bless. But he also wished they would walk the dog from time to time. But then, why have staff? They can't just sit around all day.

Akshata admitted she had more leisure time than her husband. Who would have guessed? Though what she did with it, she wouldn't say. Other than go to the odd spin class. Maybe she just puts her feet up on the sofa and manages her investments all day, so that when Rish! comes back from work saying the economy is in crisis again, she can tell him the good news that they have made another couple of million.

And that was about it. Rish! didn't have time to read. So bedtime was the same episode of *Friends* over and over again. Why bother, when you can just watch this video? This will knock you out quicker than your nightly dose of fentanyl. An exercise in sublime futility. Imagine being too boring for your new, blissed-out neighbours in Malibu.

Still, Rish! could at least console himself with the thought that he hadn't committed the cardinal error of creating news. Unlike David Cameron, who in his BBC hagiography before the 2015 election, in between saying 'Hail, good fellow, well met' to various tradesmen in Chipping Norton, let slip that he was too chillaxed for words and couldn't face the prospect of running for a third term. Much too much like hard work. Well, that ended well, didn't it?

But life can be cripplingly unfair at times. You'd have thought that Dave would have run his course after Brexit. That he had done enough damage. Time to say his byebyes. But for Dave there would be second, third or even fourth chances. For men like Dave there always are.

Lord Big Dave is now foreign secretary. Generally thought to be doing a great job. We are supposed to be grateful that he is doing us the favour. The truth is, he's much the same as he always was. It's just that the competition has become so much weaker. He looks like a statesman only because he's up against the Tory class of '24. What goes around, comes around, I guess. There's hope for Rishi yet.

The only real giveaway in Jezza's fictional budget was the despair on Tory faces

6 MARCH 2024

Was that it? Was that really it? Everything pre-briefed. No surprises whatsoever. Two percentage points off national insurance. Is that what you think my vote is worth? Because it worked so well when you knocked two percentage points off NI in last year's autumn statement. That really shifted the polls. But hey, they say insanity is doing the same thing twice and expecting a different result.

So let me bask in the giveaway that you think will make up for all the damage the government has done over the last 14 years. Feeling good? Thought not. Everything about this budget was always going to be a total fiction. And it didn't disappoint. Here we have a budget that is going to cut the overall tax burden, said the chancellor. Except it won't. Check through the small print and you will find that the Office for Budget Responsibility reckons the overall tax rate is at its highest since 1948. Every fiscal assumption that Jeremy Hunt has made is based on taxes going up.

But let's just run with the alternative reality. Take the same drugs that Jezza injects to get through the day. Just for the hell of it. After all, we aren't going to have too much more of the Tories, so we might as well enjoy them while we can. Here's how it works. You're just going to love the tax cut that means your taxes won't be going up by quite so much as they otherwise might. I mean, it's not as if the NHS and the transport system aren't on their knees. Far better you get that extra 2p than someone bothers to care for your mother with Alzheimer's. Old people are such a waste of space.

That's just the start. Because the government also doesn't want you to know that your council tax will be going up by a minimum of 5%, to go a small way to providing the services that the Treasury isn't interested in. Funny that that bit of the tax burden never got a mention.

Which leaves growth. Hunt somehow failed to mention he can only get to a positive outcome by allowing more people into the country. At the same time as the Tories are trying to break international law by offloading plane-loads of refugees to Rwanda. Go figure. Because Rishi Sunak can't.

It's just a shame that for such an elaborate fiction, we have in Jezza such a piss-poor storyteller. Remember that he was only drafted in as chancellor out of desperation. When he was the last man standing. The only Tory who looked as if he could vaguely reassure the country after the deranged 49 days of Liz Truss. He sort of looked safe. Someone unthreatening, if a bit useless. The sort of person you wouldn't mind marrying your best friend's daughter. Though preferably not your own. You would hope for more for your own child. Then Sunak took over and found himself lumbered with Jezza. Partly because there was a yawning lack of talent in his party, but also because further change would look like even greater chaos.

So Hunt got off to a slow start and has now almost ground to a halt. There is literally nothing to him. He has less grasp of economics than my dog. The country's finances are being run by a halfwit. Sajid Javid sat through the budget speech with his face distorted into Munch's *The Scream*. He looked as if he had taken an overdose of fentanyl.

For what would certainly be his last-ever budget, Jezza had invited one of his sons to watch from the gallery.

This could be construed as child abuse. It would be one of the longest, most painful 80 minutes of all our lives. There was no form, no order, no real conviction. It was as though someone had rustled up a bundle of papers and reassembled them in random order. At least, that's the only reasonable explanation for why Jezza sounded so confused. He simply had no idea what was going on.

'This is a budget for long-term growth,' Hunt began. He seemed to forget that was how he had started his last budget statement, and that we are now in recession. So he was immediately setting the bar low. He rambled his way unconvincingly through a screed of numbers that turned out to be entirely imaginary. It was like being given access to a remedial reading class. He then committed a more obvious blunder: he froze fuel duty again, having said six months ago that the only way he could meet his fantasy fiscal rules was by raising fuel duty. He must think we are as stupid as he is.

Initially, there was some sympathetic encouragement from the Tory MPs. He may be a total loser, but he was their total loser. The best they had. But gradually, a deathly silence prevailed as they realised they had just run out of luck in the Last Chance Saloon. Sunak appeared to be in agony. His face a vision of despair. Michelle Donelan looked around, searching for someone to libel. Only Victoria Atkins roared her full-throated approval. But then, it's not entirely clear if the health secretary ever really knows what is happening. Most of the noise came from the Labour benches. They hadn't had so much fun in years. 'Can you shout more quietly?' said the Deputy Speaker, Eleanor Laing.

The final humiliation came when Jezza tried to pretend that doing away with non-dom status was entirely his own idea and not a deliberate attempt to steal Labour's flagship policy. To make it harder for an incoming Starmer government. Not that Hunt really knew what he would do with the money he raised. Waste it, probably. Rish! nodded this one through. Hopefully he made sure that his wife had all her tax affairs in order before signing that one off.

At last Jezza reached the final page and could sit down. It was over. For ever. He could at least console himself knowing that his budget was unlikely to fall apart within a matter of hours. Mainly because there was so little to unravel. Every underwhelming detail had already been priced in. Everyone knew it was bollocks. The country that Hunt had described, in which everything had never been better, was one that was unrecognisable to everyone else. Jezza was no saviour rising from the street. If this was an election budget, then the election is lost.

* * *

The slow drip feed of bad headlines for the Tories didn't stop.

First, Lee Anderson defected to the Brexit Party after he lost the Tory whip over his racist remarks about the

London mayor, Sadiq Khan. Curiously, though, the Conservatives didn't feel the need to return the £10 million that donor Frank Hester had given to the party after the Guardian revealed that he had also made racist comments. I guess some kinds of racism are more acceptable than others.

Still, there had been some light relief when Liz Truss published her book, Ten Years to Save the West. Liz was the gift that kept on giving to satirists. The prime minister who had done untold damage to the country turning out 80,000 words on what the world really needed was even more of her. Self-awareness has never been her strong point.

As for Rishi Sunak, he clung on to the Easter recess as if it were a life raft. A chance to lie low. Ideally, he would have liked the break to go on indefinitely – the more people got to see of him, the further he tumbled in the polls. He just couldn't catch a break. To be fair, though, almost everything domestic was his fault. Small-boat crossings, deportation flights to Rwanda, the recession, government debt, the NHS . . . You name it, he had made it worse.

But all good things come to an end. After Easter, Sunak had to come out of hiding.

Tory MPs limp into PMQs after finally accepting their fate

17 APRIL 2024

There's something to be said for a prolonged death. It means you can get your grieving in while the patient is still alive. All the more important when that patient is you. The Tories have known the game is up for some time now. They can read the polls as well as the rest of us. They are facing electoral wipeout. It's not totally out of the question that they might even be only the third-largest party after the next election.

None of this comes easy for Tories, born to believe that they are the party of government. So there have been plenty of tears as they process their grief. The first stage in this has been denial. This can't be happening, they told themselves. These things don't happen to people like them. It is against the natural order. So they dictated their own reality. One of their choosing. The methodology of the polls was wrong. Of course it was.

Then came the anger. Messy and raw. Torrents of unprocessed rage. How dare voters even contemplate kicking them out of government? Where was the gratitude for all the government had done in making people's lives so much worse? The country didn't deserve them. Closer to the truth than they cared to imagine.

Next up was the bargaining. OK, we may have made one or two mistakes, the Tories whined. But they were very, very little mistakes. The sort that any government could easily make. So they were sorry. Sort of. Not that they could actually bring themselves to mouth the word. But look, just trust us. Vote for us again, and this time we will get it right. We will deliver untold riches. Promise.

The fourth stage was depression. Here the Tories just sat motionless, unable to raise any sort of fight. They sat largely silent in the Commons as they stared into the abyss. Those that could be bothered to make it to Westminster, that is. Many just lay in bed, with their phones switched off, only moving to let their constituency associations know that they wouldn't be standing again. Last one to leave could turn out the lights.

The grieving process has finally been completed. They have reached a state of unsteady acceptance. They have come through the worst into a parallel universe where they are neither totally dead nor alive. A half-life in which they are neither happy nor sad. Just going through the motions of an existence they are struggling to recall. To give one last performance before the final curtain.

Were you to be completely clueless about the reality of current UK politics, you might have thought that all was well with the Conservatives as they gathered for the first prime minister's questions since the Easter recess. The backbenches were almost full, and the Tory MPs managed to rise to give a throaty roar of approval when Rishi

Sunak took his place in the chamber. And Rish! looked almost happy to be back.

Only scratch the surface, and what you have is just a chimera. Nothing is quite as it seems. All smoke and mirrors. The backbenchers merely the walking dead. Sunak's ripostes not smart so much as desperate. What we were getting was not a battle of equals, but the spectacle of a prime minister who has always been out of his depth and is now getting his arse handed to him on a plate yet again. Because almost everything Rish! says is untrue. A bedtime fantasy to help him sleep at nights.

Keir Starmer went in on the Liz Truss sci-fi memoir. The gift that will keep on giving for Labour in the months to come. The Diary of an Idiot. Liz taking centre stage in her own *commedia dell'arte*. Something to put front and centre of every election leaflet. The Trusster had said that her Kamikwasi budget was the happiest day of her life. Did the prime minister know if any mortgage holder shared this ecstasy? Sunak had come prepared. Starmer should spend more time reading Angela Rayner's tax advice. He thought he was being smart. Playing to the crowd. The reality was he just sounded bitchy and peevish. His default setting.

'Mmm,' said the Labour leader. 'We have a billionaire prime minister and a billionaire peer [Lord Ashcroft] who have saved millions in tax through non-dom loopholes smearing a working-class woman over £2,000 of tax.' Is that really the rabbit hole you want to run down, Rish!?

Literally no one except the *Daily Mail* really cares. You want to look like a graceless, entitled bully, then go right ahead.

Even Sunak had the antennae to realise that this wasn't the best of looks. His trainer collection is worth far more than the tax Rayner is alleged to have avoided. So he found himself babbling in desperation, hoping that if he carried on talking for long enough, he might alight on some sentences that bordered on coherence. He had never rated Liz Truss. Truss was a loser, he was a winner. Er . . . hello. Earth to Rishi. Earth to Rishi. Is there anyone there? You actually lost to the Trusster. The Tory members preferred her to you. So this one is on you and your party. You don't get to pretend you had nothing to do with the chaos. Just grow up and take some responsibility for once.

Starmer went in for the kill. At the last budget Sunak had made £46 billion of unfunded tax cuts by promising to get rid of national insurance contributions. How on earth was he going to pay for that? Cut the NHS? Cut the state pension?

Now the bolloxometer tipped into the red. It was Labour who had put up taxes, insisted Sunak. Apparently, Labour were the ones who had been in government for the past 14 years. In any case, the NHS had more than enough money. In fact, it was over-funded. The waiting lists were just a fiction. Pensioners were also far too well-off. Truly, Rish! was a man of infinite compassion.

He ended by saying: 'Vote Conservative for a brighter future.' Yup, that will work. Because the present is so obviously shit.

The rest of the session was largely taken up with local election stuff. It was Labour's fault that local authorities were going to have to increase council tax because their money from central government had been cut. And Truss's crowning achievement had been the Australian and New Zealand trade deals that Sunak had previously rubbished. One for the ages, that.

It had been an ill-tempered and sulky PMQs. One that did the Commons no favours. But then there are few depths that Sunak has not shown himself willing to explore. The golden boy repeatedly falling from grace. As we know, though, the grieving process is rarely simple.

* * *

There was some good news for Rishi Sunak. Of a sort. It turned out his wasn't the only government in crisis. Up in Edinburgh, the SNP were determined to show they didn't want to be left out of the ongoing farce of UK politics.

Humza Yousaf's unravelling tenure shows how short and brutish political lives have become

29 APRIL 2024

It must be contagious. Just when you thought Westminster might have the monopoly on incompetence and chaos, along comes Humza Yousaf, Scotland's first minister, saying: 'Hold my Diet Coke.' Anything the Tories can do south of the border, the Scottish National Party can manage north of it. We are in a new political era, when the lifespan of politicians is measured in units of Liz Truss. Or lettuces. So Yousaf reached seven and a half Trusses – or approximately 54 lettuces. Which, all things considered, is fairly respectable. If a lot less than he had hoped.

Last Thursday, Yousaf had consciously uncoupled from the Scottish Green Party. 'You're dumped,' he had announced, looking rather pleased with himself. It was meant to be a power play. To ditch the Greens before they ditched him. A show of strength that the SNP could survive as a minority government without their coalition partner.

Only it turned out that they couldn't. The Tories tabled a vote of no confidence in Yousaf. Labour tabled a vote of no confidence in the SNP government. The Greens, horrified to find they were the dumpees rather than the dumpers, declared that they would be backing the Tory motion. It was like watching a row of dominoes collapse. The SNP leader had forgotten the first rule of politics: how to count. His political survival was balanced on a knife-edge.

Come Monday morning, Yousaf had decided the game was up. Reports of his resignation were circulating long before the announcement that he would be giving a press conference at Bute House, the first minister's official residence, at noon. So what followed was more of a formality than a big reveal. Short and not so sweet. Yousaf walked in, trying not to catch the eyes of the reporters in the audience, and placed his speech on the lectern in front of him. Last week, he had ended the Bute House agreement, he began. It had been the right thing to do. Really? Really? You still think that? Even though you're now having to quit?

It had also been the right thing for the country, he went on. He had hoped to continue working informally with the Greens, but he had failed to understand the extent of their hurt. To put it mildly. I mean, how could he have failed to see that the Greens would react badly to being dismissed in such a callous way? The only person not to see how this was all going to play out was Yousaf himself. The *ingénu*'s *ingénu*. Even so, there had been a way through all of this, he said. He was referring to a deal with Alex Salmond's party, Alba, and their one MSP, Ash Regan, that could have kept him in a job for a while longer. But to have struck one would have gone against his principles.

Hmm. Salmond had said Yousaf was still trying to hammer out a working arrangement with Alba that very morning but had been prevented from doing so by the SNP old guard, who would rather die than be in debt to Salmond. Take your pick of the truth from two not entirely reliable witnesses. So we were where we were. Yousaf would be standing down as and when the SNP had a replacement whom the Scottish parliament would endorse.

We then got the panegyric to both Scotland and himself. It had been the privilege of his life to have served as first minister. Growing up, he never got to see people who looked like him in positions of power. A fair point. He chose not to dwell on the recent troubles of the SNP – the fighting over the motorhome could come later – but instead talked up the positives. He was proud of his record on child poverty and Gaza. And he was certain Scotland was only a hair's breadth away from independence. That sounded more like wishful thinking. In his time in office, he had got to see the best of Scotland. He wished everyone could spend a day in the job. At the current rate of attrition, that might just happen. He bore no ill will towards any of his political opponents. Well, not a lot. And he concluded with a tearful thank-you to his wife and children for all they had done for him. 'My time is up,' he said, and he left without taking any questions.

His leaving became him. Yousaf may not have been the most able of politicians: the SNP wasn't in the best of shape when he took over as leader, and he did a difficult job not particularly well. But at least his departure had a certain dignity and accountability to it. That sets him well apart from any of the political resignations we've seen in Westminster recently.

Take Boris Johnson. A leader who still can't believe he was ultimately rejected by both his party and the country for lying to them. Boris always believed his dishonesty was priced into his tenure. That an exception should be made for him. He left the stage kicking and screaming that he had done nothing wrong. Despite the photographic evidence of parties and the imposition of police fines. Reality was never Johnson's strongest suit.

Then there was Liz Truss. The idiot claiming to be an idiot savant. Wholly unrepentant for crashing the economy or trebling people's mortgage payments. She, too, has never engaged in a moment's self-reflection. Or taken any responsibility. Rather, she has allowed herself to believe that the only thing that went wrong was that she was removed too soon. The answer to the pensions crisis was even more Liz Truss. A sort of inverse form of homeopathy.

And Rishi Sunak is shaping up to be a worthy successor to his two predecessors. He now gets tetchy if asked about anything except his own brilliance. People should just stop asking him when the election will be held. The riff-raff have no right to know. They should just wait and gaze in wonder. And be grateful. Especially grateful. Basically, he has done us all a favour by taking a massive pay cut to become prime minister. We are not worthy.

And what of the Disappearing Rish!? He has now taken to avoiding any unwelcome questions and criticism. His PM Disconnect events used to be open access. An opportunity for us all to see him engage with an audience. Now the TV cameras are no longer welcome, so we miss the opportunity to watch him skip down the populist rabbit hole. First with Rwanda, both a safe country and a deterrent. Now with punishing the mentally ill by cutting off their benefits. So good to have a prime minister who thinks depression is a lifestyle choice. Just pull yourself together.

Give it a few weeks and Yousaf might think he has dodged a bullet.

Electile dysfunction causes outbreak of performance politics in Commons

1 MAY 2024

There's something about the proximity of an election that sends MPs into a tailspin. Especially if they know their party will be taking a hammering. Otherwise moderately intelligent men and women – people who, on a good day, can be relied upon to dress themselves – stand up to make fools of themselves by professing undying loyalty to a lost cause. Generally, by inventing facts to suit themselves. The political wing of the Flat Earth Society. Call it election derangement syndrome. Electile dysfunction.

Even Keir Starmer and Rishi Sunak seemed to be affected. Neither was on top of his game for the last prime minister's questions before Thursday's local elections. They even forgot to personally abuse each other. That bad. Though some may think that's no big deal. Rather, they were merely focused on getting their election messages out, in the mistaken belief that someone might be listening.

This was performance politics. A largely meaningless 40 minutes, whose sole purpose was to fill dead air. Starmer got the better of the exchanges because . . . well, because he always does these days. Rish! is just his not-so-cuddly toy. A plaything. A transitional object. Sunak's real problem is that he just hasn't got a decent tale to tell about anything. Plus he's a bit useless. Everywhere he looks, he's failed.

There's a hint of desperation in everything the government is doing. The absurd publicity stunt of a volunteer offering to have himself returned to Rwanda in exchange for £3,000 in cash and five years' paid accommodation. Just to be able to say the flights have begun, when they obviously haven't. To boast 'THE PLAN IS WORKING', when it isn't. It's hardly a deterrent if people are queueing up to take advantage. Up the cash a bit, and I'm sure you could attract a fair number of benefits claimants, too.

Not to be outdone, the Home Office has released a particularly scuzzy video of detainees being rounded up for deportation. Whatever happened to the UK being a caring society? One that could afford dignity to everyone, even those whom we don't want to stay? In this new UK, refugees are just clickbait. Torture porn. Something to excite Richard Tice and Lee Anderson. Hell, why not give us a bit of tasering action for the director's cut? Next stop, public executions. Come on, you know you want it really.

Starmer began by welcoming his latest acquisition: Dan Poulter, the former Tory MP who defected to Labour last weekend, saying the NHS was not safe in Conservative hands. Rish! pretended not to care. Perhaps he doesn't. He's lost so many MPs in the last year, he's probably immune. Like bomber crews in the Second World War, he just can't afford to become too attached.

'I'm glad to see him,' Sunak said, stifling a yawn. A suggestion that Desperate Dan was a stranger to Westminster. No surprise really. There are dozens of Tory MPs who haven't been anywhere near the Commons for months. Too busy looking for another job. Rish! went on to say that all MPs talked a lot of nonsense from time to time. Hardly the best advert for his own party.

For the rest of the session, Starmer went in hard on pensions. Sunak had promised to get rid of national insurance. How was he proposing to fund the £46 billion shortfall? 'Economics is not the Labour leader's strong-point,' said Rish!. This was a hell of a cheek from someone who appointed a total innumerate as his chancellor. Poor Jeremy Hunt gets a panic attack trying to understand his own bank balance. You can see it in his eyes.

Keir zeroed in on the detail. He could understand these economics well enough. So if the Tories were going to fund the black hole, then presumably Rish! might be thinking of adopting Lord Frost's plan to raise the pension age to 75?

This should have set warning bells ringing for Sunak. Anything Frosty – the idiot's idiot – comes up with is guaranteed to be a disaster. But Rish! didn't bat an eyelid. He's in hock to these quarter-wits. So 75 it is. Hell, why not just say no one can have their pension until they've died? What could go wrong? Not that he will get to decide, because he will be in Santa Monica before long.

'Vote for me,' concluded Starmer. 'Even the Tory candidates think the prime minister is a liability.'

'Vote for me,' replied Sunak. 'Some people love me.'

To prove him right, a handful of the stupidest, most loyal members of the Praetorian Guard among the Tory moronocracy stepped into the breach. First on his feet was the heroically dim Jonathan Gullis. So hopeless that even the Reform Party doesn't want him. He spoke like a five-year-old on amphetamines. Sentences mashed up and impenetrable. Mind you, he doesn't make any more sense when you slow him down. His mind is unendearingly childlike. The suggestion that the Rwanda plan was working appeared to be what he was nudging towards. Which, of course, it isn't. Record numbers of small boats have crossed the Channel this year. Even if the flights do start, only a fraction of these people will be deported. Sunak mumbled some nonsense. He hadn't understood a word Jonny had said either.

Next up was Bill Wiggin. Another collector's item. The man with the single synapse. He was delighted that HS2 wasn't going ahead because that meant some potholes in his drive had been mended and we could all shoot badgers or something. This was why Sunak was the guy who was going to win the next election. So sweet. Not even Rish! is that detached from the real world.

Other Tories piled in. Mostly MPs unknown even unto themselves. Things had never been better; the country was winning under the Conservatives. Just imagine how happy we would be if Sunak had delivered on the other four of his five promises.

But the government was determined that this was to be a good news day. So it had lined up two ministerial statements to reassure us the country was in safe hands. First came the dour Tom Pursglove, to say he was delighted that immigration was falling because he had reduced the number of student and social care visas. So that's the universities and the social care sector screwed. Just pray no one close to you gets dementia.

Then we had Kemi Badenoch, to declare that Brexit had been a total success and that anyone who said otherwise could do one. Thanks to our deal with North Macedonia, we would increase GDP by 0.00002% over 50 years. The Comprehensive and Progressive Trans-Pacific Partnership would be a game-changer, if we were anywhere near Australia. And there was me thinking that the new inspections on goods entering the UK from the EU had just started, costing businesses money they couldn't afford. Remind me to get on message.

* * *

In early May, the country voted in the local elections. Any hopes that the polls were wrong and the Tories could snatch victory from the jaws of defeat were proved to be delusional. Even the Tory chairman, Richard Holden, a man programmed to believe in a fantasy Conservative renaissance, could not come up with anything positive. He began by saying that 2021 had been a high-water mark for the Tories, so some losses were to be expected, but even he couldn't maintain this level of stupidity. He lapsed into silence. Everyone knew what was at stake. This was just the beginning. The general election would be just as bad. (Not that Rishi Sunak had called one yet.)

To add to Sunak's woes, two Tory MPs had defected to Labour. The first, Dan Poulter, had not been that great a surprise. He had always been to the centre of the Tory party. But Natalie Elphicke crossing the floor was a genuine shock. Elphicke was so far to the right, she would have been at home with Nigel Farage and Lee Anderson in the Brexit Party. It has to be said that not every Labour MP welcomed their latest MP, but Keir Starmer felt he was on a roll. He wasn't fussy about who joined his party.

It's Labour's turn to crash and burn as party can't defend Elphicke's defection

9 MAY 2024

Defections tend to be one-day wonders. An awkward photo op with your new party leader. Thirty minutes in the limelight at prime minister's questions. And then, oblivion. Seldom to be seen or heard of again.

Take Christian Wakeford. By all accounts a decent enough bloke. But can you remember anything he has said or done since he jumped ship to Labour? He's just another backbencher. Albeit one with some explaining to do with the constituents who elected him. Likewise Dan Poulter. He was barely seen in the Commons when he was a Tory MP. Don't expect that to change much as he serves out his time as an opposition backbencher before stepping down at the coming election.

Labour must have been hoping that Natalie Elphicke would follow a similar trajectory. Another embarrassing day for the government. Tories wondering if the game is up, if Rishi Sunak can't even keep the right-wing head-bangers in his party onside. But it hasn't quite panned out like this. The reverberations of Nat's defection have continued into a second day. And the embarrassment is almost all Labour's.

Anneliese Dodds, the chair of the Labour Party, must have known she had drawn the short straw when she was allocated the morning media round. It must have been so tempting for her to have phoned in sick. Instead, she took one for the team. Keir Starmer owes her a stiff drink. Anything to blank out the memory. Normally, it's the Tories who crash and burn on these occasions. Today, it was Labour's turn.

A totally self-inflicted wound. Starmer could have told Elphicke: 'Thanks, but no thanks. We appreciate your offer but don't think you're quite the right fit. Why don't you sit as an independent for a while to process your feelings about the Tories properly? Maybe join Labour in six months' time, when you're ready.' Then the party might have claimed the moral high ground and still banked the win. Instead, it got greedy.

So there would be no tame questions on the *Today* programme about hospital waiting lists growing again. Nothing on the Ministry of Defence failing to protect the data of its personnel. Nothing on Nadhim Zahawi stepping down to spend more time with his tax return. Instead, Dodds faced a full 10 minutes on Elphicke. If she had any coherent answers, I must have dozed off.

Amol Rajan warmed up with a few matters of fact. Was Elphicke now a member of the Labour Party? Dodds didn't seem entirely certain, though she assumed she must be. She was sure all proper processes had been followed. So how did she feel about Elphicke's Damascene conversion?

It was a miracle, Dodds said. One of the modern wonders of the world. She couldn't understand why so many people were so sceptical of Elphicke's motives. Why was everyone so keen to bring up her remarks about Marcus Rashford? Her devotion – step in line, hissed Nadine Dorries – to Boris Johnson? Her constituency letter of only last week, in which she rubbished Labour? All these were merely signs of false consciousness. Some childhood trauma she had yet to process. For, deep down, Nat had always been Labour through and through. Dodds leaned closer to the microphone. Labour was a changed party. It was open to everyone. Bring me your thieves and gamblers. No one would be turned away.

That's odd, observed Rajan. Because you forced Labour's North of Tyne mayoral hopeful, Jamie Driscoll, out of the party for sharing a platform with Ken Loach. And Diane Abbott is still not allowed back in, despite having apologised for her anti-Semitic remarks. It rather looked like there was a double standard. You could be as rabidly right-wing as you liked and be welcomed, but there was a higher bar for those on the left. Dodds panicked. Unsure what to say, except the default non-answer. She couldn't say anything about Abbott because the investigation wasn't complete. Did it really take a year to complete the process? It was a very thorough investigation. Hmm.

Rajan moved in for the kill. Of her husband, who was found guilty of sexually assaulting two women, Elphicke had previously had only kind words. He was charming. Attractive to women. Really? I remember him as the previous Dover MP. He seemed utterly charmless and unappealing. Nat saw things differently. He had been trapped by these women. He wasn't really guilty. Was someone with so little empathy for the victims of sexual assault really the kind of MP Labour wanted?

To be fair to Dodds, this question should have been put to the Tory party years ago. Nat's support for her husband is nothing new. But maybe everyone has lower expectations of the Tories. Sexual assault is no big deal in Toryland. She was just being a loyal wife. Family values.

But Dodds had no answer at all. There was no place for this kind of behaviour in the Labour Party. Except there is now. Was that the time? Dodds had places to go, people to see. Starting with her therapist. Nat was seeing hers. In the afternoon, she was strong-armed into an apology.

Later in the programme, Gillian Keegan sounded elated by Elphicke's defection. Couldn't believe they had finally got rid of her. Too toxic even for the Tories. Just another

150 or so more to go and she would have her party back. What the education secretary really wanted to talk about was free speech. Which is odd, because Sunak is actively working to shut it down. Say what you like about David Cameron, Theresa May, Boris Johnson and Liz Truss, but at least they could handle scrutiny. They welcomed all lobby-accredited hacks to their public speaking events. Not Rish!. Rish! can't handle being made fun of by some sketch writers. He is too thin-skinned. So he limits the number of reporters from each media organisation to just one: the political editor. In the last 12 months, I've been admitted to only one event. Democracy in action.

Meanwhile, almost nothing was happening in the Commons. It seldom does these days. The government has almost given up doing anything. Just wasting time before the election. Even Penny Mordaunt looks washed up. She used to use her weekly Thursday session at business questions as her personal leadership campaign. To remind Tory MPs what they could have had. Might have yet. But, today, even she looked beaten. Flat. Her jokes died on her lips. Her heart wasn't in it. This must be the end of days.

Starmer takes it step by step in the phoney war that is a general election campaign

16 MAY 2024

Call it the phoney war. The government has long since stopped governing. Politics is now conducted entirely through the prism of a general election campaign. The Tories go through a weekly relaunch in a desperate hunt for credibility. Something that might allow them to at least save some face. Losing has already been factored into everyone's calculations. But still we don't have a date, as Rishi Sunak hangs on for a miracle. At this rate, by the time the election is announced we're all going to be thoroughly knackered.

On Thursday, it was Labour's turn for a dry run. A no-holds-barred launch of its general election campaign that isn't, because it hasn't officially started. If you get my drift. A chance to meet the government-in-waiting, which looks more like a government than the one that is in office.

It's an upside-down world we live in now. Nothing is quite what it seems. We're just waiting. Waiting. A state of both imminence and immanence. Creeps in this petty pace from day to day. Till the last syllable of recorded time. The way to dusty death.

The difference in ambition between the Tories and Labour could not be more pronounced. Sunak had given

106

his relaunch 7.0 in a tiny room with just a handful of hacks present. He might as well have been in a bunker with his two remaining believers. It felt unhinged. Whoops Apocalypse! If that is the best Rish! has got, he should give up now. At the same time, Esther McVey was upstaging him by declaring war on coloured lanyards. Finger on the pulse, Esther. Finger on the pulse.

Labour's launch at the Backstage Centre in Purfleet was altogether on a bigger scale. Yet somehow far more human. These were ideas and people with whom most could connect. The politics made personal. Though not without its glitches. No one has yet found a way of assembling the entire shadow cabinet and a few assorted guests on a stage without making everyone look as if they were starring in their own hostage video.

This was to be more of a greatest hits concert – each performer got a five-minute slot – played out under a banner of 'My First Steps for Change', alongside a portrait of Keir Starmer, looking every inch the 1980s catalogue model. Check out those slacks. Though whatever you do, don't call it a 'pledge card'. Any resemblance to 1997 was entirely coincidental.

First up was Angela Rayner. 'This is Labour's first steps,' she began. Just in case we had missed this. First Steps, mind. As opposed to the First Missions, which Starmer launched more than a year ago, and which most of us could barely remember now. Though the missions had not been entirely forgotten. Just, shall we say, somewhat superseded. An occupational hazard in a never-ending election campaign. Let's call it a 'refocus'.

Thank you and goodnight, said Angela, as she introduced Rachel Reeves to tee up step one. This amounted to a commitment to not crash the economy. It's a sign of how far we've fallen as a country that a promise not to make everyone worse off provokes an outburst of gratitude from voters. Tears of relief that we won't all become destitute. Stability is no longer boring; it's a lifestyle aspiration. But that wasn't all. We still hoped to become the fastest-growing economy in the G7, but let's just take one thing at a time.

Cut to the video screen. A property developer and the Boots CEO declaring their undying love for Rachel. And why not? Even I would look like an economic god compared with Jeremy Hunt. Then it was Wes Streeting's turn. Normally, Wes can work a crowd, but maybe he felt confined by the format. His delivery was strangely detached as he promised to reduce hospital waiting lists.

The impressive list of guests continued with Nathaniel, a teacher with a terminal cancer diagnosis who had also done a turn at last year's Labour Party conference. He was the first to get a proper standing ovation. Then Mike Tapp, the Labour candidate for Dover. He could talk border security. And perhaps reassure everyone there was life after Natalie Elphicke.

Then came Ed Miliband. He, too, spoke with passion. Not to mention a sense of déjà vu. Images of the Ed Stone must have been flashing through his mind. If only he had tempted hubris. But then 2015 was a lifetime ago. Just stick to energy, Ed. Cheaper and greener. Job done. Yvette Cooper and Bridget Phillipson were equally competent as they talked through their first steps. No great flourishes. Just sticking to the scripts. This was no place for prima donnas.

Just as it felt as if the tempo was about to flag, the volume got turned up. A video of Keir in various Action Man poses, an introduction from a former Tory voter, and then the man himself. The jacketless, tieless Keir with rolled-up sleeves. Poised to deliver for the country. It wasn't subtle. There were no big arguments here. Those have long since been fought and won. He has already persuaded more than enough people that the Tories are not fit to govern.

This was all about getting the message across. It was like listening to the news on the radio. First tell everyone what you are going to tell them. Then tell them what you want to tell them. Finish by telling them again what you've already told them. Because what we got were the First Steps spelled out all over again, twice. Along with the word 'change'. Time for a change. A leader with his shadow cabinet literally behind him. Something of which Sunak can only dream.

Starmer ended with questions from the media. In the past, this has been where he has been at his most awkward. Now he seemed entirely relaxed. Happy with his team, confident in his message. Ready to take questions from anyone. Unlike the Tetchmeister. Was he being ambitious enough? Read his lips. These were just the First Steps.

What had happened to the more Labour policies, like workers' rights? He was here to park his tanks on the Tories' lawns. Most of his six First Steps were what any government would aspire to. He was here to get elected, not join a protest movement. Wasn't it all a bit Tony Blair? He should be so lucky. Blair had won three elections on the bounce.

Ninety minutes in – an age for any normal political shindig – and people were getting restless. Starmer wrapped things up. Time to head home. The Tories may be falling apart, but Labour now had all its ducks in a row. Bring on the election. Bring on the real war.

* * *

Weird. You wait months – years even – for a general election that you know is coming, but when it is called you are still blindsided. It had been widely assumed that Rishi Sunak would hang on for as long as possible before announcing a general election. Into the late autumn at least. It wasn't as if he was ever going to get another chance of being prime minister, so why not get a full two years in Downing Street on your CV rather than just 18 months?

But Rishi surprised us all. No one knew quite why. There was no secret polling suggesting the Tories were closing the gap on Labour. Nor was anyone predicting the Conservatives would slump to an even worse defeat in November. Rather, it seemed as if Sunak had just had enough. Fed up with delaying the inevitable, he chose to put himself and his party out of their collective misery.

Cringing in the rain: soggy Rish! kick-starts his farewell tour

22 MAY 2024

Things can only get wetter. The humiliation. Even when Rishi Sunak is totally down on his luck, he can't buy an even break. This was meant to be his last hurrah. The prime minister's final act of pomp and circumstance, standing at the lectern outside Downing Street to inform an ungrateful nation that he was calling a general election for 4 July.

Only it wasn't just raining. It was chucking it down. Soak the Rich. Soak the Rish!. Sunak was determined to front it out. To not give in and miss out on his photo op. But he looked fed up even as he appeared at the front door. Five minutes later, he looked thoroughly miserable. Borderline catatonic. His suit drenched, his speech in rags. And all the while Steve Bray played Labour's 1997 election theme song, D:Ream's 'Things Can Only Get Better', at full volume.

Call it an admission of defeat. The moment that Rish! realised he had run out of road. All hope gone. It wasn't meant to be this way. Only good things had ever happened to him up till now. The boy in the gilded cage on whom success and wealth had been endlessly bestowed. Being prime minister was supposed to come easy to him. For 18 months Sunak had been hoping against hope. Praying for a miracle. If only he believed hard enough, he could turn things around. But on Wednesday he realised the game was up. There was no cavalry coming to the rescue. Wishing it could not make it true.

He had planned to wait till November, but now that just seemed pointless. With his luck, the country would be in an even worse state by then. Even the IMF thought there would be no room for tax cuts in the autumn. All he could offer was more pain. So he'd get out while he was still young. He had no real friends here. Certainly none among his MPs. The rest of the summer in Santa Monica lay ahead. California Dreaming.

Rish! peered towards the cameras through the sheeting rain. The optics couldn't have been worse. A desperate man for desperate times. Cosmic synergy. He started by reminiscing about the Covid years. How he had single-handedly saved the entire country. Yes, and some gratitude would be nice. He seemed to think Covid had been a happier time for everyone. When everyone had pitched in together. Apart from Lady Mone. Sunak seemed to have forgotten that tens of thousands of people had lost loved ones. That this had been a time of great unhappiness for many people.

'I would never leave you alone in your darkest hour,' he said. Though he seemed happy enough, in a despairing kind of way, to leave us now. For he was about to kick-start his farewell tour in politics. He would disappear with little trace. A prime minister of almost no significance. A footnote in the history books. Alongside Liz Truss.

Sunak came to the bit where someone had written: 'Try to look a little bit cheerful.' But he couldn't even manage a hint of a smile. This was a speech to be endured through gritted teeth. It's not every day a prime minister gets to broadcast his own death knell.

The economy. Hey, that wasn't as bad as everyone had feared. I mean, borrowing might be at near record levels, but inflation was down to 2%, which meant we were all getting more and more broke a little more slowly. Rish! had never quite got his head around the fact that prices didn't go down when inflation did. But this was a prime minister who delivered for the people. That's why he was proud to say that his was the first government to have lowered living standards over the course of the parliament.

'My plan is working,' he mumbled. No attempt made to keep the disbelief out of his voice. To think that we're going to hear this rubbish on repeat for the next six weeks. His plan is working very well. For him. His family have racked up another £120 million over the last year. Enough to make him richer than the King. But perhaps not so well for the rest of us. Maybe we should all have tried a bit harder. As should he. He's kept only one of his five promises. And that was with no help from him.

Then the scary bit of the speech. The world was completely fucked. We were all going to die. And all Rish! asked for was to be allowed to carry on for another five years. Or less, if civilisation as we knew it ended before that. This was just weird. Sunak had taken no interest in global security until he discovered it last week for his seventh relaunch. So if everything was that terrible, why hadn't he done something about it before?

Now Rish! was just desperate to get to the end. To get indoors, out of the rain and the cold. It was all he could do not to shiver. To burst into tears. All pretence at coherence had been long abandoned. Because after telling us how dangerous the world was, he tried to persuade us that everything was amazing. We were stopping the boats. No, we weren't. There are far more than last year. People were going to Rwanda for extended holidays. Someone, talk him down.

We limped to the end. Labour had no plan, he said. Well, that's odd. Because anyone with a memory could have sworn Keir Starmer had launched his pledge cards only a week ago. And the Tories had taken them so seriously that they had sent out a press release with some fictitious costings for them. Not for the first time over the last two years, Labour has been way ahead of the Tories. And not just in the polls. But then we have long since slipped through the looking-glass. Sunak is an unwitting truth-teller. Guilty of the failings he describes in his opponents. He ground to a halt. The rain had won. He turned his back to go inside, and the country felt a mixture of indifference and relief. Indifference to Rish!'s exit, relief that we were to be put out of our misery.

Moments later, Starmer appeared on TV bathed in two Union Jacks. This was his time. The waiting was over. He was ready. We were ready. Bring it on. Meanwhile, in another corner of London, Paula Vennells couldn't believe her luck. Her worst day at the Post Office inquiry had just been erased from the public consciousness. Much like her memory.

* * *

The death spiral had begun. A six-week election campaign with only one outcome. It wasn't long before many Tory MPs decided that enough was enough. They could sense the public mood and chose to stand down as candidates. Far better that than go through the humiliation of losing a seat they had represented for years. No one wanted to be the Michael Portillo moment.

Meanwhile, Nigel Farage was considering his options. To stand as a candidate or just watch from the sidelines.

Nige had previously fought and lost seven seats, and his ego couldn't stand another loss. But his Reform Party was polling well, taking support from the Tories, and he didn't want to miss out on his big moment, if and when it came.

Rish!'s warehouse visit takes the biscuit for talking down to voters

23 MAY 2024

A psychotherapist would have a field day with Rishi Sunak. His pathology isn't quite as obvious as with Boris Johnson or Liz Truss, but it is there nonetheless. Scratch the heavily defended surface and you will find a suitable case for treatment. There's the overbearing sense of entitlement, combined with a constant craving to be noticed. A man with so little self-worth his only validation comes from others. There's his persistent tetchiness; the irritation at not being properly understood. He needs to be appreciated. Needs people to be grateful to him. For everyone to realise they only exist so he can do them a favour. That is our purpose in life: satellites to orbit Rish!.

But the real work is to be found in Sunak's self-hatred. Forget the failing upwards. Forget the £750 million in the family kitty. Those are mere distractions. What you are left with is a paradox. Why has the man who could have anything made it his life's ambition to do something at which he is so obviously unsuited? One where his short-comings are so ruthlessly and publicly exposed?

As prime minister, Rish! has yet to find something he can do well. Not being Truss no longer really counts. That only bought him a six-month honeymoon. Of his five pledges he has failed on four, and the other one was nothing to do with him. Yet still he cannot let go. Carries on feeding his illness under the umbrella delusion of public service. Relies on the non-existent applause to mask his self-loathing. The kindest thing any of us could do is vote him out of office.

But for now there is the general election that cannot be won. The election Sunak reluctantly called because he had run out of options. Backed into a corner by his own uselessness. Things may be utterly shit now, but they would probably be even more shit in the autumn. The election that almost no Conservative MP wanted right now. They needed all the time they could get to line up future employment.

Sunak looks like a man alone. At his opening event in the toilets of the ExCeL centre in London on Wednesday evening, his cabinet lined up behind him. All looked lost in their private grief. Like mourners at their own funeral. They were all in shock. They had always known their political careers were coming to an end; they just hadn't expected it to be this soon. None was capable of speech. Falling, falling, falling into the existential abyss.

The last person standing on Team Sunak is Sunak himself. His self-hatred urging him ever onwards to his final immolation. So first thing on Thursday he was out and about on the airwaves, trying to find the best version of himself. Predictably enough, it all ended in tears as his irritation got the better of him. He just couldn't bear it when Nick Robinson started contradicting him. When his obvious lies were mirrored back to him. That he imagines he is going to win the TV debates is yet another manifestation of how deluded he is.

Still, there was always a ride in a private jet to cheer him up. The UK's carbon footprint is going to take a hell of a beating from Sunak over the next six weeks. So, an hour or so later, Rish! found himself in a biscuit distribution centre in Ilkeston that had been in security lockdown since Monday in anticipation of the prime minister's visit. Sunak's contribution to national productivity.

Nothing had been left to chance. Especially the audience. Alongside a few miserable-looking employees – no one likes to be associated with failure – Tory HQ had packed the 25-weak crowd with a few Tory activists disguised in hi-vis jackets and meant to look like ordinary workers. Rish! went into his default campaigning mode. That's to say he started up the condescending, entitled nasal whine. He may be his very own mini-me, but he has yet to find someone to whom he doesn't automatically talk down. He can't help himself.

Let the patronising begin. It was like this. Right? OK? Are you listening, little people? Well, let me talk a little slower because you're all probably a bit thick. You are from up north, after all. Do we want to go back to square one?

Er, no. That's why Labour are 21 points ahead in the polls. It was your lot that put us at square one. Do you think we are halfwits? Actually, don't answer that one.

We need a bold future, and I'm a bold kind of guy, he said. That's why I've come up with a Rwanda plan that doesn't work. And 15 other European countries have decided to leave the EU and refuse to recognise the European courts by declaring unsafe countries to be safe. It's hard to know what is worse. That he believes this shit. In which case he needs urgent help. Or that he's just utterly cynical.

Having basically delivered the standard stump speech he had given twice the day before, there was just time to take questions from the stooges. Still, he's nothing if not equal opportunities, because he treated them like halfwits too. I've brought in the smoking ban, he said. No, you haven't. The bill has fallen because you called the election. For a man desperate for a political legacy, he's his own worst enemy.

Then it was time to stretch out his legs in the private jet for a trip to Glamorgan for more of the same. This time in a brewery. Piss-ups and all that. Obviously, it was a car crash. Mr Man of the People managed to alienate everyone by forgetting that Wales hadn't qualified for the Euros. Next stop Scotland, and then Northern Ireland tomorrow. By which time he will have hacked off the entire UK. Great start, Rish!.

Meanwhile, Keir Starmer was kicking off Labour's campaign at Gillingham Football Club in Kent. He, too, gave his usual election number, with a subtle difference. Where Sunak had been all about 'Give me your vote, vote for me or I won't exist,' Starmer was more collaborative. This was our vote. So use it to effect your own change. It made a pleasant change to be treated like a person.

Down in central London, the Reform leader, Richard Tice, was grappling with his own internal contradiction: that one of the most off-putting things about the Reform Party is himself. Dicky is instantly dislikeable. He looks untrustworthy. The sort of man who you might find on the shopping channel, trying to flog you an air fryer that would fall apart within a week.

Even Nigel Farage can't be arsed with Dicky any more. He won't be standing as a candidate and may drop in for an hour's campaigning one day if it's sunny and Donald Trump doesn't need him. Still, Reform looks likely to take chunks out of the Tory vote. So Dicky has his uses.

Jimmy Dimly shows us how to serve by fronting up latest Tory gimmick

26 MAY 2024

When the BBC announced its line-up for Laura Kuenssberg's Sunday politics show, there was a large blank beside the Tory part. To be confirmed, it said ominously. Hardly a surprise these days. At the current accelerated rate of attrition, it must be increasingly hard to find a cabinet minister or Conservative backbencher who has definitely decided to stand for election again.

On Wednesday, Michael Gove had declared his wholehearted support for Rishi Sunak's surprise election announcement; two days later, he had decided to spend more time with his crack den. That's our Mikey. On brand to the very last. Saying one thing, doing another. Treachery runs in his veins. Even the prime minister looks as if he isn't sure whether to fight this election. His body language during the first three days of the campaign has suggested a man yearning for Santa Monica. He only gets out of bed through a misplaced sense of duty.

So there was an air of excitement on Sunday morning to see who was going to turn up for the Tories. Come 8.25 a.m., the home secretary walked into the Sky studio. James Cleverly had decided – for now, at any rate – that he was still onboard for this week of the campaign. He might as well get his futile gesture in early on. Plenty of time to quietly drop out later.

Still. Call it a win for the Tories. Hard to believe, but Jimmy Dimly is something of a catch for the government these days. Obviously, he's not very bright – which of them is? – but he's tenacious and has an air of confidence that can only come from someone unaware of just how desperate the situation is. He's also incredibly loyal. A natural-born follower. A slightly more charismatic Tom Pursglove. Someone who treats his synaptic disorders with homeopathy. It's the closest to memory he gets.

Jimmy D was wheeled out for Trevor Phillips on Sky and Laura Kuenssberg on the BBC. Both interviews started with questions on the Tories' latest gimmick: the return of national service. Truly, the idiocracy has excelled itself this time. You can sense the desperation in Tory HQ. SOS! We need a policy to attract Reform voters. Something that will remind the over-80s of VE Day. But save bring back hanging for when the polls get even worse.

For reasons best known to themselves, Trevor and Laura insisted on taking national service seriously. Rather than a badly thought-through gimmick that would never see the light of day. Private Jimmy Dimly stood to attention. This was the nation's chance to serve. To make good on the divisions the Tories had created in society over the past 14 years with some mandatory volunteering. Rather sweetly, he was totally oblivious to the contradiction.

Here's how it would work. Some 18-year-olds could make up the numbers in the armed forces, which the Tories had depleted, with a year's service. Obviously, there weren't enough military personnel to train these new conscripts, so they would have to learn to discipline themselves. And those who didn't fancy killing people could maybe learn to be paramedics or join the police for 25 weekends a year. Unbelievably, Jimmy D managed to say all this with a straight face.

Try to think of it this way. Most 18-year-olds are merely criminals in waiting. We all know they are going to be guilty of something sooner or later, so why not punish them in advance? For thought crimes, if nothing else. So this way they got their 'Community Payback' service in early. Credit in the bank. And the genius of the scheme was that as special constables, they would be well placed to arrest themselves. An ingenious way to lower the crime statistics.

Talking of which, Laura pulled up the figures. Knife crime up 7%, gun crime up 7%, shoplifting up 37% and robbery up 13%. That was all because of Sadiq Khan's London, Dimly insisted. Er . . . these are national figures, Kuenssberg pointed out. Jimmy D just ignored her, repeating that this was all London. Most shopkeepers in Tooting had given up trying to get customers to pay for anything. They just had signs saying: 'Come and nick what you want.' Nor could you move in Hyde Park without people stabbing one another.

You cannot argue with this level of stupidity. Though by now JD was on a roll. The fact that more and more small boats were crossing the Channel was a sign that the Rwanda deterrent was working. Sometimes we all just have to face facts: the home secretary isn't very good at basic arithmetic. Or anything really.

Later on Kuenssberg, we got the shadow chancellor, Rachel Reeves. A brief oasis of calm and sanity. Laura tried to get her to make some unfunded spending commitments, but Reeves stuck closely to her brief. Which was to look normal and not commit any news. Job pretty much done.

Rachel didn't say anything remotely memorable. She just reminded everyone that the country was in a far worse state than when Labour had come to power in 1997, and people shouldn't expect miracles. Labour promises to do the basics well. More hospital appointments and more teachers. After that, we'll see where we are. It beats lowering living standards over the course of a parliament.

Over on Sky, Phillips looked horrified as Nigel Farage went full-on racist. Not the kind of thing you expect before 10 a.m. on a Sunday morning. Every problem the country faced was down to the Muslims. None of them loved the place. They were the worst kind of foreigners. People who didn't even bother to speak English. Nige has never found a Muslim to whom he could speak.

Stuck in traffic? That's all down to the Muslims. They come over here, have the cheek to buy cars and then clog up our streets, bringing our towns and cities to a stand-still. Waiting for an operation? It's because Muslims have queue-barged their way to the front. Muslim doctors were prioritising Muslim patients.

Farage looked across at Phillips. You lot are OK, I sup-pose, he shrugged. You West Indians speak English and like cricket. He's clearly never met a Pakistani or Indian. Yes, West Indians would be allowed to stay, Nige conceded graciously. But Reform was committed to eradicating Muslims from the UK.

Trevor tried to remind Nige that he had been respon-sible for Brexit and that immigration had soared since the referendum. But Nige has never taken responsibil-ity for anything. He's just an unpleasant gobshite. If this is the Reform message, then the election is going to get a lot more toxic yet. The sooner Nige moves to the US the better.

Lights, camera, Farage: Nige just couldn't bear to be left out

3 JUNE 2024

Alas, poor Dicky, I knew him well. Richard Tice and Nigel Farage had already given two press conferences the previous week. Both times they had been given equal billing. Even though everyone but Dicky T knew who the real star was. On Monday, all pretence had been pushed aside. Out came the op note. Nigel Farage was to make an 'emergency election announcement'. Tice wasn't even mentioned as an afterthought. Even though he was probably paying for the pleasure.

Dicky was determined not to be left out, though. The man with no charisma or personal warmth relegated once more to Nige's warm-up act. The man on the downward trajectory. Soon he will be relegated to doorman. I'm not sure if Tice even convinces himself. His patter is all third-rate Farage. The sort of thing you might get if you typed 'Write me a bad Nigel speech' into ChatGPT. Reform was 'moving into eighth gear', he said. Really? Some of us were losing the will to live.

Then the ultimate humiliation. Dicky tried to sound upbeat as he revealed that Farage was to take over as leader of the Reform Party. Most people outside Westminster probably assumed he already was. In reality, if not in terms of job description. Just watch the body language. You couldn't miss the pathos. A boardroom coup as Nige realised Tice wasn't up to the job. Deep down even Tice knew he wasn't. People just don't like him. Don't warm to him. He even had to hand over his debit card to Nige.

Moments later, Farage took to the stage. Lights, cameras, action. These are the moments he lives for. Right at the centre of things. He'd be lost without them. Imagine going to a pub and no one recognising him. The unbearable lightness of his being. Nige began by doing a reprise of the speech he had given at the same venue last week. The election was boring. Labour was going to win. He hated them. The Tories were useless. He hated them, too. Most kids didn't know what D-Day was. Like he would ever have enlisted. His patriotism has its limits.

Time for the reveal. The worst-kept secret. He was going to stand as a candidate in Clacton after all. So what had changed? 'I felt guilty,' he said. Guilty that he was letting down all the little people who couldn't survive without him. Who had been begging him to get involved. Guilty that he had left the Reform Party in the hands of a bunch of charmless nonentities. He was the talent. The celebrity. The star of his own movie. Lie back in the warm bath of his narcissism. He just couldn't bear to be left out. To be ignored.

Thereafter his speech rambled somewhat. He didn't have any more to say, but he wasn't going to let that stop him. Every media outlet was waiting on his every word. He was going to spin this out for as long as possible. Nothing worked. Everything was in decline. Curiously, he never mentioned how he would kick-start the economy or fix the NHS. Other than by stopping immigration and being unpleasant to Muslims. That should do it.

But Nige was in his happy place. All stardust and no responsibility. He's quite happy to break anything, less keen to mend it. Happy to channel the disaffection with empty promises. He would be the official opposition in the next parliament. The biggest party in five years' time. Yup, with Dicky as chancellor and David Bull as foreign secretary. The men in orange. Can't see the problem. Though Rishi Sunak could. This was his worst nightmare. A Reform Party with Nige at the helm was a far more worrying proposition. A Tory meltdown was now on the cards.

From one narcissist to another. What is it with Kemi Badenoch? What makes her so angry? Even the smallest challenge sends her spiralling into an uncontained fury. Put her in front of a mirror, and her reflection will start yelling: 'What are you looking at?' It can't be any way to live. Where are the beta blockers when you need them?

Kemi is something of an outlier. While other MPs at some point reluctantly come to terms with their limitations, Badenoch never gives an inch. She has never met anyone whom she didn't think to be much stupider than her. And she never hesitates in telling them. She has yet to be wrong about anything. Hers is a binary world.

Like almost everyone with a massive ego, Kemi has very little self-worth. Her arrogance is her shopfront, set up to conceal her insecurities. Because she's not nearly as bright as she thinks she is. So her default mode of communication is talking down. To belittle people in a one-way conversation. She can't help herself. She does it to other MPs in the Commons. Presumably she also does it to cabinet colleagues. She certainly does it to the little people. Charm school is a foreign country.

Unbelievably, though, Badenoch is the favourite to replace Sunak as party leader after the election. There again, of late the Tories have had something of a love affair with psychologically damaged leaders: Theresa May, Boris Johnson, Liz Truss and Rish! himself. Mr Tetchy. The ultimate abusive, codependent relationship. So maybe Kemi will fit in just nicely. Though it will make a change to have a leader whose natural talent for winning over voters is to insult them.

Like so many of her cabinet colleagues, Badenoch had been sidelined for the first week and a half of the campaign. Whether this was because Rish! couldn't stand the competition or because he was dimly aware of her toxic reputation is anyone's guess. But whereas most have been happy to let Sunak be the fall guy for the inevitable disaster, Kemi has been raging about being sidelined. Deprived of her chance to seek out new ways of being rude.

Come Monday morning, Badenoch was unleashed onto the airwaves to talk about the latest Tory promise: a change to the Equalities Act. And the unfortunate person on the receiving end was Mishal Husain, on Radio 4's *Today* programme. It was combative from the start, Kemi seemingly furious that Husain had actually done her homework. Badenoch did not want to be engaged on the details of the proposed changes. She appeared not to have given them a moment's thought. Of more interest to her was a quick soundbite in an ongoing culture war. To create a wedge between her party and Labour. Though in reality Labour and the Tories are not so far apart on trans issues these days.

Kemi got angrier and angrier. Husain never less than polite. 'You're trying to be difficult,' Badenoch snapped. Mishal wasn't. She was just curious how the law was going to be enacted without any legal paperwork. Were people going to be able to determine sex solely on the basis of their personal prejudices? They were. We finished with Kemi calling Mishal 'trivial and unserious'. Code for 'I'm out of my depth and I can't admit I'm wrong'. Husain sighed and ended the interview. She had taken one for the team.

Keir wins the applause in the TV debate, while the audience openly laughs at Tetchy Rish!

4 JUNE 2024

It was another night of broken sleep. Fever dreams of Nigel Farage tormented him. That wide crocodile smile. Siren promises to the disaffected. The narcissistic orange glow.

Worse, Rishi Sunak had even woken to the man himself being interviewed by Mishal Husain on Radio 4. Would no one rid him of this turbulent fraud? Now Nige sounded irritable. Angry that someone was daring to ask him about policy details and not just blowing smoke up his arse.

Rish! forced himself to get out of bed and made a coffee. He checked the news headlines. The latest catastrophic polls predicting a wipeout for the Tories. Still, it wasn't all bad. Jeremy Hunt and Grant Shapps looked on course to lose their seats. Good. He had never rated them. They were just all that was left in the talent puddle. Then there had been the latest party political broadcast. Another total fuck-up. What clown had put the Union Jack the wrong way up? The distress signal. There had been too many Freudian slips for his liking.

His ruminations were interrupted by the arrival of Oliver Dowden, here for the final preparations for the first televised debate, which would take place that evening. Olive was supposed to be role-playing Keir Starmer. It hadn't been going well. Rish! detested Starmer because . . . because he had the air of a winner. Men like him weren't meant to succeed. And try as he might, he couldn't bring himself to have any feelings for Dowden. He was just too wet. Too useless.

'I have a plan that is working,' he said. 'Starmer will take us back to square one.'

'You're so right,' mumbled Olive. 'I will take you back to square one.'

'You're not meant to be agreeing with me . . .'

'I'm sorry. I just can't help being a sycophant.'

This wasn't going well. It was time for a last pep talk from Graham Davies, his motivational media coach. The man who had worked wonders with Kemi Badenoch. Had managed to turn her from the woman whom almost everyone disliked to the woman whom everyone disliked. Result. Graham gave him a reassuring hug.

'How are you feeling?' asked Graham.

'I have a plan that is working . . .' said Sunak.

'Yes. Quite. But how are you feeling?'

'Um . . .'

'I get it. You're nervous. That's understandable. But try to reframe it. Look at this as an opportunity. At present no one believes a word you say. This gives you an enormous freedom to say any old crap. You have nothing to lose because nobody is going to vote for you anyway. Especially after Nigel . . .'

'Don't mention that word.'

'Sorry.'

Rish! gave a half-smile. He was as ready as he would ever be. Time to dig out his extra-short lucky trousers. The Tory spinners were already saying he had won the debate before it had even started. In the spin room situated in the *Coronation Street* Experience – write your own soap opera gags – Victoria Atkins tried to claim that Sunak was 'actually very funny'. He keeps it well hidden.

Cue . . . action. The opening credits rolled to reveal a set more suited to a game show. Keeping it real. Starmer behind a lectern on the left, Sunak on the right, host Julie Etchingham to one side.

First, the opening statements that we've all heard dozens of times before. Keir saying 'change' every other word and reminding everyone that the Tories' record over the last 14 years is indefensible. Sunak saying that he has a plan and that it is working. Even he didn't sound as if he believed it. Cutting taxes by increasing them. Cutting waiting lists by increasing them.

Then to the questions. First Paula from Huddersfield on the cost of living. Rish! insisted that he knew the strain people were under: £700 million doesn't go quite as far as it used to. A brief mention of the furlough scheme – the last time the country liked him. A plea for gratitude. Forget Liz Truss, forget your misery. Trust the plan. Labour were going to increase taxes by £2,000 per family.

Weirdly, Starmer didn't refute this figure till much later in the debate, allowing Sunak to repeat it six times. What he did have, though, was empathy. He understood how hard it was. He also delivered the killer line. If the plan was working, why didn't Sunak delay the election until we could see the benefits? The reality was that things were about to get worse.

The next 45 minutes descended into something of a free-for-all, despite Etchingham's best efforts to maintain control. Good telly, but a crap debate. It was almost inevitable that Tetchy Rishi would make an appearance. That version always does when he's under pressure. Being found out. He started getting snippy, continually talking over Starmer. It was a terrible look. Far better to have turned off Sunak's microphone for a bit.

We raced through questions on the NHS, education, tax, defence and climate change. Keir got far more of the applause, while Rish! died a death as the audience groaned and openly laughed at him. First on health, then on national service. His only tactic was to keep saying that he was the one with the ideas. Even if they were all completely rubbish. Designed to make headlines for a day. Not to be implemented. Heaven forbid.

It was something of a relief when it was all over. Performative politics, nothing more. Light entertainment. Sound and fury, signifying nothing. Both sides would say they had won, because that's what always happens. As far as the studio audience was concerned, Starmer shaded it. But most of the country was probably watching Netflix.

No more Mr Nice Guy: Rish! is embracing Boris Johnson's brand of making stuff up

5 JUNE 2024

It reeked of desperation. There again, Rishi Sunak has a lot to be desperate about. Two weeks into the election campaign, and there's no shift in the opinion polls. If anything, they are getting worse for the Tories.

So the prime minister has reached the point where any old lie will do. Not bothered if it all falls apart the next day. Anything to grab a headline in the right-wing press. Fooling some of the people some of the time is now as good as it gets for Rish!.

Sunak used to pride himself on being Mr Integrity. A politician you could rely on to tell the difficult truths. That Sunak has long since been discarded, and his credibility is on the line after an increasingly unattractive display from the prime minister in Tuesday's televised debate, which saw him at his tetchiest, constantly talking over Keir Starmer and the host, Julie Etchingham.

Maybe Rish! thought his luck was in, as Starmer took half an hour to engage with his accusations that Labour had planned a £2,000 tax rise on every family. But even when Keir did wake up from his comatose start, Sunak kept up the attack. These were tax rises that had been verified independently by civil servants working in the Treasury, he said. Again and again. He even sounded as if he believed it. Mostly because he needed to. He feeds off scraps these days.

Nor is Rish! too bothered about who he takes down with him. Any collateral damage is a price worth paying in the futile endeavour of trying to stay in power. He has long since stopped thinking of his cabinet ministers as people. They have been reduced to pawns in a losing game. Apparatchik automata sent out to destroy their own reputations as well as his. The energy secretary, Claire Coutinho, must have been devastated to find out she was the chosen lamb to the slaughter for Wednesday's media round. Of all the days to have been given. Obliged to indulge in the fantastical. To celebrate the magnificence of all things Rish!. The man who could do no wrong.

In fairness, there is no real malice to Claire. She isn't a Michael Gove-like character. But then there isn't very much of anything to Claire. Her rise through the Tory ranks has been shrouded in mystery. The kindest explanation is that she isn't as unpleasant as her peers. Though neither is there any discernible ability. Her synapses are so few, you can hear them rattle. Departmental questions are an ordeal for her and everyone else. It's like watching a car crash. She does, though, have the loyalty of a particularly dim pet. If Rish! has told her that Rish! is brilliant, who is she to argue?

Shortly before 8 a.m., Coutinho was talking to the BBC's Justin Webb on the *Today* programme. The only real topic of conversation was the £2,000 tax lie. Claire's limitations quickly came to the fore. Starmer had taken a while to deny the claim, so therefore it must be true.

Please, someone put her out of her misery. A lie does not become true just because someone doesn't refute it. That's not how the world works. All it proved was that Keir hadn't been quite as quick-witted as most of the viewers.

Webb was just getting started. The figures had been cobbled together using dodgy information supplied by Tory spin doctors to make them look as bad as possible. Not at all, said Nice But Dim Claire. She had been specifically told that Treasury civil servants had decided of their own free will to investigate random Labour policies. And had asked the permanent secretary – the top civil servant in the Treasury – to sign their figures off. Something the permanent secretary was more than happy to do as he was intensely relaxed about breaking the civil service code and pissing off his future employers in the Labour Party.

'The thing is,' said Claire, failing to realise she was dying on her feet, 'if anything, everyone had fallen over backwards to portray the figures in the best possible light.' As you do. If anything, the £2,000 was an underestimation. So what was the real figure? Coutinho hummed. Maybe twenty ten thousand. Justin also pointed out that the £2,000 was spread over four years – something Sunak hadn't mentioned. Ah, yes. But a leap year came every four years, so it was like a year really. It was as if we were dealing with a halfwit.

Coutinho went on to praise Jeremy Hunt for his brilliant handling of the economy – something no one said ever; Jezza is the least serious chancellor in living memory – before getting confused as to whether energy bills would be going up in the autumn. They would, but somehow they wouldn't. Yeah but no but yeah but no. Something tells me that is the last time Claire ever appears on the *Today* programme. A relief for all of us. But for her in particular.

But her ordeal was not quite over. There was still an appearance on *Good Morning Britain*, by which time a letter sent to Labour by the permanent secretary, James Bowler, had been leaked, saying his staff had been forced to do the costings under duress, based on dodgy data. That the figures were totally unreliable and he had never signed them off. In short, Sunak had lied through his teeth. And forced Coutinho to do the same.

Coutinho's response was to pretend nothing had happened. The letter wasn't a letter. It was a mirage. Bowler hadn't known what he was writing. He had been unwell. Just because everyone in the Treasury disowned it and the working assumptions were all made up, it didn't mean the figure of £2,000 wasn't entirely accurate. I'd hate to see the state of her family's finances.

Yet again Sunak had proved himself to be the politician who can't do politics. By telling one of the most egregious lies in any election live on TV, he has made himself vulnerable for the remaining four weeks of the campaign. The first question will always be: 'Are you a liar?' To which the only answer is: 'Yes.' His honesty is now up for grabs. His reputation little better than Boris Johnson's.

For his part, Rish! has temporarily abandoned the campaign for the D-Day commemorations. He read out Montgomery's address to the troops from 80 years ago about sacrifice and service. Something Sunak knows little about. If war broke out, you couldn't imagine Rish! being in the first wave of the Normandy landings. He'd be at home on his computer, betting on a crash on the German stock exchange. Keeping it real.

* * *

June 6th marked the 80th anniversary of D-Day. An important day of national commemoration. A day on which normal election campaigning would be suspended. Rishi Sunak had a simple job: to show up, pay his respects to both the living and the dead, and stand side by side with the leaders of the other nations that took part in the Second World War. It turned out that Rishi couldn't even get that right . . .

There's no distance these Conservative heroes won't travel to serve . . . themselves

6 JUNE 2024

Just for one day the election campaign took a back seat as the country's eyes turned towards northern France, where the commemorations for the D-Day landings and the Normandy campaign were taking place. A time to remember both those who came back and those who didn't.

No one came out of the war unscarred. My dad could never speak of the horrors he had witnessed, nor the gallantry that won him a Distinguished Service Cross. Here were the last survivors of the war generation, most of them 100 years old or more. They had fought for our freedom. A freedom that many now take for granted.

So what better time to step back and honour a couple of Conservative heroes who have overcome similarly insuperable odds to become candidates in this election? Men who have made the ultimate sacrifice for their party. Men who have laid down their friends for their lives. We will remember them.

Step forward the Conservative Party chair. Up until a few weeks ago, Richard Holden had been the MP for North West Durham. Luckily for him, his constituency got swallowed up in the boundary changes. Otherwise he would have been forced to defend a seat he was almost certain to lose, with only the prospect of a peerage giving him solace. So, since then, Rich has been biding his time. Waiting for somewhere reasonably safe to become available.

With just two days before all the candidates had to be nominated, Rich turned up unexpectedly in Basildon and Billericay. Much to the annoyance of the local constituency association, whose members would much rather have appointed someone who knew the area. 'Hi,' said Rich. 'I'm sorry to say that the other two candidates that CCHQ have put forward – Dicky Holding and Ricky Holdup – can't make it tonight. So it looks like you've been lumbered with me.'

At which point most of the Basildon and Billericay Tory association left in disgust. They wanted no part of any stitch-up. That left the association's executive officer, Richard Moore, to go through the formalities of the nomination.

'Right,' said Moore, reluctantly. 'We might as well get this over and done with. So why don't you tell me a bit more about your political career? Start at the beginning.'

'Well, as you probably know . . .' Rich smirked.

'I don't. I couldn't care less . . .'

'I started off as special adviser to both Chris Grayling and Gavin Williamson.'

'Two of the most useless cabinet ministers of all time . . .'

'Yes. On my watch Chris handed over a government contract to a ferry company that didn't have any ferries, and Gavin leaked top secret briefings from the National Security Council.'

Moore buried his head in his hands and started sobbing quietly. Eventually, he managed to pull himself together.

'And what about your career as an MP?' he said.

Holden became animated once more. 'I like to think of myself as a go-getter,' he said. 'An attack dog. The sort of guy that gets things done. It was me that led the campaigns to get Keir Starmer done for Beergate and Angela Rayner convicted for tax fraud.'

'Er . . . but the people investigated both of these and found there was no case to answer in either of them.'

'Yeah, but it caused a bit of trouble. That's the main thing.'

'So you're the kind of man who likes to instigate damaging witch-hunts on innocent people for no good reason?'

'Absolutely.'

At this point Moore paused and checked his notes.

'Tell me about your convictions,' he said.

'What convictions? Who told you I had convictions? The jury found me not guilty of sexual assault . . .'

'I meant convictions as in principles. What drives you?'

'Oh, I see,' said Rich, calming down a little. 'I think my biggest strength is my loyalty.'

'Quite. I remember you saying you would always be loyal to the north-east.'

'And now it's my turn to be loyal to the south-east. We are in the south-east, aren't we? Had a hell of a time trying to find my way here. Thing about loyalty is, it's always best if it's shared around. That's the Conservative way.'

'OK,' said Moore, changing the subject. 'In your role as party chairman, it was your job to secure donations. Do you feel it was right to take a further £5 million off Frank Hester? You don't think we should have handed it back?'

'Absolutely not,' said Rich. 'We needed the dosh. Besides, Frankie Boy is a thoroughly good bloke, despite a bit of violent, misogynistic and racist language.'

Moore looked down at his list of questions. This was pointless. He might as well wrap it up.

'Are there any questions you have for me?' he said.

'Just the one. Is it safe?' replied Rich.

'Well, like many towns these days we have our problems. Some parts of the centre I'd advise against visiting on a Saturday night . . .'

'I'm not bothered about crime,' Holden interrupted. 'You won't see me for dust if I'm elected. What I wanted to know was whether this was a safe seat. I don't want to waste my time on a place where I'm going to lose.'

Moore started tapping out an email to CCHQ. Just this once Basildon would rather have no Tory candidate at all. 'Too late,' came the reply.

And now for the second honourable Tory. Step forward Douglas Ross, leader of the Scottish Conservatives in Holyrood. Not so long ago, Wee Dougie announced he would be standing down as an MP, saying he wanted to spend more of his time with his colleagues north of the border. With just 24 hours until the nominations closed, Dougie had a change of mind. He now quite fancied the new seat of Aberdeenshire North and Moray East. A seat previously held by another Tory, David Duguid, who was at home recovering from spinal surgery.

'I don't think you're well enough,' said Wee Dougie.

'I think you'll find I am,' Duguid replied.

'Well, tough. It's mine. CCHQ have rubber-stamped it. I need the £85,000. You can just bugger off.'

Charming. In the distance a trumpeter sounded the Last Post.

Slanging matches and soundbites: TV debate delivers seven ways to make time drag

7 JUNE 2024

Not another one. We've only just recovered from the last election debate. A fairly tawdry head-to-head between Rishi Sunak and Keir Starmer, in which all we learned was that the prime minister would tell any lie to try to stay in Downing Street. He's even moved on to lying that he isn't a liar. We're now in Boris Johnson territory.

But the debates come thick and fast, and it was now the BBC's turn. This was a seven-way debate between the leaders of Plaid Cymru and Reform, the co-leader of the Green Party and the Scottish National Party's Westminster leader, along with the Labour and Liberal Democrat deputy leaders and the Conservative leader of the House of Commons. It promised to be a 90-minute shouting match in which almost no one had the time to talk in anything but soundbites. And who would be watching anyway on a Friday night?

One person who definitely would not was Rishi Sunak. He would be in a padded cell. The first person in history to section himself. It's hard to imagine a worse prime minister. Nostalgia plays tricks with the mind, but Liz Truss would have made a better fist of it. She may have looked stupid and out of her depth, but at least she would have stayed for the duration. And every minute away from Downing Street would have been one where she couldn't tank the economy. Win–win.

But Rish! knew better. He always thinks he does. Comes with the combined brain power of Isaac Levido and James Forsyth. Two men in search of a connecting synapse. Rish! had come up with the bright idea to brave his way through the British D-Day commemoration – a bit of a yawn for him – but then to shoot off home and miss the big international service of remembrance.

In 1944, tens of thousands of terrified men had crossed the Channel, knowing that many of them would not come back. Eighty years on, and with just a handful of survivors still alive, Rish! had taken the first helicopter out of Caen. Just imagine if the troops had all taken the easy option. *Au revoir, mes braves!*

But our heroic D-Day Dodger had things to do. Speeches to write on the importance of national service. And he didn't want to have to hang around for all that EU glad-handing. Hugs with Joe Biden, Olaf Scholz, Emmanuel Macron and Volodymyr Zelenskyy. Leave that to *collaborateurs* like Keir Starmer. There was no way he was going to stand to attention through the 'Ode to Joy'. That was for losers.

Come Friday morning, Rish! had had a rethink, after he had been slated for sneaking off home to give an interview to ITV about why it was OK to lie about being a liar. So it was a very chastened Sunak who gave a brief statement to Sky News. The classic non-apology apology. Just meaningless, charmless words. Words without affect.

He was sorry but . . . his diary had been booked up weeks ago. He just couldn't see the problem. D-Day was a time for doing the bare minimum. He'd gone to the Brit bash. Surely that was enough? He didn't seem to realise that Zelenskyy had found time to attend while in the middle of a war with Russia. And other parties shouldn't politicise his absence. Said the man who had disrespected his own nation, dishonoured his office, by bunking off to give a campaign interview. We look forward to his next moves. Murdering pandas in London Zoo. Demolishing Battersea Dogs Home. Exiling Judi Dench. Closing all hospitals. Hanging Paddington Bear.

Penny Mordaunt seldom smiles at the best of times. But she looked grimmer than usual as she took her place in the line-up for the debate. Sunak's afternoon flit may well end her parliamentary career. Portsmouth is a naval town, and marginal with it. Inevitably, the first question was on Sunak's no-show. Cue a Mordaunt pile-on from everyone. Penny tried to go all Thatcher but fell flat. Left chewing wasps. She couldn't defend Rishi, and her only attack was to dare Angela Rayner to press the nuclear button to prove she was hard enough. Give me strength.

Believe it or not, that was more or less the high point of the debate. The rest was turgid fare, notable mainly for being simultaneously deadly dull and extremely bad-tempered. Niche TV. From time to time, Rayner and

Mordaunt would have a slanging match, in which Penny shouted louder and longer to less and less effect. She will be embarrassed when she watches this on catch-up. If she has a sense of shame.

But otherwise you could have predicted what everyone was going to say and when, as we raced through questions on the NHS, housing, the cost of living, the climate crisis and trust. Nigel Farage was his trademark Smuggy McSmugface, banging on about foreigners at every turn while exposing his complete lack of a plan for running the country. Just the unpleasant voice of protest. Rhun ap Iorwerth was almost a total nonentity. Not even the host, Mishal Husain, wanted to hear from him. Carla Denyer, Daisy Cooper and Stephen Flynn sounded the most reasonable. But then they had the least to lose. They can afford to be honest.

Time began to drag. The audience started checking their watches. We were getting nowhere. The final thoughts of each contestant were almost devoid of thought. It was over. A relief for us all. Over on Channel 4, midway through the second half, England were losing to Iceland. Happy days.

Rish!'s bargain-basement manifesto offers anything you want if you just vote Tory

11 JUNE 2024

Round and round in circles. The wheels coming off. Skid marks everywhere. Crashing out at the first corner. Getting lapped. Stalled at the start. The pits. Burning up fossil fuels. Mired in sex scandals. You can write your own jokes here.

Someone in Conservative headquarters must really have it in for Rishi Sunak. Either that or Isaac Levido and James Forsyth are secret Labour stooges. Why else would the Tories have chosen Silverstone as the venue for their manifesto launch? Surely someone must have foreseen what was coming. Or maybe everyone is now just along for the roller-coaster ride. Leaning into the mother of all car crashes.

In the main hall – a cavernous, soulless room that could have been anywhere, not a racing car in sight – Tory aides were spotted removing several rows of chairs. Clearly short of numbers. Over in the media pen, a waiter was explaining why the coffee wasn't really coffee. It was just hot water in a jug marked 'coffee'. Piss-ups and breweries came to mind.

We waited. And we waited. Staring at the words 'Clear Plan. Bold Action. Secure Future' on the stage backdrop.

Empty, meaningless slogans. Symbolic tokens of Tory failure. There isn't a person in the country who really believes them. Not even Rish!.

The event was meant to kick off at 11.30, but it was 11.45 before most of the cabinet shuffled in. Those we haven't loved. Nothing works as it should in this country any more. Kemi Badenoch grim-faced. There under duress, biding her time. Michael Gove spaced out. No sign of Penny 'Penelope Pitstop' Mordaunt. She was planning her parliamentary afterlife. The others merely grinned sheepishly. Lambs to the slaughter. Like the politburo at Stalin's funeral. Unsure of whether to laugh or cry.

First to the stage was the education secretary, Gillian Keegan. 'I never dreamed that one day I would introduce the Tory party manifesto,' she said. You and me both, Gillian. Don't worry. It will never happen again.

Then came the Teesside mayor, Lord Houchen. Or Ben, as he likes to be called. A peerage from Boris Johnson is a devalued honour. 'I've known Rishi for nine years,' he said. So that's all fine then. Vote Labour and get Armageddon. Bring it on. It can't be any worse than the last 14 years.

So please stand and give a big welcome to . . . the prime minister. The cabinet reacted as if they had been electrocuted. It's a measure of just how disaffected and disengaged they all are that no one wanted to be seen to be openly disloyal by being last to stand. The guilt trigger. The applause in the room bordered on the hysterical.

The Tory party really are losing it. But nothing happened. There was no sign of Rish!.

Again we waited. Eventually, somebody unlocked the door and let him in. That, too, was worth an extra round of applause. Finally, calm. And then Sunak delivered what must be his most demotivational speech yet. Almost a resignation statement. Just 20 minutes of everyone's time they will never get back. A speech devoid of affect. You could sense the despair in every sentence. Just chucking as many bribes as he could think of into the air, knowing they were all meaningless. His credibility is shot. We know it. He knows it. There's no longer any attempt to disguise his shortcomings. We're just filling in time until the final curtain. We're here because we're here because we're here.

'We've turned a corner,' Rish! smiled wanly. We had all come to Silverstone just to hear that one lame metaphor. The manifesto was about bold actions, he went on. Except it wasn't. It was one long panic attack. A last, desperate throw of the dice. Sunak can no longer pretend that the Tories haven't fucked things up. All he can do is offer a less than heartfelt apology on behalf of five prime ministers and the empty promise that everything will be better in the future. You'd need to be lobotomised to go along with that. And if your latest policies are so good, then why didn't you implement them earlier?

On we went. Part dirge, part threnody. The last rites. The world is an unsafe place, he said. Then why did you dismantle so much of the armed forces? 'We need to stand with our allies.' Of course we do. So that's why you did an early flit back home from the D-Day celebrations. Because nothing says brothers in arms like turning your back on your friends.

After that it was bargain-basement time. Everything must go. A meditation on failure and greed. People could have whatever they wanted. Anything. Just please vote Tory. Don't like foreigners? Then the flights to Rwanda would start in July. Really? In which case why didn't you wait till after the summer to call an election. This was shameless and completely lightweight. Not even the Tories are falling for this. Don't like the ECHR? Then we could rip up international treaties. Be more like Russia and Belarus. Such a good look.

Then on to the tax cuts. Free money for everyone. It's a wonder he didn't just start handing out £50 notes to everyone in the audience. We were operating in a total intellectual vacuum. The week of magical thinking. Only last week Sunak was accusing Labour of being dishonest about the economy. Now he had found £17 billion to give away. Roll up, roll up. And how was this to be paid? By cutting the number of civil servants – most of them were lazy – and cracking down on tax evasion. The fantasy of the magic money tree was back. Huge public service cuts were coming. We would all be broke. It was like Liz Truss had never gone away.

Rish! tried to mitigate the disaster by taking questions only from what he hoped was the largely friendly media.

Except no one is friendly any more. He and his government's credibility is totally shot. All people wanted to know was why anyone should believe anything he said. No one even bothered to refer to the manifesto costings as everyone in the room agreed they were all imaginary.

'I'm proud of my record,' he said. How sweet. No one else is. Certainly not the Tory party. Everything is on its knees. Now Rish! got tetchy. Annoyed that all these idiots were daring to question him. Why couldn't the world bend to his will? He even tried to say his was a family steeped in small business. Must have forgotten his wife and father-in-law.

That was that. Things to do, places to go. The launch was dead on arrival. Tory candidates who had been waiting on a miracle left to confront a bleak reality. The cabinet rose to give a final round of applause. They shook hands with each other. A form of goodbye. It would be the last time many of them would be in the same room together.

* * *

There were moments in this election campaign that felt like performance art. Like the Tories were on a mission to self-destruct. Not content with losing, they wanted to lose as badly as possible. Fail. Fail Again. Fail Better.

There are strict rules on gambling with insider knowledge. Yet, strangely enough, one Conservative insider who had allegedly been informed of Sunak's decision to call the election before it had been announced decided to place a bet on a July election.

Winning a bet may be the best it's going to get for Rishi and his team

13 JUNE 2024

You win some, you lose some. This week, both Labour and the Tories will reckon they've struck lucky with the timings of their manifesto launches – though for very different reasons.

It's always hard to know which is the best launch slot. To go first and set the agenda, with the anxiety that everyone will have soon forgotten what you are about. Or to go late and risk your manifesto lingering in the memory for all the wrong reasons. This year, both the main parties – if the Tories can still be called that – will reckon they judged it perfectly. For the Conservatives, this may be the only thing that has gone right in this campaign.

That was, until Craig Williams's stunning 5/1 bet. Who would have guessed that Rishi Sunak would call a July election on a Wednesday afternoon in May at 5 p.m., just three days after placing the bet? That had to be worth £100 of anyone's money. Especially Craig's. Though you would have thought that such a gifted political clairvoyant might also have warned the prime minister that it would be a spectacularly bad idea. Hey ho. Might as well cash in while he still can. Things Can Only Get Betting.

The Tories launched their manifesto at Silverstone. The kindest thing that can be said about this collection of empty promises is that it was dead on arrival. Not even David Cameron, who was given a peerage on the condition that he said nice things about Sunak, has felt able to be complimentary about it.

As it turns out, everyone has now forgotten the Tory list of pledges. Yesterday's recycling. An irrelevance that was never going to happen anyway. Something new has come along to take its place: the Labour manifesto. And Keir Starmer and his party will be happy to talk about it for weeks and months to come.

No disasters. No idiot pratfalls. This was a launch that went about as well as anyone could hope. Coherent. A philosophical subtext. And clear measures to improve people's lives. For ages, Labour has been saying it is a serious party again. Now it actually looks as if its leaders believe it.

Where the Tories had to remove chairs to disguise the empty spaces at their launch, it was standing room only in the vast atrium of the Co-op headquarters in Manchester. Half an hour before the start and there were already hundreds of people looking on from the balconies above. There was a buzz in the hall that had been absent from the other launches – the attraction of being tantalisingly close to real power.

With minutes to go, copies of the manifesto were handed out. Photos of Starmer on almost every page – shades of Boris Johnson in 2019. Even one of Keir with Volodymyr Zelenskyy in Normandy. Another reason for Sunak to kick himself for coming back early.

Next, the shadow cabinet trooped in to huge whoops and cheers – surely a first – and took their places stage left. They smiled and waved. Unlike their Tory counterparts, they hadn't been dragged away from their unwinnable constituencies for the day. They could afford their time in the sun.

Finally, we were ready to start. First up was Angela Rayner. She kept it short and sweet. Hope. Change. Hope. Change. Hope. Change. You can probably spot a theme here. When even Angela remains relentlessly on message, you know the election is in the bag. Just try not to look as if it's a done deal.

Hard to do when your next speaker is Richard Walker, the CEO of Iceland. A political weather vane, Dicky hates not being on the winning side. Not so long ago, he was on the candidates list for the Tory party, happy to endorse Johnson and the lockdown parties. For him to switch, you know it's game over for the Conservatives. Anyway, Walker whispered sweet nothings. A knighthood is probably in the bag. You can't say he hasn't worked for it.

Then came various party members. Daniel, living in a bedsit with his wife and children. Nathaniel, a cancer patient who will never know for sure if the long wait for chemotherapy has cost him his life. Holly, an 18-year-old A-level student voting for the first time. She didn't say if she was thrilled at the idea of doing national service. But I think we can assume not.

A short video of Keir doing Keir-like things – kissing babies, raising the dead – on the campaign trail to a heavy-metal soundtrack. And then we got the man himself. Cue another prolonged ovation. He didn't disappoint. Well, not much. Let's face it, Starmer is never going to be an electric performer, the sort of speaker who can carry you along on a tide of emotion. You can't conjure charisma out of nothing. But this was very definitely Keir doing Keir's best version of himself. A man at one with himself. Someone who has risen from shouting on the sidelines to genuine prime ministerial material. Ready to assume the responsibility of the office. Longing to get on with the job. The next three weeks can't pass quickly enough for him. He spoke with clarity and conviction. Passion, you are never going to get.

A few minutes in, there was a brief interruption from a young woman, protesting that Labour had given up on her generation. It wasn't clear what more she expected. Not so long ago, Starmer might have been unnerved by this. Now he just brushed the distraction aside. 'We used to be a party of protest,' he said. 'But I have changed the party.' All the room applauded.

There were no big revelations in the speech. Keir was at pains to point out that he wasn't in the business of panic-selling election bribes like the Tories. If you wanted pantomime, there was always Clacton. Everything in the manifesto had long since been costed. The tax rises and offers had long since been priced in. Instead, what we got was more of a mood board. Yes, things were shit now – 14 years of Tory government had seen to that – but things could be so much better. Immerse yourself in Labour's warm bath. Allow yourself a ray of positivity. Things could change. Don't worry about a thing. The days of wealth and plenty were coming back. Economic growth would spark a British renaissance. Meet him in a land of hope and dreams. OK, 'growth' was doing a lot of heavy lifting here. Some were saying it was unachievable and that spending cuts were unavoidable. But at least it was a clear pitch. Something by which the party could later be judged.

It was soon apparent Starmer wasn't the only one who thought he was a prime-minister-in-waiting. Most of the media did, too. They deferred to him in a way that they no longer do with Sunak. Yesterday's man. Keir is the man of the present. GB News wondered how we would cope under a one-party socialist state. To which there was only one answer. A lot better than under a Tory rabble.

* * *

One way of judging how well a campaign is going is to check out the support that erstwhile colleagues are lending their party leader. Almost everyone appeared to have abandoned Rishi Sunak. Not even David Cameron – who had Sunak to thank for his undeserved peerage and short stint as foreign secretary – could be found speaking up for the prime minister. The only person who could be found to defend the government on the daily media round was the business secretary, Mel Stride. He became an almost daily feature.

Meanwhile, as his friends deserted him, Sunak became increasingly tetchy. Whenever he was asked a tricky question, he seemed to be within a heartbeat of losing it with journalists.

On the Hunt for Jeremy, the Tories' invisible man in this election

16 JUNE 2024

Send out the search parties. Sound all the alarms. It's been more than three weeks since Rishi Sunak called the general election and still no sightings of Jeremy Hunt. Just a couple of unconfirmed reports of a sad-looking man roaming the streets of Godalming with his dog, knocking on doors that never get opened. The sense of pathos is overwhelming. That such a titan should be reduced to near invisibility.

You'd have thought that Sunak would have wanted the chancellor to be by his side for at least some of the campaign. The brains behind the economic miracle of the past two years. The man who has overseen a recession, a cheerleader for the current 0% growth. And when better to unleash him than now? The forensic economic mind to pick holes in the Labour manifesto.

It's almost as if Rish! no longer has faith in his right-hand man, the linchpin of his cabinet. Has he begun to wonder if Jezza isn't a miracle worker, as he has led us to believe? Or maybe it's Hunt's own decision to make himself invisible. After nearly two years of cosplaying the role of chancellor, the strain has begun to take its toll. He can no longer maintain the pretence that he knows what he's doing. When in truth he never did. He's tested the pretence to self-destruction. Now he can scarcely raise his head from beneath the duvet. Either way, we should be concerned for his well-being. Pray for Jezza. A minute's silence for the still-suffering Jeremy.

So this week it was left to Mark Harper to do the BBC and Sky Sunday politics shows. To which many will quite reasonably say: 'Mark who?' What possible reason could the government have for sending out its transport secretary? Had potholes become the most pressing concern in the election? Or have we just reached the point in the campaign where Harper is the only member of the cabinet still willing to go out and defend the government? Were we all supposed to be grateful that we weren't having to make do with Chris Philp? Laura Kuenssberg and Trevor Phillips could barely contain their disappointment at having to interview someone who is anonymous to most and irrelevant to all. This is not to be harsh on Marky. He always comes across as one of the more decent, more personable Tory politicians. It's just that he's both unremarkable and barely functioning.

The highlight of his career was standing for the leadership of the Tory party in 2019. He had just one campaign event: a speech in a tiny room in Westminster that drew an audience of 10. Of which I was one. Happy days. He was one of the first to be eliminated from the contest. No one could quite understand why he hadn't been *the* first. Break out the champagne. It's all been downhill from there onwards.

But the show had to go on. Laura and Trevor are nothing if not old pros, so if Mark was the man the Tories had put up, then Mark it had to be. Kuenssberg got things under way by observing that many Conservative candidates appeared to be embarrassed by their party's brand. Andrea Jenkyns' electoral promo material even featured a photo of her with Nigel Farage. Not at all, said Harper. This was all perfectly normal. Nige was an extremely handsome man.

'Isn't it a bit desperate for the Tories to now be trying to terrify the electorate that Labour were on course to win 450 seats?' Laura continued. Mark shook his head. Every move CCHQ made was being done from a position of strength. All the Tories were interested in was making sure that voters got what they wanted. And if, as seemed likely, the electorate really did want to give Labour a super-majority, then that was fine by him. He wasn't about to start quibbling.

Harper did want to make some claims about all the tax rises that Labour had already ruled out but which he suspected might be introduced anyway, but he was quickly reminded of his party's own shortcomings in that area. The highest tax burden since the 1940s. Marky looked crestfallen at this. It was almost as if this had come as a shock to him. Why had no one told him?

By the end of the 15-minute slot, Laura was almost beginning to feel sorry for Harper. No disrespect, she said, but can you explain why I am talking to a nonentity such as yourself? I got the feeling that she was also having the same feelings of anxiety – borderline panic – about the missing Jezza. Maybe he had been kidnapped. Presumably by CCHQ.

And what about Lord Big Dave? At this rate, Cameron would have picked up a peerage for a couple of months' first-class travel round the world. No one could think of any positive contribution he had made to anything as foreign secretary. Except looking like a shiny person. Couldn't he defend Rish! at least once on the TV? Apparently not. Lord Big Dave has his limits. Marky just shrugged. He couldn't help being so useless

Phillips was every bit as brutal. Time and again, Harper urged Trevor to forget the past. Boris Johnson, Liz Truss and Rishi Sunak had never really happened. We were living in the continuous present. Our minds are a *tabula rasa* to be rebooted with fresh nonsense every 30 seconds. Under Labour there would be endless tax rises. So, much like the Tories then.

'I'm up for the fight,' said Marky. He didn't look like it. He looked battered. A man who can't wait for the election to be over. Voters were still undecided, he maintained. Undecided as to whether they merely dislike the Tories or whether they actively detest them. Somewhere in the depths of Harper's psyche he knows that the game is up. He just hasn't reached that higher level of consciousness yet.

Also on the morning shows was Labour's Wes Streeting. One of the most exhausting politicians around. A motormouth on speed dial. God knows what he would be like if he were on the same drugs as Michael Gove. Wes is not someone who is ever going to die wondering. He opens his mouth, and the sentences are fired like machine-gun bullets. Shoot first, ask questions later. Still, he's an effective performer. If only because he doesn't allow the interviewer to get a word in edgeways.

Wes fired off his soundbites. Fully costed. Manifesto just an opening gambit. Growth would take us to sunlit uplands. Junior doctors' strike bad. Don't give the matches back to the arsonist. A point that Harper had also made. Albeit accidentally.

Raging Rishi – or maybe his avatar – gave us an object lesson in how not to win friends

20 JUNE 2024

They seek him here, they seek him there. That damned elusive Sunakel. We need to talk about Rishi. Has anyone you know seen him recently? Is he checking out schools in Santa Monica? Has he been abducted by aliens? Is he at home studying the spread-betting odds on a Labour landslide along with the rest of his campaign team? Face it, that's about the only thing any of them are likely to win in this election. When Rish! says, 'Can you afford to gamble on Keir Starmer?' he means for you to take him at face value.

Sunak has gone missing in action. Some claim to have caught fleeting sightings of him over the last week, but none has been confirmed. Not so long ago, you could be guaranteed to see a prime minister at a press conference every day during an election campaign. Not to mention regular trips to different parts of the country, where they would kiss babies and be nice to dogs. OK, so they would tend to make the same dreary stump speech wherever they went, but it was easy to tune out. What mattered was that at least they were visible.

More recently, prime ministers have become more selective with their engagements. The daily press conference binned. Replaced by operational notes sent out to lobby journalists the night before, inviting them to turn up to some stage-managed events attended by hand-picked Tory cheerleaders who would whoop and cheer at every banality. Theresa May and Boris Johnson were particularly keen on these and would do at least two or three a week. They could pretend they were meeting real people even when they weren't.

But it's been more than a week since Rish! last did one of these. Not since his manifesto launch has he turned up to an event to which more than one hack has been invited. It's as though he has gone undercover. A unique style of campaigning whereby the prime minister seeks to make himself invisible. You could argue that this was a question of shame, Sunak unable to face the country after 14 years of Tory government that academics have defined as the worst ever. Only that doesn't quite stack up, as Rish! doesn't do shame. It's us who owe him, not the other way round.

The truth is stranger than you think. What's happened is that Sunak has been replaced by an avatar with faulty AI. You thought the Maybot was bad? Then hold my beer, because Rish! is even worse. Let's examine the evidence. First, there's the sheep. We caught a glimpse of someone resembling Sunak on a farm in Devon. Only the sheep sussed him out. They stayed away from him, even though he was offering them food. They knew he wasn't real.

Now the clincher. Only bad AI could be as consistently woeful as Rish!. By the law of averages, a real human would have the occasional day when he was moderately less useless. Do something almost normal. Not Avatar Rish!. He hasn't put a foot right throughout the campaign. From the rain-soaked speech to D-Day to the piss-poor manifesto to the gambling, he's screwed everything up. It's like the Tories have bet the house on losing the election and didn't want to leave anything to chance. Nearly there, guys. Nearly there.

Just two weeks to go. Along with some more pointless debates. Starting with BBC *Question Time* on Thursday. What better way to cheer yourself up after England have fumbled to a scratchy draw than two hours of the party leaders answering the same questions they've been asked hundreds of times before? First up were Ed Davey and John Swinney. Presumably because if they'd gone last, then we unhappy few who were watching would have switched over for the second half of Spain vs Italy. The Liberal Democrats and the Scottish National Party were very much the evening's supporting cast. Not that the audience gave either an easy ride. Davey struggled on tuition fees and the Post Office Horizon scandal. Swinney prevaricated on what constituted a mandate for a referendum. He at least got some applause for being genuine.

Keir Starmer got off to a nervy start as he was asked to explain why he had said Jeremy Corbyn would make a great prime minister during the 2019 election. Hardly surprising, as it's generally not a good idea to admit that you were lying through your teeth when playing the election game. But thereafter he looked more assured, despite frequent interruptions from Fiona Bruce, who decided her own questions were more interesting, and he got out more or less alive.

But then the moment the audience had clearly come for. To give the Tories a kicking. Out walked Rish! – or possibly his avatar – with a forced smile. The smile of a man who wanted to punch someone. This wasn't just Tetchy Rish!, it was Angry Rish!. He had no time for the little people bothering him with their stupid questions. Why couldn't they accept he was Mr Integrity, Professionalism and Accountability? Hell, no one ran a better gambling ring inside No. 10 than him.

The Avatar was now completely out of control. Furious that the only applause was for the audience's questions. Furious that there was not more gratitude for him. Furious that no matter how patronising and condescending he became, no one warmed to him or believed a word he said. At one point he was even laughed at. The billionaire Avatar was now just a standing joke. Stop the Boats. Stop the Bets.

It was an object lesson in how not to win friends and influence people. The only explanation for the performance is that the Avatar is a secret Labour supporter. His gift to the country the destruction of the Tory party. If only more people had been watching.

The Farage faithful know he's a fraud but they don't care

27 JUNE 2024

Call it confirmation bias. The media were the ones who wanted endless debates – the public would have been happy with one or two at most – and so it was inevitable that the media would declare them to be important way-points on the campaign trail. But were they?

Sure, the debates were picked over forensically, but strip out the sound and fury and you're left with very little we didn't already know. Rishi Sunak might have been even more thin-skinned and tetchy, and Keir Starmer rather more wooden, than we might have imagined, but this is all surface trivia. Nothing new in concrete policy terms was revealed. Just the familiar half-truths and evasions with which we are all too familiar. Manifesto pledges that almost certainly won't stand contact with reality.

Time and again, Rish! has played the trust card. The country can rely on him to tell the truth. Sometimes you can only think he is taking the piss. Has a masochistic urge to self-destruct. Because within minutes of him bleating on about integrity, the Tory press office was masquerading as 'Tax Check UK' on Twitter, pumping out fictitious claims about Labour's policies. The man who wants to be believed has no regard for the truth. He just looks needy, corrupt and desperate.

Meanwhile, Nigel Farage can hardly believe his luck. Having started the campaign as very much the outsider, not even planning to stand as a candidate, he is now living his very best life. Things could hardly have gone better.

With the Tories lurching from crisis to crisis – insulting the veterans at the D-Day commemorations and then the insider gambling ring – and Labour offering a don't-rock-the-boat, safety-first approach, the campaign has been low on energy. A low-wattage endurance test. Hell, no one said politics was meant to be fun, but some hope would be nice. Promising to make things a little less shit doesn't really cut it. And there's no vacuum into which Nige won't jump head first. Anything for some attention. He's learned his narcissism at Donald Trump's knee.

The queue outside the Rainton Arena in Houghton-le-Spring, near Sunderland, snakes back at least 100 yards. And this is at 11 a.m., an hour before the start. While Sunak and Starmer have gone out of their way to meet as few members of the public as possible – one or two strictly controlled photo ops per day – Nige adores an old-fashioned rally. And it seems this crowd in the northeast are also more than up for it. They are looking for a politician who will make them feel good about themselves. One who talks to their insecurities and plays on their prejudices. Forget the policies, stay for the LOLs.

After brief warm-up acts from two local Reform candidates, Farage takes the stage to some loud techno music
pumped out through some ageing speakers, flashing
lights and an indoor firework display. The audience rise
to their feet to join in with the fun. Nige just stands there,
lapping it up. He can't get enough of the applause. It's
what nourishes him. He's not here to make a difference.
He's here to feel whole. Without a crowd he's uncertain
whether he actually exists. Deep within what passes for
his soul there is an emptiness that can never be filled.

But there is undeniably a connection. One that Sunak
and Starmer would kill for. One that allows Nige to
get away with almost anything. Because you'd expect
a crowd like this to have worked out Farage long ago.
A posh, establishment boy with no real interest in the
north-east. Just another politician passing through. Yet
their scepticism is put on hold. They appear to buy into
his act entirely. They know he's a fraud, but they don't
care. At least he's an entertaining fraud. A voice of disaffection. They like him not for what he is but for what he's
not. He's not a Tory and he's not Labour.

Let the show commence. And this is a show more than
a speech. Nige's time working the neocon circuit in the US
over the past four years has paid dividends. He now has
the air of a televangelist who you know will be arrested
for tax evasion in a matter of hours. Asides to people
in the front row. Conversational rather than oratorical.
You half expect him to interrupt his flow and make an

appeal for donations to his favourite charity – the Bank of St Nigel. And it would have been no surprise if half the 1,000-strong audience had handed over their credit cards.

He talks for well over half an hour. No notes needed because this is a greatest-hits event. All to celebrate his own greatness. He can't believe the arena packed out in a matter of days. A humblebrag. He'd have been devastated if no one had turned up. He really connects with the young people. Only the crowd looks almost entirely middle-aged or older. He has always been right about everything. Nige is never slow to say 'I told you so'.

Then into his familiar tropes. The country wasn't working. You couldn't move without someone wanting to rob or kill you. Probably a foreigner. Farage would be devastated to find out that most people aren't afraid to walk the streets. People should be proud of their history, he says. Though not confident enough in it to question it. Nige doesn't do critical thinking. Not his style. Keep your prejudices and hatreds mainstream.

Immigrants. Too many of them. He'd always said so. Even when there had been very few. Leave the ECHR. Join Russia and Belarus. 'We must not set people apart from one another,' he says. That's literally what he does. Then a few vague promises. Pay less tax. Though no mention of how he would pay for anything. Brexit, though with no apology for his part in its failure. Doubles down on Ukraine, but skips over his apparent support for Putin (although he has denied this, saying he dislikes Putin and is opposed to the invasion). It's all deeply unpleasant stuff. Nige in his element. The thrill of power with no responsibility. He'd be devastated to find himself prime minister.

Come the end there are no questions. Nige likes it best that way. And so does the audience. Because questions might puncture the mood. Because very little of what he says bears examination. In that respect, he's even worse than the career politicians he claims to despise. At least Starmer and Sunak try not to deal in fantasies. Well, not all of the time.

But you can't deny the numbers. You may hate it, but Nige is reaching parts of the country that no other party is. And it is all about him. If Dicky Tice were still in charge, Reform would be also-rans. People like him because he legitimises their anger. Gives voice to their discontent. He tears things down with no thought for a rebuilt future. Next week he will be in parliament. Don't say you haven't been warned.

Johnson appears on campaign trail at last – to dance on Sunak's grave

2 JULY 2024

Cast your mind back to 22 May. You probably wondered not just why Rishi Sunak had called an election at all, but why he had chosen a six-week campaign. It wasn't as if he had anything new to say in that time. The economy wasn't suddenly going to make a miraculous recovery. Hundreds of refugees weren't going to volunteer to fly themselves to Rwanda. Patients weren't about to take themselves off hospital waiting lists.

Rish! told us he had a plan. And it's turned out he knew exactly what he was doing. Six weeks was what it would take. Six was the perfect number. Six weeks is what it would take for the Tories to lose their minds completely. The past five and a half weeks have just been a warm-up act of low-key events, idiotic policies such as national service – we haven't heard so much about that recently – allegations of gambling with insider knowledge and the 'Leave Them on the Beaches' retreat from the D-Day commemorations. Now, the *pièce de résistance*, the moment the Conservatives jumped the shark.

Tuesday morning was the perfect cluster-fuck. A threnody of national shame. Future generations will look back at Election 2024 in despair. How could we have sunk so low? The day dawned with a new Tory campaign video. A man waking up to yet another power cut. Albeit one where the electric alarm clock and the kettle are still working. Go figure. The bloke in the video walks down-stairs in the dark. Picks up a paper to find that Rachel Reeves has put up taxes and the stock market has crashed. Then he wakes up and finds it's all a dream. This is so bad it's almost laughable. To be effective an ad must at least be plausible. But this is the sort of disaster scenario more likely to occur under the current government. You could only conclude that the advert had been made by some teenagers who had failed their social media studies GCSE. Presumably they are the only people left in Tory central office.

Then there were the letters sent out to random voters around the country, supposedly written by their future selves in 2044. Saying how they understood why they had voted Reform 20 years previously and that they had been badly let down by the voting system. Just bonkers. The first time the Tories have ever been known to make the case for electoral reform.

All this happened while you were asleep. So it's likely you woke up to the half-witted Maria Caulfield making the same claim made by Grant Shapps and other Tory ministers that Britain was no longer safe should Russia choose to invade after 6 p.m. on a Friday.

'Starmer was planning to work a four-day week,' she said. This from a woman who has achieved so little she might as well have worked a two-day week. From a party that gave us the laziest prime minister in history in Boris Johnson. The man who missed five COBRA meetings. This made the new attack advert look sophisticated. The politics of the kindergarten.

Coordinating all this – someone must have been – was Sunak himself. On a whistle-stop tour of what, before this election, were rock-solid Home Counties Tory strong-holds. No one is even pretending Rish! is going to win any more. It's all damage limitation. Here, the existential futility has been ramped up to new levels. Has there ever been anything quite so pointless as a 5 a.m. visit to an automated Ocado centre?

'Are you voting for me?' pleaded Rish!.

'No,' said the robots in unison.

From there it was on to speak to almost no one in a supermarket owned by one of the few remaining Tory donors. A collector's item, that. Then to a farm in Banbury. Just to say he had been there. To prove to himself that he was dynamic. Mr Testosterone. Not like Keir 'Sir Sleepy' Starmer. It was desperate, desperate stuff. Fooling no one. A prime minister has seldom looked so alone.

We ended in Chelsea. Sunak's second appearance in this upmarket constituency in as many weeks. This is no triumphal march. Five years ago, Boris Johnson had concluded his campaign in the Olympic Park, in front of an adoring crowd. This was more of a wake. One where the family had had plenty of time to process the death while the relative was still technically alive. The queue outside the National Army Museum had long since rattled through the five stages of grief. The mood was acceptance.

'Of course we've lost,' said one man.

'Yes, we lost the moment we got rid of Liz Truss,' replied his friend.

I'm not sure they were quite in tune with the mood of the country.

There was a helicopter hanging from the ceiling, below which a crowd of 400 people were gathered. Half of them security guards. The Saigon jokes wrote themselves. Sometimes I think the Tories are running the campaign for my benefit. After half the cabinet – including a rare sighting of Jeremy Hunt and Lord Big Dave – had taken the stage (Mel Stride was inexplicably nowhere to be seen), Michael Gove stepped out. His speech was totally deranged. The Tories had a proud record in government.

You could see his former colleagues – Mikey is out of here, out of it – blanch. Don't mention the war. The whole reason the Tories might finish third behind the Lib Dems is because of the last 14 years. Then he was rushing on his run. He might as well have said Labour would kill your babies. Worse, they would kill all dogs. They would make you homeless.

Eventually, the Govester fell over, to be replaced by . . . Johnson. It's almost as if the Tories want to lose this election by even more than predicted. Who to bring out but the man the Tories themselves had concluded was unfit to govern? The man most of the country is happy to forget? The audience went wild. 'Boris, Boris,' they cheered. Louder than for Rish!. Natch.

What followed was classic Boris. He really doesn't care. He appears to hate Rish!, and so the only reason he would bother to appear was because he wanted to dance on Sunak's grave. He said he had been working tirelessly throughout the election. By going on holiday. He looked terrible. Wherever he's been, it's done him the world of harm. He rambled on about his own achievements for about 10 minutes. Not a word of praise for Rish!. The two did not appear to even exchange a glance. Let alone shake hands. He ended by saying that Starmer would not stand up to Putin. It would have been laughable if it hadn't been so tragic.

Finally, we got Sunak. There was no great love for him. The cheers were half-hearted. 'It's great to have the Tory family back together,' he began. It didn't look that way. And where was Truss? No funeral is complete without her. His speech then petered out. It was the same stump speech as always. And just as ineffectual. Then he wandered off back into the night.

Not with a bang but a whimper.

* * *

It had been a long six-week slog. Endless pointless debates. Countless contrived media appearances. One stunt after another from Ed Davey. Anything to fill the void. But, finally, election day had arrived. The country was about to get a new government.

The seconds ticked by to 10 p.m., when the people's will would be revealed

5 JULY 2024

It felt as if the world were coming to a standstill. Time was slowing down the closer we got to 10 p.m. The waiting became almost unbearable. In the ITV studios, presenters, pundits and reporters nervously rehearsed their lines. Filling in time before the moment when the polling stations closed and the exit poll was announced. Democracy can be surprisingly tense. That one point in the cycle when the power resides with the people, not the politicians.

The exit poll is rarely wrong. It's never yet failed to predict the largest party. Only in 2015 was there a small glitch, when it failed to predict a Tory overall majority. These days, it is treated with the reverence afforded to a holy relic. It shapes the narrative of the whole night. The defining verdict on the accuracy of all the other polls conducted over the previous weeks and months. The last word on the ambitions of the party leaders. From zero to hero. And vice versa.

Slowly, the clock ticked round. The minutes feeling like hours. After the last chime of Big Ben, Tom Bradby ended the suspense. A Labour landslide, with a majority of 170. Labour predicted to win 410 seats. The Tories just

131. A good night for the Lib Dems on 61. Reform on 13. The SNP almost wiped out with just 10.

It may not quite have been the wipeout the Tories had feared, but it was a disaster nonetheless: the worst result in their history. Ed Balls tried not to look too smug. As did George Osborne. He still has scores to settle with the Tory ranks. Then the post-mortems began. A pallid-looking Osborne – he's been on an anti-sunbed – laid into Rishi Sunak, Boris Johnson and Liz Truss. He can't help protecting his own legacy. Starmer had taken on the extremists in his party. Sunak hadn't.

Bradby turned his attention to Nicola Sturgeon. There was an ongoing police investigation into the SNP, he said. That can't have helped. Ouch. Nicola gulped and wondered why she had accepted the invitation to come onto the programme. Meanwhile, Tom was having the time of his life. He hadn't seen so much excitement in years. On to the seat predictor. Jeremy Hunt, Grant Shapps and Penny Mordaunt all lined up as toast. The country could breathe a little bit easier. But Rish! couldn't. We cut live to his seat, where it was reported he was planning to stay up all night. The man's a masochist. Just reach for the fentanyl.

Angela Rayner was first up for Labour. Hardly a ray of sunshine. Clearly under orders not to look too thrilled. She was here to serve, etc. But the odd smile wouldn't have gone amiss after 14 years in opposition. She did at least have an umbrella to keep the rain off. Labour had promised change, and Angela had just delivered. No drowned rat for her.

It took a while for the first Tory to make an appearance. Step forward a sad-looking Robert Buckland. Also not long for this parliament. He launched a furious attack on the Tory right for its brand of knee-jerk populism. He hoped his party wouldn't disappear down the Reform rabbit hole. Hold my beer, said an email from the neocons of Popular Conservatism that landed in my inbox. They plan to do just that. The Tory party seems hell-bent on tearing what's left of itself apart. Happy days.

Deeper into the night, we had an interview with Neil Kinnock. Quite the moment. He wears his heart on his sleeve and, like many of us, had wondered if he would ever see a Labour government again. Dreams do come true from time to time.

Meanwhile, Nicola had gone almost silent. Once bitten, twice shy. Maybe her lawyer had texted to remind her to say: 'No comment.' This won't be a night she cares to remember. Nor was it plain sailing on the other channels. Moments after pollster-in-chief John Curtice had put a health warning on Reform's predicted 13 seats, the BBC panel decided Reform was the big story of the night.

Mmm. Not so sure about that. The real story is that we have a new government with a landslide majority. Reform might have helped, but the people who voted for them knew what they were doing. They weren't that bothered if they put Keir Starmer in Downing Street. More than that, they were delighted.

If you wanted aggro, then Channel 4 was the place to be. Alastair Campbell and Nadine Dorries were at each other's throats from the start. Mainly arguing about Boris Johnson. Still, it made a change from talking about Thursday's election.

As the night wore on, the pace quickened, though the BBC seemed to miss many of the counts as its present-ers preferred the sound of their own voice. Viewers may have thought otherwise. Things just kept getting better and better for Labour and the Lib Dems. Paul Waugh did parliament a favour by defeating George Galloway in Rochdale. George threw a strop and didn't even bother to turn up for the declaration. Rochdale won't miss him.

Defence secretary Grant Shapps went down in Welwyn. One of the dangers of getting one of his alter egos to stand against him. Justice secretary Alex Chalk lost in Cheltenham. Gillian Keegan and Jeremy Hunt also looked in danger. Iain Duncan Smith managed to hang on in Chingford as the left did battle with the left. Never change, never change.

Finally, we got the first sighting of our new prime min-ister, as Keir Starmer turned up for his count. Whisper it, but he raised his eyebrows and forced a smile. You might even say that he looked happy. Almost. Welcome to the Pleasuredome. The future starts now.

Rishi Sunak departs with a brief nod to his achievements – mostly imagined

5 JULY 2024

It ended as it began. With Downing Street under leaden grey skies. Someone's idea of a cosmic joke. Only this time, rather than a torrential downpour, the rain had eased to a light drizzle. If you're a Tory, you take your blessings where you find them on days like these.

First to leave was Jeremy Hunt. The walk of shame from No. 11 with his wife and children into the back of a grey people carrier. No more government limos. The change of government can be brutal. No hiding place for the defeated. He managed the odd half-hearted smile towards the press. Nothing remotely convincing.

Only his dog looked thrilled to be returning to life in the Home Counties. The walkies are so much better in Godalming. Nicer smells. More sticks. Jezza may have been a distinctly average chancellor – the numbers and the spreadsheets were always beyond him – but his departure had been a model of graciousness. His winning speech at his declaration pitch perfect.

In time Jezza may get to appreciate the relative obscurity. Steve Baker claimed to be gagging for it. Couldn't wait to be rid of Westminster. 'I'm outta here,' he said. He'll get '4 July' tattooed on his arm. Hard to know if this was just another manifestation of his never-ending midlife crisis.

Meanwhile, Liz Truss departed this political life amid a flurry of indifference towards her constituents. The feeling was mutual. She was slow-handclapped at her count. A dismal end to a dismal former prime minister. But I'll miss her nonetheless. Where will Popular Conservatism be without the woman who made it so Unpopular? Her unknowing sense of the absurd was comedy gold.

Still, not entirely good news for the Tories. Much to the disappointment of his colleagues, Richard Holden won by 20 votes in Basildon and Billericay. No greater love hath any man than this, that he lay down his friends for his seat.

Shortly before Rishi Sunak stepped out of No. 10 to make his own resignation speech, you could hear a faint ripple of applause from inside. It was either his staff showing their appreciation or an ovation for Larry the cat, who was adding yet another notch to the doorpost. This is the fifth prime minister he has seen off. Larry is one of politics' great survivors. Been there, seen it, name on the T-shirt.

Near the security gates, you could just hear a few protesters singing 'Goodbye, auf Wiedersehen, adieu'. It felt more like a Pavlovian response than heartfelt dissent. They were there because they were there because they were there. Not long after, Rish! appeared from No. 10 for the last time. Followed by his wife. Being the partner of a high-profile politician can be demeaning. Reduced to the status of a trophy.

Nothing became Sunak quite so much as his departure. He began with an apology. Several apologies, in fact. To the country, for having messed up. For having allowed the division and decline to continue. To his Tory colleagues who had had their careers ended by his own shortcomings. Though, to be fair, many of them must also take responsibility for their actions. They knew the party was lurching to the unelectable right and yet they chose to do nothing. There was a brief nod to his own achievements – mostly imagined, but we can allow him a spell of denial at such a time – before he reminded us of the destruction of the Boris Johnson and Liz Truss administrations. Realistically, there was no coming back from those once Rish! had failed to disown them at the time.

Finally, some kind and thoughtful words about the innate decency of Keir Starmer and his pride in the country. Where had this Sunak been for the last 20 months? Had we seen more of this gentler Rish!, we might have been more inclined to give him a break. We might even have got to like him a bit. Instead, he played the tetchy right-wing provocateur, and we all saw through him.

There was silence as he made his way to the waiting car. This was a personal grief on which no one wanted to intrude. 'Oh dear, oh dear,' said the King, when Sunak made his final trip to the palace. There wasn't much else to say.

Two hours later, the Union Jack umbrellas were out in force as Labour staffers lined Downing Street. The media operation was in overdrive. This wasn't just a landslide for those who had voted Labour on Thursday. This was a government for the whole country. No one would be left behind. Everyone was welcome. Fourteen years of austerity, infighting, partying, incompetence and division had come to an end. The country could once again be proud of itself. Allow itself to believe in a future. Give hope a chance.

Then the ultimate kick in the teeth for Sunak. The sun came out. Of course it did. Poor Rish! has never managed to buy an even break. Crowds lined the streets. Waved flags and cheered as Starmer returned from the palace after being invited to form the government. It was a moment when you just knew that England were going to beat Switzerland 3–0 in the quarter-finals of the Euros on Saturday. New Starmer, new England.

It took an age for Keir and his wife, Vic, to shake hands with and hug his supporters inside Downing Street. Starmer even managed to break into the occasional smile. About as close to happy as he gets. Though his main emotion was relief. This was the culmination of four and a half years' hard work. Turning a beaten, unelectable party into a potential government. Power, not protest. And for the last six months he had known he was so, so close. But not quite daring to believe. Now he could relax. Not just a majority, but a super-majority. The moaners could moan, but the numbers spoke for themselves. The country had got what it voted for. Dreams do come true.

This was to be a good day for speeches. You wait ages for one, and then three come along at once. Starmer was modest, inclusive. Not a hint of triumphalism. No 'I told you so's. His mission wasn't to reach out to his supporters; it was to make the non-believers believe. Dignity, respect. Stability, moderation. A government unburdened by dogma. No more noisy performance. Keir would tread lightly on our lives. It's been an age since we've heard a prime minister talk to us like that. He may have campaigned in prose. But in his first hour in office he had governed in poetry.

More hugs, more cheers. Then Keir and Vic went inside. There was work to be done. The future started now.

* * *

Time waits for no one in politics. There is no graceful period of reflection. Rishi Sunak had been forced to leave Downing Street within hours of conceding defeat. We were thrust into a new era. One to which it would take us all time to adjust.

The Tories had been in government for 14 years. I had started as the Guardian's *political sketch writer in January 2014 and had only ever written about Conservative prime ministers. It would take a while to get the measure of the new Labour government. I rashly wrote that it felt as if the grown-ups were back in power. Time would tell how accurate that proved to be.*

Less is more from Starmer and Reeves, in contrast to Tory sound and fury

8 JULY 2024

For much of the last week of the election campaign, Rishi Sunak chose to portray Keir Starmer as something of a slacker. A man who would allow a country to invade the UK if it interrupted his Friday-night TV viewing. As for weekends, you could forget it. A write-off. Keir needed his lie-ins, and his phone would be switched off. Call back on Monday after 9.30 a.m.

On the basis of the last 72 hours, the Tories should have taken a leaf out of the new prime minister's book. Because it turns out that Keir can get a lot done while he's in bed. Or when he's sleepwalking. The somnambulist's somnambulist. Some might even argue he's achieved more in three days than the Tories managed in the last 18 months. There's been an energy to Starmer's slumber from which we could all learn. The dialectics of slackerdom. The more effort you put into appearing to do nothing, the more effective you become. Less is clearly more.

Forget Rish!'s tight-suited 1980s yuppie vibes. All sound and fury, signifying nothing. During the hours normally dedicated to his sleep, Keir has made some inspired appointments – viz. James Timpson – visited all corners of the UK and made it clear to the country that he is happy to be judged on his actions rather than his promises. Unusually, we have a prime minister with a sense of personal responsibility. Maybe we can all now get on with our lives, rather than waiting for the next clusterfuck from central government. That would make a change.

Nor is Starmer alone in his anti-work ethic that could so easily be confused as a work ethic. Most of his cabinet seem to have spent their entire weekend inside their new departments. Getting to know the layout and finding out what horrors lie in wait in their in-trays. None more so than Rachel Reeves. She has been personally going through every drawer of every desk, searching for a stray £10 note. Anything that might help balance the books and go towards 6,500 more teachers. But, after an exhaustive search, she had come up with nothing. Just one IOU, dating back to the Boris Johnson years, from one staffer to another for the Friday-night booze run to the Co-op, and three maxed-out credit cards. Not even a note saying there was no money left. At least Liam Byrne had had some manners back in 2010. The Tories were just rude.

Monday morning found Reeves back in the Treasury, delivering her first speech as chancellor. In the front row were half the cabinet. All for one, and one for all. It will take time for civil servants to get used to the idea of collective responsibility in government again. It might even catch on. It must also be especially unusual for Treasury staff to now have a boss who sounds as if she knows what she's doing. For the last couple of years they have had to put up with Jeremy Hunt, a man chosen for his affability rather than plausibility. A chancellor who seemingly understood less about economics than most of the rest of the country. There were moments during his budget statements when he seemed so out of his depth he was on the verge of tears. At least he had the integrity to have impostor syndrome. We take our comforts where we find them.

Reeves is never going to be an inspirational speaker. But so long as you've had three double espressos – Michael Gove can make his own pre-loading arrangements – it's usually worth listening to what she says. In fact, being a bit soporific provides its own reassurance. I long for the economy to become a somewhat dull niche pursuit again. For too long, all any chancellor had told us was how we were lucky not to be even more broke than we already were. That it was a race to the bottom to see if we could die before our mortgages were paid off. Assuming we were fortunate enough to own our own homes. Beneath Reeves's surface dullness there lies real hope.

We began with the government's own health warning. She had been through the books – something Jezza had never dared to do – and everything was just as bad as she had feared. The economy was in its worst shape since the Second World War. She would explain more when she gave a statement to the Commons later in the month. It will be interesting to see what whoever happens to be shadow chancellor at the time has to say in reply. 'We're proud of our record' probably isn't going to cut it.

Reeves praised the Bank of England and the Office for Budget Responsibility for their work – a reminder that her pre-election fiscal rules still applied – and said she would be giving her first budget in the autumn. Then to the nitty-gritty. To stimulate economic growth, she was changing the planning regulations to get more houses built. One and a half million over the course of the parliament. Something that even Tory think tanks and housebuilders had been crying out for. There would be more onshore windfarms too. Green energy a go-go.

You couldn't help thinking that Reeves had achieved more in one speech than Jezza had ever managed. The one drawback could be that the housebuilders may not have the skilled workers to actually do any building on this scale. It takes about six months to find someone to fix your roof these days. Still, I suppose there are a lot of unemployed ex-Tory MPs, so maybe they might like to retrain for the construction industry. I can just see Liz Truss as a plasterer. Jacob Rees-Mogg as a chippy.

It wasn't all sweetness and light in Labour land, though. Emily Thornberry isn't taking being overlooked for the attorney general's job lying down. She hasn't even been made a minister of state in another department yet. Her statement was a model of passive aggressions. She was 'sad and sorry' not to have got the call, she said. Make that totally furious. Still, with a majority of over 170, Starmer can afford to piss a few people off. Or maybe he just nodded off and forgot. It's long past everyone's time for a few zeds.

PopCons reassemble, and Jacob Rees-Mogg is the sanest person in the room

9 JULY 2024

I'm waiting near the front door of the Emmanuel Centre in Westminster, drinking a coffee. A well-dressed man leans in and whispers: 'Did you manage to get your MP over the line?' I've been mistaken for one of the last men – and they are almost all men – standing. A true believer. I don't want to upset the man, so I just mumble that we did get our woman over the line. I don't mention that the woman was Labour's Rosena Allin-Khan. It might break him completely.

This is the second gathering of the Popular Conservatism group. At the first, earlier in the year, there was a distinct buzz. Liz Truss was the star speaker, and Nigel Farage and Lee Anderson were in attendance, soaking up the vibes. We even had a star nonentity,

Holly Valance, an ever-present at batshit-crazy right-wing events. Those were the days when the Tories still mattered.

Now, not so much. The speaker line-up is a list of deadbeats and never-wases. No sign of Thick Lizzie. The organisation that seemed to have been formed for her coronation is now without its queen. Ever since she lost her seat last week, Truss has been having the mother of all sulks. Won't answer the phone, won't even get out of bed. Though she will keep drawing the £110,000 a year that gets handed out to ex-prime ministers.

Half the auditorium has been roped off, and by the time the conference – if you can call it that – kicks off, there are barely 200 people there. Still, there are 14 people waiting to follow proceedings on YouTube. So that's something. In the background, Gerry Rafferty's 'Get It Right Next Time' is playing through the PA system. At least someone has a sense of humour. It won't be long before they need to rethink the Popular bit of their Conservatism.

Annunziata – Nancy to the riff-raff – Rees-Mogg makes the introductions. 'It's wonderful so many of you have come,' she says. Hard to know if this is sarcasm or whether she's just relieved that everyone in her WhatsApp group has turned up. We mustn't celebrate colleagues who have lost their seats, she adds. But hey, if you must. Clearly, there's no love lost between her and her brother Jacob. Nor are we here to apportion blame. Could have fooled me.

Next up is Mark Littlewood, former head of the Institute of Economic Affairs and the brains – if you can call it that – behind Liz Truss's economic miracle. He sets the tone of delusion perfectly. Now is the start of the great rebuild, he declares. This is not a time for a leadership hustings. Just as well, because the only sitting MP in the room is Wendy Morton, and she's not being allowed to speak. Imagine being considered too much of a liability by the PopCons.

The tone is relentless. The Tories have been too woke, too left-wing. To listen to this lot you'd imagine the last 14 years had been a socialist paradise. Cameron, May, Johnson and Sunak had all been leftist extremists. Double agents dedicated to the destruction of the Tory party. David Starkey even thought that Margaret Thatcher was a closet lefty. Though he'd settle for a dead Maggie over a live Rishi.

'Are we learning from the catastrophe?' sobs David Frost. Er . . . the idea that Frosty the No Man might learn from anything is the ultimate category error. That would require the cognitive faculties of a three-year-old. Bizarrely, in right-wing circles Dave is considered to be something of an intellectual. A man who confronts the hard truths. To the rest of us, he seems barely able to dress himself. Frosty's unconsidered opinion is that the last Tory government betrayed the Conservative Party. One day, he might realise he was actually part of the government. Maybe this is just his way of saying how much he hates himself. The only man to perform acts of passive aggression on himself. Needless to say, he goes on to complain about the Brexit deal that he helped negotiate. He just can't stop himself. I suppose we ought to feel sorry for him.

On a pre-record from Washington DC, Suella Braverman literally just phones it in. She also seems to have lost the plot entirely. Happy to fill the vacuum left by Liz on the lucrative neocon speaking circuit Stateside. She sounds as if she would be delighted if she never had to come back at all. A loss to the US, but our gain. There are no lengths to which she wouldn't go to destroy the Tory party and see it out of office for at least three terms. Purge the One Nation softies, split the Tories and return it to its lunatic base.

You know your conference is in trouble when Jacob Rees-Mogg is the sanest person in the room. We're an irrelevance, he says. No one is listening to us. Apart from some sketch writers in search of some laughs. Though his sanity is short-lived. His advice is for the party to merge with Reform so that it can remain in opposition in perpetuity. Just remember that it's our members who give us the best leaders. That would be Thick Lizzy again. The woman who sank a thousand ships.

To see what a genuinely popular party looked like, you only had to turn to the Commons, where the 412 Labour MPs had gathered en masse for the election of the Speaker. Poor old Pat McFadden was left skulking in the shadows behind one of the exits. The shift in power hasn't been so graphically illustrated since 1997. The new cabinet were all smiles. They've waited a long time for this. It's a tradition that the Speaker has to look reluctant to take up the office. With Lindsay Hoyle, it was the other way round. He loves the job, would be bereft without it, and he was the one dragging Cat Smith and David Davis to the chair. He couldn't get there fast enough.

Then came the speeches. Keir Starmer paid tribute to Hoyle and called for an end to the self-obsession of some MPs. Dream on. He also squeezed out some hollow words on Diane Abbott's elevation to mother of the house. Awks. It was Starmer who had been trying to prevent Abbott from standing in her Hackney constituency.

Rishi Sunak, in his last few weeks – months, maybe – of standing in as leader of the opposition, cut a forlorn figure. This must be torture for him. But he is more gracious in defeat than he ever was as prime minister. Almost likeable.

More than could be said for Nigel Farage. These party leader speeches are supposed to be gentle and non-political. Funny, if possible. Nige failed on all three counts. Never one to read the room. He droned on about John Bercow and the betrayal of Brexit. And lied about his party having no experience in parliament. Lee Anderson just about counts. But then with Nige everything is always about Nige. Start as you mean to go on.

* * *

It would take everyone time to get used to the new world order. Not least Keir Starmer. Several times at PMQs he would refer to Rishi Sunak as prime minister. There were also hundreds of new MPs – both Labour and Tory – who were struggling to find their way round the corridors of Westminster. To get used to the quirks and customs.

But not everything was all change. The Tory party was still in crisis. And for those of us who enjoy that spectacle, we were about to be treated to another leadership contest. Bring it on.

Finding Labour a bit dull? Fear not, the Tory fun factory is gearing up again

25 JULY 2024

Go on. Admit it. There's a small part of you that has missed the psychodramas. Not necessarily the existential angst of lying in bed each night wondering what fresh hell the government was going to unleash on us the following day. But certainly the infighting. For the last five years or so, watching the Tories implode, with little help from the opposition parties, became one of the country's favourite spectator sports.

The general election put an end to that. Most of us had forgotten what serious government looked like. Ministers going about their business in a calm and capable manner.

No major crises. No meltdowns. Even seven Labour MPs losing the whip over the two-child benefit cap blew over in a matter of 24 hours. Hardly a ripple.

Of course, it's early days, so not too much can have gone wrong. Labour are spending as much time uncovering hidden Tory horrors as they are getting on with their own programme. At some point, it's inevitable that things will go tits up. They always do. No government is perfect, and something always comes back to bite you. But we're not at that point yet. Keir Starmer has made a confident start on both the global and the domestic stages. And if it all feels, well, a bit boring, then he will settle for that. Prime ministers like boring. The country needs a bit of boring. It means that things are going reasonably well. Long may it continue.

The good news, though, is that the Conservative fun factory is back up and running. As in, fully dysfunctional. The even better news is that this time the fun comes with no jeopardy to the country. Because whatever the outcome, none of it really matters. The Tories are no longer – for the next few years at least – a danger to anyone. Except themselves. They are an irrelevance. They now exist purely as entertainment for entertainment's sake. An amusing diversion for lovers of political theatre.

Nor is the fun time-limited. This one is set to run and run. OK, the Tory leadership contest officially ends in early November, but the reality is that the show will extend for months. Years even. Because it's in the nature of the party's rules that the only possible result is a leader who will inevitably need to be replaced before too long. It is the Tory party membership who have the final say, and they – there is no easy way of sugar-coating this – are all completely mad. Only interested in electing someone who is as crazy as they are. Someone the country would never consider putting in government. It's win–win for the neutral.

Given the nature of the contest, it was only fitting that the first person to announce that they would be running was a joke candidate. Step forward James Cleverly. Now I dare say that to some new Tory MPs – there are a few, I promise – Jimmy Dimly might seem impressive. Quite the catch. Former foreign and home secretary. So one or two might have been tempted into nominating him. But step back and think about it. What exactly has Jimmy D ever done in government? Your mind is probably blank. Because the answer is, very little. Apart from turning left into first class when boarding aeroplanes on government business. As home secretary, he was worse than useless. His was the chronicle of a death foretold. As foreign secretary, he showed a rare moment of insight by declaring the Rwanda plan to be 'batshit crazy'. So it was just his luck to be put in charge of implementing it. With inevitable results. The thing to remember about Dimly is that he's not very bright. A born follower. Something of a drawback in a leadership contest.

Next to put his name forward on Thursday morning was Tom Tugendhat. The trouble with Tom is that he comes with way too much baggage. He is officially one of the few sane Tory MPs left, someone whom, polls suggest, people outside the padded cells of the Tory membership would consider as prime minister material. This obviously makes him a complete non-starter. No one thought to be borderline sensible has a viable role in the modern Tory party.

To be fair to Tom, he has been doing his best to prove that he, too, can be a full-blown mentalist. So he wrote a piece for the *Telegraph* in which he promised to take the UK out of the European Convention on Human Rights, if necessary. A clear pitch to the Tory membership that he was willing to be as mad as they were.

Only his heart wasn't really in it, because on the morning media round he couldn't commit to what he had put in print. He knows it's a bad idea to turn the country into an international pariah. To give up so much of value in search of an illusory, short-term gain. He also knows it's not what most of the UK wants. So, even if he were to make it to the last two, then the membership would reject him. There again, he did back Liz Truss, so you never know.

A little while later, Robert Jenrick also announced his candidacy. The former immigration minister who resigned because he wasn't good enough. With Honest Bob, you can judge the man by the company he keeps. It was Honest Bob who eased through the planning permission for Tory donor and pornographer Richard 'Dirty'

Desmond. And Honest Bob's campaign manager is none other than Danny Kruger, a man with so little judgement that he makes a habit of attaching himself to losing, lunatic right-wing causes.

It is Honest Bob's belief that the reason the Tories lost the last election was because they weren't right-wing enough. He has yet to realise that losing the country's trust, crashing the economy, destroying public services and leaving everyone worse off might have played a part. He probably never will. Some things will always be a mystery to him.

There again, the same applies to most of the other contenders. We have Priti Patel: sacked for breaking the ministerial code and running her own foreign policy agenda. Erstwhile best mate of Nigel Farage. Suella Braverman: sacked for breaking the ministerial code, and who has been trying to reinvent herself this week as the compassionate face of bigotry. Kemi Badenoch: the most divisive woman in politics. A woman who hates the electorate almost as much as she hates her colleagues. And herself. She could start a fight with her reflection. Lastly, Mel Stride. We began and end with a joke. A man who has confused his own electoral survival with importance. The Mark Harper of this leadership race.

So, as we head towards recess, let's allow ourselves time to enjoy the spectacle. Blue on blue. A race to the bottom. Let the fun begin.

Reeves and Hunt come to brink of fisticuffs over mysteriously absent £22 billion

30 JULY 2024

The timing could have been better. For much of the last few weeks the Tory party has been dancing on eggshells around Labour. As if in awe of their majority. Still suffering PTSD from 4 July. Bunkering down. Even at their one prime minister's questions before the recess, Rishi Sunak chose to ask about Ukraine, a subject on which everyone agrees. It was as though everyone was just trying to somehow make it through to the summer break vaguely intact.

It had all been going so well. Then, on Monday, it all kicked off, with Rachel Reeves accusing the Tories of covering up a £22 billion black hole in the public finances. Jeremy Hunt angrily denied this. Well, as angrily as a man who doesn't really do anger can. Jezza has never been big on feelings. Wouldn't recognise one if it bit him. Let's just say he was quite hurt. Disappointed even. But even this was a bit half-hearted. Parliamentary procedure dictated that punches be pulled. You must never call a liar 'a liar' in the Commons. But neither Reeves nor Hunt could quite let it go. They were both up for some afters. Somewhere they could make their real feelings known. So, on the last day before recess, both were on the morning media rounds, kicking the shit out of each other.

On balance, you would have to say the chancellor won on points. But only because everyone beats Jezza on points. He's the ultimate posh-boy beta male. Whose career-defining moment was to be the head boy of a minor public school. Nothing has ever been so good since. Nor ever will be.

Reeves wasted no time in going for the jugular. Hunt and Sunak had deliberately misled the country. Had been handing out unfunded tax cuts that the UK couldn't afford. Had already spent the year's emergency reserves three times over in just three or four months. In short, they had lied.

Here it got somewhat confusing. Because it wasn't immediately clear if this was the £22 billion black hole that we had all expected. The one for which the Institute for Fiscal Studies (IFS) had prepared the way. Or whether that black hole was now mysteriously accounted for and Rachel had discovered an entirely new one. Not even the IFS or the Office for Budget Responsibility (OBR) has been able to solve that one. Both have issued statements saying there were all sorts of things in the books that they hadn't anticipated. Though, confusingly, not the full £22 billion. This one will run and run.

It fell to Mishal Husain to pick the bones out of this on the *Today* programme. So, she began, at least some of the £22 billion can be accounted for by Labour's public sector pay awards? Now it was Reeves's turn to get narked. All she had done was accept the recommendations of the pay review board. It wasn't her fault that the previous Tory government had set the parameters so high.

OK, said Husain. So if it had been down to you, the government would not have settled on a 20% rise for junior doctors? Er . . . Yes, no, yes, no. We were where we were, and she was sure the doctors were worth it. Possibly. So would the nurses and other public sector workers be getting a 20% rise? That was a category error, Reeves snapped. Not keen on this particular line of logic, she changed the subject. What Mishal and Radio 4 listeners had to accept was that the Tories were very, very bad people. It wasn't Rachel's choice to be the Ministering Angel of Death, but it wouldn't be fair to the country were she to pretend that everything was OK.

She wasn't sorry that she had to cancel the 40 new hospitals. But then neither was anyone, as they had never existed in the first place. Only in government do you get rewarded for creative accounting by cancelling something that was never going to happen. Nor was she sorry she was introducing means testing for the winter fuel allowance for pensioners. It would do some of the old people good to get a bit cold.

Same with social care costs. People with dementia couldn't expect any favours from a Labour government. There were fiscal rules for a reason, and she was going to stick to them. Unlike the Tories. If people started dying, it was on the Tories. Not her. She wasn't going to do a Liz Truss and start making unfunded spending commitments.

Her job was to keep saying no to everything. The IFS and the OBR seemed to broadly agree.

That just left Jezza in the more than capable hands of Justin Webb. Though even he seemed to take pity on the shadow chancellor. Rather too late in the day, some people have only just realised what most of us already knew: that Jeremy simply isn't that bright. So when he claimed that he hadn't deliberately lied about the state of the economy, I was inclined to believe him. Because to have done so would have been to assume that Jezza knew what he was doing. Which he didn't. The only reason he was put in charge of the Treasury was because he was the last person standing in the Tory party who looked like a chancellor.

Justin didn't bother to interrupt. Or even to ask too many questions. Far easier to let Hunt implicate himself. There's so little that he does seem to understand, it's hard to know where to start. Jezza didn't seem to grasp that the reason the original estimates were different from the revised estimates was because the revised estimates had been . . . well, there's no easy way of saying this . . . revised. That's rather the point of revision. You get to have another look.

We moved on to the unbudgeted £6.4 billion for housing refugees. That wasn't fair, said Jezza. Because the government had literally been on the verge of sending 60,000 refugees to Rwanda. So, put like that, the real costs were zero. It was quite sweet really. The bear with little brain. 'I'm not profligate,' he concluded. He seemed to have forgotten the 4% cut in national insurance. A cut that, curiously, was worth £22 billion. Just saying.

More normal service was resumed in the Commons, where we had been expecting some fireworks between Angela Rayner and Kemi Badenoch during the housing statement. All we got were damp squibs. Angie made a few jibes about the Tories losing the election, but Kemi could hardly be bothered to respond. Most unlike her. Normally, she is up for any fight. Even with herself, if necessary. Now she just seemed subdued. Maybe she is trying to present a new, softer side to Tory MPs during the leadership election. Maybe she's overdosed on joyless decadence. Too much time hanging out with Michael Gove.

Keir's had his holiday ruined, so he's ruined ours – by telling us everything's hopeless

27 AUGUST 2024

Nothing screams the end of summer more than a prime minister giving a speech marked 'state of the nation'. Especially when that speech could just as well have been made a week later. To give us all a chance to enjoy the start of the Paralympics. Feel the last warmth of a cooling sun. Not think about how hopelessly shit everything is for a few more days. We could all have done with more of a break. Maybe it was revenge. Keir Starmer had his holiday ruined, so he was determined to ruin ours.

It wasn't as if Starmer had anything new to say. He's spent much of the past seven weeks telling us that things are even worse than he had imagined, and Tuesday's speech was basically more of the same. By now we have all lost count of the number of black holes he has found in the country's finances.

Was the £22 billion shortfall the same as last week's £22 billion shortfall? Or was it a completely different £22 billion? After a while all the numbers start merging into one another. God knows where we file the extra £5 billion spent on servicing debt. And we've known for some time that a punishment budget is coming down the line. So why keep reminding us?

Then again, politicians are a different breed to the rest of us. When we go back to work, we do so silently. We don't feel the need to make a big song and dance about our return. The reappearance of a slumbering hero. Expecting thanks and applause for bothering to come back on the day we said we would. To do the job we are employed to do. Not so the governing class. They live in fear that people will assume they are doing nothing, unless they keep up a running commentary on their latest manoeuvres. They trust neither us nor, it seems, themselves. They demand our attention. They only know they are doing their job if they can read about themselves in the papers.

So Starmer's speech was as much for himself as it was for us. More so, in fact. We would have been quite happy to do without it. He would have been devastated to miss out on the opportunity. For a man who is often so critical of performative politics, he is quite the performer. It rather goes with the job. Still, at least he can stay in role. When you're being told the country is dying on its feet, it's reassuring that the messenger has the natural demeanour of a professional undertaker.

Just after 10 a.m. the prime minister stepped out into the Downing Street garden. Carefully stepping round the broken swing that has been rusting for several years. Trying to avoid the smashed vodka bottles. After a moment's prayerful silence, Starmer began speaking. The location was no coincidence. Fifty members of the public and the media were gathered in the garden to remind us we had moved on from the sleaze and indulgence of the Tory government. From now on the garden would be a place of solemnity. A very serious garden. A symbol of service. A place from which frivolity would be banned. No smiles allowed. Keir was here to show he meant business. Everything he did, he did it for us. Very Bryan Adams.

Things weren't just worse than he had imagined, he said. They were even worse than he hadn't imagined. So much so that things were going to continue getting worse before they could get better. This is really the undiluted truth that only a prime minister with a landslide majority can express in their first few months in office. He sounded like the builder who says you need a completely new roof, after you'd called him in to clean the gutters. Too much more of this and some Labour MPs will start to get twitchy. This wasn't exactly the message during the general election campaign.

Still, Keir did have some good news. He had at least identified the cause of all the problems. The Tories. They had left the country flatlining in A&E. Their cheap populism had been behind the recent riots. He had been left with a prison service that didn't even have enough room for all the offenders. So he would have to inflict more pain on the country to make things better. He was sorry about pensioners losing their winter fuel allowance, but old people would have to choose between keeping warm and having a functioning NHS. Right now, they couldn't have both.

'Look,' said Keir, 'this isn't the position I wanted to be in.' Him and us both. But we were where we were. The budget was going to be painful. Higher taxes for sure. Probably some public sector cuts thrown in. It was all a bit reminiscent of the early days of David Cameron and George Osborne. And look how the country ended up after them.

Come the end, there was time for a few questions from the media. Most focused on the forthcoming budget. Where were the tax rises going to hit? Keir gave these short shrift. He had been quite clear. There would be no increases to income tax, national insurance or VAT.

So that clearly meant the rises would be piled onto everything else. Duh! Hardly a surprise.

With that, Keir was off. A good morning's work for him. Even if the rest of us would rather he had remained on holiday. We get it. Honest, we do. Everything's rubbish. And is going to get more rubbish. Salvation is a long way off.

No one cares who will lead the Tories next, not even them

9 SEPTEMBER 2024

Yet another day in the land of shadows. Where politics goes largely unseen. If not totally unheard. Providing you can read the puffs of smoke. This is the new world order. All the big decisions taken away from the public gaze. All we are left with is a puppet show embedded in interpretive dance. Even in Westminster the show must go on.

Take the Tory leadership contest. Now into its second phase, with Priti Patel last week consigned to oblivion. Here the blind are leading the blind. There are no more public events in which the game-show contestants can road-test their policies. Instead, we are in the realm of a private hustings for Tory MPs' eyes only.

Except not even the Lucky Five remaining candidates seem to have a clue what is going on. It was only when they turned up shortly before 4 p.m. that they discovered the event was actually starting at 4.15 p.m. and what the format was going to be. The organisers had obviously decided to keep them out of the loop. Keep them on their toes. On a need-to-know basis. Or maybe if the 1922 Committee didn't even know what was going on, there was less chance of the contestants coming prepared. Piss-up and brewery came to mind.

There again, low-key seems to be the order of the day. There was a faint buzz of expectation when the Tory leadership contest began. Though possibly this was the last heaving breaths of a dying party. Now reality has resumed. There is no great interest in the Tory party – let alone in the rest of the country – in who takes over from Rishi Sunak. Because it's, by and large, an irrelevance. A formality to be observed. Someone to shout from the sidelines.

It wasn't always that way. Back when being Tory leader was a big deal – think of the various contests to replace David Cameron, Theresa May, Boris Johnson and Liz Truss – you couldn't move for Tory MPs and lobby journalists. People would arrive early to get a good seat. Now, just 10 minutes before the start, the committee room was totally empty. By the scheduled start of 4 p.m., there were barely 10 MPs. A few more turned up in dribs and drabs over the next 20 minutes – clearly disappointed not to have missed the opening credits – but there was no sense of excitement. Most had chosen to have a snooze – opposition is good for that – rather than bother to turn up to hear what their next party leader might say. When push comes to shove, they just aren't that interested.

Outside the committee room, the five candidates just stood around looking awkward. Tom Tugendhat nervously tried to engage James Cleverly and Kemi Badenoch in desultory conversation, but they proved largely monosyllabic – more interested in their Instagram feeds. Mel Stride just seemed a bit bewildered. Understandably. Even he has finally got round to asking the question everyone else is asking: what is the point of Mel Stride? If the answer is Mel, you're asking the wrong question. There again, the same could be said of all the Lucky Five.

One man stood further apart from the others. Robert Jenrick. Not even pretending to get on with his colleagues. No one is still any the wiser as to whether he's been secretly rubbishing Kemi to the media, or if Kemi has been rubbishing herself. Both are equally possible. The Tories are that deranged. Somehow or other whoever eventually gets elected has to unite the Conservatives. No one can see exactly how. They all seem to hate each other as much as the country hates them.

All this was observed by me and two other journalists. Without us, the Tories wouldn't even have known they were really there. Call it a public service. At about 4.15 p.m., sensing there was not going to be a late surge of Tory MPs, the chair of the 1922 Committee summoned the Lucky Five into the room. They still didn't really have a clue what to expect. There was some polite banging on the desk – more a Pavlovian response than genuine enthusiasm – and then the first question: why are we here? No one had a clue. Tomorrow the Lucky Five become the Lucky Four.

Meanwhile, Labour was going through its own private rituals. First in cabinet, where it was revealed that there had been 'zero dissent on the withdrawal of the winter fuel allowance'. Somehow that was not reassuring. More the feel of a Stalinist politburo, in which everyone is terrified, than an outbreak of warm-hearted consensus. There was to be no concession. No change. Everyone must be happy. Rictus smiles. All a bit forced. Just like Labour's hope that everyone would take up pension credit instead. Thereby saving the government precisely nothing. From a cut that was designed to save money.

Still, Rachel Reeves did make the token gesture of addressing Labour MPs late in the day. A stroke of largesse from the Ministering Angel of Death. Not that she was there to change her mind. More to let everyone know that she wouldn't. But also to say that she really wanted to do her bit for pensioners. So every speech she made from now on would be accompanied by a phone number for the Samaritans helpline. If you have been affected by any of the issues raised in this sketch, call 116 123.

Over in the Commons there were a few brief signs of normal political life. But ones that showed the opposition is in even worse shape than previously imagined. It really doesn't have a clue how to effectively oppose. It's heard of this thing called an 'urgent question' but has no idea what to do with it. On Monday it was the turn of the shadow health secretary, Victoria Atkins, to make an idiot of herself. She had asked for a UQ on Wes Streeting's decision to ask former health secretary Alan Milburn for advice. 'Er, hello,' said Wes. Unlike the Tories, he wasn't too proud to ask experts for help.

'The health secretary should know what they are doing,' Atkins replied. 'I always did.' Cue a major pile-on, as Atkins had been a spectacularly poor health secretary. Though not noticeably worse than any of her Tory predecessors. It was an open goal for Streeting, who went on to list the more egregious cases of Tory cronyism. Believe it or not, Atkins reckons she is in with a shout of becoming shadow chancellor if Honest Bob becomes leader. Rachel Reeves's job just became a whole lot easier.

Starmer's NHS offering: no more gaslighting, but no more money either

12 SEPTEMBER 2024

Attention all citizens. This is a public service announcement. Stop what you are doing and listen. For your own safety you are advised not to get ill any time in the next

10 years. If you feel a heart attack coming on, then just take a few deep breaths and ignore it. If you are worried you may have cancer, take two aspirin and go to bed. If you aren't dead within six months, you will know it was a false alarm. If you think you need mental health services, just pull yourself together. Just stop it. Thank you for your time. There will be further updates in due course.

Having spent the first weeks of his time in Downing Street examining the state of the public finances – far worse than he thought – and the prison service – far worse than he thought – Keir Starmer has now turned his attention to the health service. This, too, is far worse than he thought. We're definitely seeing a pattern here. In fact, it's a miracle that many of us are still alive. Or not stuck in the permanent limbo of A&E. The only reason no one had complained was because everyone was too busy waiting on hold, hoping to get an appointment with their GP.

Speaking at the King's Fund after the publication of the Darzi report, Keir was happy to cosplay as the Grim Reaper. We few. We lucky few who had beaten the odds and survived. Spare a thought for those who had fallen along the way. The undiagnosed. The misdiagnosed. The diagnosed-too-late. But don't ever relax. The apocalypse is coming for all of us sooner or later. None of us will get out of this alive. No one has ever beaten the system. All we can do is try to stay one step ahead of eternity for as long as possible.

Weirdly, there was something rather uplifting about all this. And not just because Starmer is a natural undertaker. If being prime minister doesn't work out for him, there's a job waiting for him as mourner-in-chief to the deceased with no known relatives. The eulogy for the unknown person. Sad face. Sincere face. What was most welcome was the reassurance. The Grim Reaper was telling us what most of us instinctively already know. Our experience tells us that the NHS is on its knees. That doctors and nurses are fighting a losing battle. That a thousand everyday kindnesses – staff going the extra mile – cannot compensate for a system in collapse. That waiting lists are interminable. That A&E can be a war zone. That hospitals are falling to bits.

So to have a politician acknowledging reality comes as a relief. At last there is someone serious in charge. Someone who isn't gaslighting us or trying to persuade us that any failures are minimal. Transient. Insisting that 40 new hospitals have been built when we all know that at best one waiting room may have been refurbished. We can move on from a state of cognitive dissonance.

Starmer leaned on his scythe. Everything was bad. Worse than bad. It was terrible. People were dying unnecessarily everywhere. Dropping like flies. Cardiovascular and cancer outcomes were far worse than in other comparable countries. Our children were fatter, our adults were iller. Mental health patients in cells, with only mice for company. And the blame lay squarely with the last government. Fourteen years of underinvestment and neglect. The pandemic a smokescreen. During Covid our patients were dying off far quicker than elsewhere. One person was singled out as especially worthy of blame. Step forward, Andrew Lansley, David Cameron's first health secretary, whose top–down reforms had almost single-handedly wrecked the NHS.

Needless to say, Lansley's reward for this act of destruction was a seat in the Lords. Establishment politicians like him are only ever allowed to fail upwards. A more fitting punishment would have been to make him an unpaid car park attendant at St George's hospital. Instead, he remains untouched by his own incompetence and ideology. He now whiles away the hours, collecting his £361 daily attendance fee and advising companies on health policy as a side hustle. Presumably people have learned to do the opposite to what he suggests.

Unusually, the Grim Reaper chose not to leave it there, the audience left in a state of terminal despair. Because his minders have now instructed him to leave room for a glimmer of optimism. The faintest gamma ray of hope. So there was a solution, he said. Labour could fix this. Though not with more money. Because there wasn't any. See above, and previous sketches. Though he did get through this speech without mentioning the £22 billion black hole. Probably an oversight. But a collector's item nonetheless. Nor would he be raising taxes, as working people couldn't afford this. Watch his lips. Instead, he was going to reform the NHS back to health. Making everything digital. Cancer surgery via AI. Treating people in the community. Stopping people getting ill in the first place. Sorting out social care for good. Allowing doctors and nurses time to do their job rather than hunt for beds.

It all sounded wonderful. Though how any of this was going to happen without more money was rather glossed over. Just trust the process. Want to believe, and it will happen. Still, it was a change to hear a prime minister who was on nodding terms with the reality of the NHS and a desire to improve it. The bad news was that it was all going to take 10 years. Not all of us were going to live that long. Though our sacrifice would not have been in vain.

Just under an hour later, the health secretary, Wes Streeting, was on his feet in the Commons, saying much the same thing in his ministerial statement. Though, Wes being Wes, it was said with rather more force. It was the Tories wot wrecked the NHS. Lansley and the rest of them had blood on their hands. What they had done was unforgivable. The least they could do was say sorry.

An apology was the last thing on the mind of the shadow health secretary, Victoria Atkins. Rather, she wanted to let people know that the NHS wasn't really in that much of a state. Its shortcomings had been exaggerated. People should enjoy their 40 new hospitals. Be grateful for Lansley. And if people had been dying off more quickly than they should have been, then it was their fault. Lack of moral fibre.

The thing about Vicky is that she's not that bright. Not something that prevents her being a high flyer in the current Tory party. It would be a start if she could learn to read the room. The Speaker shut her up mid-sentence. An act of kindness.

* * *

To be fair, there had been excuses. The Southport riots had dominated much of the summer. Then there had been a long holiday period in August. It had felt as if everyone was in need of a break. Politics had been a full-on business for years. It was a relief not to have to go to bed worrying what catastrophe the government would trigger while you were asleep.

That said, you couldn't avoid the conclusion that Labour didn't appear to have done that much in their first few months. It was as though all their energies had been focused on winning the election, and not much thought had been expended on what they wanted to do once the election was won. There was the hint of a vacuum, into which negative energy would spill. Sure enough, the first scandal was not long in coming: Keir Starmer and Rachel Reeves taking clothes and makeover freebies. The sort of thing that was evidently a no-no to everyone else. But politicians don't seem to be able to help themselves.

With a lust for freebies and hobbled by infighting, Labour look like the Tories 2.0

19 SEPTEMBER 2024

During the last election campaign it was hard to escape the impression that, whatever his other faults, Rishi Sunak just wasn't very good at politics. The charge sheet included getting drenched announcing the election and leaving D-Day veterans on the beaches. And insisting that black was white: that he was stopping the boats, that the economy was in good shape, that the Tories were on course for victory.

Just a couple of months later, it very much feels like Keir Starmer and Labour are saying: 'Hold my beer.' Keen to prove that they, too, are amateurs at the political PR game. It's almost as if there is something about being in government that makes fools of everyone. Though few would have imagined that Labour could manage it quite so quickly. A period of grace would have been more fitting.

Take the freebies. And Keir has. The Arsenal tickets. The Taylor Swift tickets. The suits. The designer glasses. The clothes for his wife. Starmer's big shtick was that he was going to do politics differently. The antidote to Tory corruption and scandal. A man who could be trusted. He was one of us. So why put yourself in a position where you can so easily be criticised by the right-wing press? If you want to set yourself up as a model of propriety, then you can't start making exceptions. Especially not so early on. A couple of years in, and people may not notice so much. You have to be above reproach. Yes, it might be a loss not to go to the football. And you might resent having to buy a few more suits for yourself. But that all rather goes with the job. Being prime minister may be a career highlight for a politician, but you have to take the downsides.

Perhaps Starmer has been too honest for his own good. Maybe he should have been more like Boris Johnson. Keir has made himself accountable by listing his freebies in detail. We know exactly where all the money went. With Boris, we are largely in the dark. He took whopping gifts from all sorts of undesirables, and we aren't entirely sure of the details. Being prime minister was a licence for Boris to cash in. No one expected any different from him. He never pretended to be on the side of the angels.

Then there is the question of Sue Gray's pay. You could say that someone should have suggested that Sue take a £4,000 drop in salary just for appearances' sake. So she earned less than the prime minister. Maybe throw in a clothes allowance and an events expense account to make up the difference. No one will notice. Surely. I guess she is a tough negotiator. One of the reasons she was made chief of staff.

But all this is not really the point. The issue is, why is the Labour Party indulging in open feuds with itself by leaking the story in the first place? We were promised a government of service, and yet it already appears to be totally dysfunctional. It's as if Starmer has taken the Tories as his role model. How did it come to this, that half the No. 10 top team hate the other half? And vice versa. Couldn't someone have just got a therapist in? Or at the very least established a workplace culture where people talked to one another? Or – and here's a thought – paid junior staff the proper rate?

Still, Keir isn't entirely a slow learner. There's a tradition that prime ministers do a media round of regional radio stations on the Thursday before a party conference. But, after the last two years, when Liz Truss and Sunak each had an hour they would rather forget, Starmer decided to reset the format to pre-recorded outings, where he hoped there would be less room for disaster. All the interviews would be released at 5 p.m., when he hoped no one would be listening.

So it was left to the business secretary, Jonathan Reynolds, to do the morning media round. An experience he would rather forget. Reynolds comes across as a decent man, but too much more of this and he will find himself as Labour's answer to Mel Stride. The minister who gets to do the rubbish jobs that no one else will. In future, at times like this I am sure he will learn to put his phone on mute and not take calls from the No. 10 comms team. It's early days, I suppose.

On Times Radio, Aasmah Mir cut to the chase. Why did Starmer accept so many freebies? Reynolds forgot to engage his brain. It was like this, he said. Politicians get invited to events all the time, and it would be rude not to go. It was the way people tried to engage with decision-makers. Sure thing. That's why it was vital for Boris Johnson to accept a freebie to Evgeny Lebedev's party in Italy. And a Taylor Swift concert is a prerequisite for stopping the winter fuel allowance.

It very much sounded as if he was talking about the perks of the job, said Mir. Oh no, replied Reynolds. Far from it. Perish the thought. Just that politicians worked extremely hard and deserved a little downtime. Especially if they didn't have to pay for it. The thought occurred that if Starmer was desperate to see Arsenal, he could have afforded the cost of a seat with the corporates. It was just strange that all these dazzling freebies were never offered to the rest of us.

Over on Sky, Kay Burley was outraged by the size of Gray's salary. One wonders what Burley's wedge is. I'm not sure she would get out of bed for £170,000. She would consider that an insult. But I'm sure that's not the point. Even so, Reynolds still couldn't think straight. Why not just say that Dominic Cummings and other former Downing Street heads of staff would have been on a similar sort of salary, if you allowed for inflation. The same people outraged now were not outraged then. It could just be that £170,000 is the going rate for the job and that it is the prime minister who is underpaid. A thought.

So the nonsense will continue into the Labour Party conference, starting this weekend. And Labour really doesn't have anyone to blame but itself. Freebies and staff pay should have been headed off ages ago. And maybe it doesn't matter if we have a government that is bad at politics if it gets the big calls right. After all, the chances are we'll be talking about something else in a month's time. Head down and onwards and sideways.

* * *

Parliament took its annual break as the parties went on their conference recess. It proved to be a strange three weeks for all concerned: the Lib Dems trying to build on their election success, which had made them the third-largest party with more than 70 MPs; the Tories trying to get used to being in opposition; and Labour similarly trying to come to terms with being in government.

First, though, we had Reform. A party that, like its leader, traded on grievance and struggled to come up with any real policies.

Reform's conference is all blame, grumpiness – and no idea how to fix things

20 SEPTEMBER 2024

From the railway station, you take the emergency stairs down to the perimeter road. Walk half a mile round the back of the vast hangars of Birmingham's NEC. Get to a fork. To the right, the Bear Grylls Adventure. To the left, the Reform Party conference. Decisions, decisions. A day out being macho and talking the Alpha course with Russell Brand. Or having reality twisted with Nigel Farage and his crew. Come to think of it, there's not much difference.

More than an hour before the start the queue for Reform snakes back 100 yards from the entrance. Fair to say neither Labour nor the Tories will get a crowd this big for their conferences over the next 10 days or so. Inside, the merchandise stall is doing brisk business in Reform coffee mugs. No one seems that interested in the Richard Tice turquoise ties. Strange. Looking like the sales rep for a sunbed company is very much on brand for the upper echelons of the party.

Near the entrance to the auditorium are two stalls. One for the TaxPayers' Alliance. The other for the Free Speech Union. Even the Institute of Economic Affairs has stayed away. I speak to a delegate. He explains how he used to be a member of the Revolutionary Communist Party, before he realised there were too many immigrants. What he really wants to talk to me about, though, is the fact that John Lennon was killed by an assassin acting on the direct orders of George H. W. Bush.

Inside the hall, the 4,000 members get to their feet as Nige takes his place in the front row, surrounded by minders and snappers. A chant of 'Nigel, Nigel' bounces off the walls. It's a curious mix of a Billy Graham revivalist meeting and a Nuremberg rally. This is a party that has come to party. It may have been playing the same tunes for the last 10 years, as UKIP was followed by the Brexit Party and now Reform, but its supporters are ever hopeful. They believe their time is coming.

The suspiciously tanned David Bull gets proceedings under way. No one knows exactly what Dave does, but he acts like one of the chosen ones. The inner circle. He runs through a few old favourites. Immigrants. Loud boos from the audience. Keir Starmer taking freebies. More loud boos. Just wait till they all find out how many freebies Nige has taken in his career. This is rapidly turning into a pantomime act. Brexit has been stolen from them. No one here is taking any responsibility for the Brexit they campaigned for.

Then James McMurdock. The Reform MP who only got elected because he signed the wrong papers. He thought he was joining the party, when in reality he was applying to become a candidate. He had been in the party less than two months when he became an MP. 'I guess I should introduce myself,' he says. Good. Maybe he was about to reveal how he was imprisoned for domestic violence. On second thoughts, maybe not. The truth is mutable for Reform. Bewilderingly, he concludes by saying that if you vote Reform, then you get honest and skilled MPs. He is exhibit No. 1, I guess.

Next we were promised one of the most famous people in the country. Instead, we got Ann Widdecombe. A woman too unpleasant even for the Tory party. Imagine. She doesn't even try to keep her hatred of immigrants in check. Sink the boats. Do whatever you like. They aren't real people to her. Imprison them in rat-infested squalor. Send them to any old country. As long as they aren't here. She has no idea how to achieve any of this. Nor any interest in international law. But neither has the audience. They all believe that foreigners belong anywhere but here. She gets a standing ovation.

Believe it or not, Ann was comparatively sane compared with Ant Middleton, who followed her. The kindest thing to say about him is that he's not very bright. Only capable of a stream of unconsciousness. Since being thrown off *SAS: Who Dares Wins* for being a total dick, Ant has come to believe he's the Messiah. He specialises in confessional motivational speeches that are complete and utter bollocks. Maybe he thought he was at the Bear Grylls centre.

'They are out to get you,' he confided from the front of the stage. We never got to find out who 'they' were. But it sounded like the establishment. In which case, beware of Nige and Dicky Tice. They are more establishment than most of the government. And beware all foreigners. He loved his country, and it was being stolen from him. British culture was Christianity. Any unbelievers had to be eradicated. This was too much even for some of the audience. Imagine being too out there for Reform.

During the lunch break, the professionally grumpy became even grumpier as half the food concessions were closed and some of the queues were 200 or so punters deep. Then we settled in for the afternoon. Basically, a long list of grumpiness. Everything was broken and everything was someone else's fault. No ideas how to fix it, other than Nige would come up with something sooner or later.

MP Rupert Lowe sounded like a golf-club bore as he listed his pet hates. Rainbow lanyards, Covid vaccinations, the Office for Budget Responsibility, the BBC, taxes that affected wealthy people like himself. He even confessed to hating democracy. Lee Anderson continued along the same lines. Vegans, net zero, Sadiq Khan, Black Lives Matter. All evil. The only person he did like was Jim Davidson. He got a standing ovation for ripping up his TV licence reminder. Free the 30p Lee.

It was all getting a bit tedious. Repetitive. Worse was to follow with the personality-free Dicky Tice. A man desperate to be loved but so hard to trust. He took the afternoon by storm by insisting Britain was dominated by the three cults. At least, he meant to say 'three cults'. He actually said something much more Anglo-Saxon. It's a view, I suppose. Zia Yusuf came and went in a sea of indifference. He didn't seem to realise that the Battle of Arnhem had been a historic disaster.

Finally – to a soundtrack of Eminem and fireworks – the man himself. Big Nige. The rock'n'roll politician. Allegedly. Only for much of the time it felt as though he was just phoning it in. A greatest-hits compilation of reality-bending dishonesty. Everyone to blame for Brexit but himself. He was exempt from changing the country for the worse.

Farage went on about the need to democratise and professionalise the party. But it felt distracted. As if his heart wasn't in it. He tried to sound engaged, but it was as though he was bored. He'd made this speech hundreds of times before, and even he had had enough of it. Imagine. Maybe he had reached peak narcissism and could take no more. Can see through his own bullshit, even if others can't.

After half an hour of mindless talking, he checked the time and wound it up after going through his pet grievances. NatWest. The Tories, useless. Labour, useless. Nothing positive to add. No vision. Just him at the centre of the universe. Cue more fireworks and some balloons. Just to remind people that they had been in the presence of greatness. Apparently.

Forget Orwell's Two Minutes Hate – let's try Labour's Two Minutes Hope

24 SEPTEMBER 2024

Forget George Orwell's Two Minutes Hate. The new world order for the current government is the Two Minutes Hope.

Having spent much of the last three months telling everyone how rubbish everything is and that there's even less money than they imagined, the Labour Party have now realised that many people had lost the will to live. Had decided there was no coming back from the chaos and scandals of the Tory years. So now we are all commanded to obey the Two Minutes Hope. To stop what we are doing at midday precisely and try to think of something we are vaguely looking forward to. It's harder than you think.

On Monday we had Rachel Reeves. She's not a natural. The best she could come up with was that at least we are all still here. Apart from those that had died in the last 24 hours. On Tuesday it was Keir Starmer's turn, in his first conference speech as prime minister. He got round to the hope bit about two-thirds of the way through and sounded far more convincing about it than his chancellor had. Though it was still going to be hard work. And not all of us would make it. But hey, it was a start. And that was progress.

Waiting for the speech to start, the list of constituencies that Labour had won rolled up the screen like the opening sequence of a *Star Wars* film. All we were missing was the Jedi Knight. We didn't have long to wait. After a brief video clip that included the BBC announcing the exit poll – drawing some of the longest and loudest cheers of the afternoon – Keir entered, stage left. Arms raised, thanking the audience. The first and most essential act of communion.

Starmer has got a lot better at these gigs. Maybe it's the media training. Or maybe he no longer suffers from impostor syndrome. He believes he has earned the right to be the star turn. Just three or four years ago, when he became Labour leader, his delivery was awkward, hesitant. He couldn't land a punchline. Looked terrified he might lose his place at any moment. Now he commands the stage. He is at ease. Has one-liner riffs on hand for any unwanted heckles. Enjoys the glitz and the drama.

The only real downer is his scripts. It's become the accepted norm that a leader's speech should last an hour. Otherwise it's somehow deemed insubstantial. But there's no point putting yourself and your audience through the ordeal if you don't have enough material. Better to leave people wanting more. Especially as much of the speech appeared to have been lifted from last year's effort. Conference is not a place for a repeat episode. Worse, there was a lack of coherence. Almost as if someone had accidentally scattered the 15 pages of the speech on the floor and stapled them back together in the wrong order. No wonder most of the audience looked a bit bemused and comatose for the first half-hour. The standing ovations more of a Pavlovian reflex to trigger words – Nationalise railways! Workers' rights! – than a conscious response to detailed argument and rhetoric.

'We have had the hope beaten out of us,' Keir declared early on. True. But not the greatest of starts. Or what people had come to hear. Starmer has never been one for triumphalism – it's one of his more endearing qualities that he only ever really gloats about Arsenal victories – but the audience looked as if they could have done with just a little more celebration. If you can't have a party after a landslide victory, then when can you?

You could sense people struggling to keep up. Trying to follow the logic as Starmer sidestepped from idea to idea, before being as surprised as any of us that he had inadvertently found himself back where he started. The pauses by Pinter. The words by Beckett. The deconstruction by Derrida. Maybe this was a masterpiece after all, and we just hadn't realised it. Keir included. Could this have been a game-changing paradigm? The model on which all future party leaders will be based?

At one point during a random paragraph on the Middle East, Starmer demanded the return of all 'sausages'. It was tempting to believe this was a breakout moment of postmodern theatre of the absurd, rather than a mangling of the word 'hostages'. We were well beyond the conventionally prosaic. He also called for an end to hostilities between Israel and Lebanon and an immediate ceasefire in Gaza. It doesn't appear as if anyone in the region was listening.

Then there were the occasional mentions of the five missions. Leitmotifs to anchor us to reality. Except even Keir can't quite remember what they are. We can all still recite Rishi Sunak's five promises, which he never kept, but the Labour missions are still viewed through a glass darkly. And in the midst of all this, a random shout-out to a holiday in the Lake District. The point of which escaped everyone. Probably just comic relief.

For the last 20 minutes, it suddenly all began to hold together. Its meaning mystically revealed. The vibes finally taking shape in more or less the right order. The audience perked up. Opened their eyes to the heavens. Stood up and cheered. Now they began to see the point of Keir. The point of their existence.

Things were difficult. Things had been broken by the Tories. Starmer reclaimed 'Take back control' from Brexit and applied it to migration. He nicked 'We're all in this together' from David Cameron and made it sound as if it might be true. Something Lord Big Dave had never managed. There were tough times ahead. Code for 'tax rises imminent'. Nimbys would just have to get used to the idea of pylons in their eyeline. Not even a lone Gaza protester could distract him.

We ended in a fugue state of ambition, hope, defiance. Hope, defiance, ambition. Defiance, ambition, hope. There was a light at the end of the tunnel. Even if access to it was strictly time-limited.

The last few minutes were drowned out by a standing ovation. Keir acknowledged the crowd but didn't milk the applause. A quick hug with his wife, and he was off. Back to a government of service. The rest of us had been given our instructions. The Two Minutes Hope starts here.

* * *

If the Labour conference had felt more like a work in progress than a gathering of an established government, it was a model of professionalism compared with the Tories' annual get-together. When it comes to master-minding failure and embarrassment, the Conservatives are in a league of their own – especially when in the midst of a leadership contest.

Moderation out and madness to the fore in the Tories' Birmingham echo chamber

29 SEPTEMBER 2024

See it from the point of view of the Fearless Four. You've already seen off the mighty challenges of Priti Patel and Mel Stride, latter-day Tory titans both, so now you're through to the Birmingham eliminator. You've disappeared through the wormhole into the mephitic swamp where any intelligent life comes to die. Where only the clinically deranged and terminally deluded are to be found. Where the sanest voice is Michael Fabricant's rug, pleading with its owner to be allowed to go home. Welcome to the Tory party conference.

But this is your big moment. Four days when the Tory party has nothing better to do than turn its gaze in on itself. Four days when you can take centre stage. When your narcissism can go unchecked. You've been dreaming about this for weeks. People actually pretending to be interested in what you have to say. Just for this week your existential futility is kept in check. In Birmingham, reality is put on hold – that whichever mediocrity becomes the new leader, they will still be an irrelevance. A stopgap at best. The new Michael Howard. The deadbeat's deadbeat.

You've spent the last couple of weeks preparing. Writing speeches. Buying clothes. Or finding someone to buy them for you. Anticipating hostile questions. Killer one-liners. Most importantly, you've ratcheted up the madness. It's almost ancient history since anyone won a Tory leadership contest through moderation. Now you have to be full-on batshit crazy. No idea can ever be too idiotic for the Tory members who have the final say.

Then you make it to conference and find that the maddest possible thing has already been said. Nothing you can say could possibly trump it. And it hasn't been said by any of the four hopefuls. It's been said by Boris Johnson, in the serialisation of his almost entirely fictitious memoir. The one that is written so badly it could have been done by ChatGPT. As ever, Boris has done the least amount of work possible, and still he outshines those he has left behind. When it comes to attention-seeking sociopathy, he has no equal.

Desperate for a headline, Johnson declared that he – along with Bear Grylls and Ant Middleton – had intended to invade the Netherlands during the Covid pandemic to steal a lorry-load of vaccines, which they would then take back to the UK on a submarine. Having first annexed Germany and stormed the European Parliament in Brussels. Hell, what was the point of Brexit if we weren't going to declare war on all our former allies? Keep mainland Europe British. It's what they want.

Here's the thing. We all know these are lies. Boris knows they're lies. But they still get published because they're more fun, more interesting than reality. There's no one else who could get away with this. The only leader the Tories have really liked in the past 10 years is one who is congenitally unable to tell the truth. Read the other so-called highlights of the serialisation – the *Daily Mail* have been robbed blind – and the lasting impression is that Johnson regrets nothing. He just wishes he had dared to tell even bigger porkies.

Which has left the Fearless Four in something of a quandary. They are boxed in. Nowhere to go. Their madness will look only half-arsed. Too tame for Tories given new hope by the thought of starting a third world war fuelled by Covid dreams. So all the hopefuls could do was go through the motions. They were beaten before they had really got started.

If the answer is Robert Jenrick, then it's odds-on you have been asking the wrong question. But whether the Tories like it or not, Honest Bob is the clear favourite to win the leadership contest. And he was the first out of the blocks on the Sunday-morning media round. He won't count this as his finest hour. Not just because the former immigration minister can't point to any career successes – failure is no bar to entry in this contest – but because he didn't really have anything to say. He failed the insanity test by sounding almost normal. He didn't even back Donald Trump. He hasn't got the hang of this.

At least the Tories have Kemi Badenoch. Having implied that immigrants should be barred from entry to the UK for not liking Israel, KemiKaze went for broke by insisting that all women who had babies were basically spongers. Only getting pregnant to hoover up maternity pay. Despite the fact that just five years ago she was extolling the benefits of her maternity leave. Sometimes you wonder if, for all her hatred of others, the person she hates the most is herself. The Tories are flirting with danger. This prompted a small reaction from the other three, all of whom said she had gone too far. Though if Boris had said this – and hell, he's had enough experience of partners on maternity leave – they would probably have cheered.

Honest Bob tried to up the ante by claiming it was the EHRC that was responsible for small-boat crossings. He still hasn't worked out that the 'E' in EHRC stands for European. Neither James Cleverly nor Tom Tugendhat really got a word in. Jimmy Dimly tried to claim that having done the jobs of home and foreign secretary badly qualified him to be a bad leader of the opposition. Tug was just left to hawk his artificial spray tan from his concession stall. The best news for the Fearless Four is that all this took place inside an echo chamber. Compared with previous years, the conference is a ghost town. The security is to keep people inside the compound, not to stop the unwanted coming in.

The main event of the afternoon was a session entitled 'Dispatches from the Election Campaign'. It was hardly a truth and reconciliation committee. More a coming together of the weak and the fallen, trying to console themselves that the public still loved them really. It's not you, it's me. The Tories haven't quite grasped that no one gives a toss what Penny Mordaunt and Daniel Hannan have to say any more. If they ever did.

We also got through a full hour without anyone mentioning Liz Truss, Partygate or Brexit. Reform UK was dismissed in a single aside. It seems the Conservatives have a way to go before the collective synapses interact. The biggest queue of the day was for Rishi Sunak. Here for one day, only to show slides of his summer hols in California. Says it all, really.

* * *

The Tories have often had a weird obsession with the past. Those who are not pining for Margaret Thatcher's magical return from the dead are holding on instead to the more recent memories of Boris Johnson. Anything to eradicate the pain of the present, I guess.

But one of the more inexplicable features of the current Tory party is its ongoing fascination with Liz Truss. You'd have thought they would have gone out of their way to forget her. It was her 49 days of carnage that sealed the deal on their oblivion. And yet, for reasons I still can't fathom, Truss was the biggest draw at the party conference. A 90-minute queue for her one-off appearance. Go figure.

Please stop Liz Truss making public appearances. Not for our benefit, but for hers

30 SEPTEMBER 2024

Sooner or later, someone is going to have to call a halt to Liz Truss's public appearances. Not for our benefit, but for hers. We've nearly reached the point where we've tipped over into the Theatre of Cruelty. A freak show where audiences turn up just to see what mad thing she says next. Where she is egged on to make herself look ever more ridiculous. Hard to believe, I know. But every time you think you have reached Peak Trusster, Liz is there to say: 'Hold my beer.'

It would somehow feel less grubby if Liz were in on the joke. If she were aware that her residual value is as a washed-up end-of-the-pier entertainer. Someone long past her best, churning out her greatest hit. A song that reached Number 73 in the charts several decades ago. But Liz is totally unaware. Blissfully ignorant. She actually believes she is still relevant. Not only to the Tory party, which just wishes she would disappear under a rock. The electoral disaster whose name strikes fear among relatively sane Conservative Party members. Must be PTSD. Not even just to the country, which she has still not forgiven for bringing about her graceless resignation. But to the entire world. The Trusster's stated mission is now to save Western civilisation. Liz Truss.

Most striking of all, Liz actually means this. She believes the fate of the Western world resides solely in her hands. She wakes up every morning, stares at a map of the globe and plots her next move. First she takes Manhattan. Then she takes Berlin. Something like that. For narcissistic endeavour, she outdoes Boris. A genuine contender for the world's maddest person. Even Napoleon had less of a Napoleon complex. Where are her shrinks when she really needs them? They have a duty of care. Truss needs to be protected from herself.

Ninety minutes before the Liz Truss fringe event is due to start, I join a pioneering group of hacks in the auditorium. No one wants to miss this. At a party conference whose sole function is as a beauty pageant for the Fearless Four, this is the top attraction. Or distraction. Above the stage there is a screen advertising the talk, with a QR code that allows audience members to send in questions. Everyone tweets this. We're then turfed out for the next hour and made to queue.

When we're allowed back in, the QR code has mysteriously disappeared from the overhead screen. Perhaps too many random people had submitted questions that were considered off-message. Like 'Could you please explain the best way to get promoted well beyond your capabilities?' or 'Don't you ever suffer from impostor syndrome?' I'm sure you all have variations on these questions that you would like to see answered. You will be waiting a long time. Because nothing approaching these topics is allowed. There is an *omertà* on any suggestion that the Trusster could ever have made a mistake. Something that applies throughout the party conference. The Tories just want to pretend that Truss never happened. There is a 49-day hole in the Tory collective memory. Liz is a mistake they can never learn from because it occurred only in a parallel universe. A different space–time continuum.

It's best to draw a veil over Liz's 45-minute appearance. Mainly out of decency. The Trusster shouldn't be allowed out without a responsible adult in attendance. Someone to advise her to say: 'No comment.' Because whatever medication she is on – and it must be a lot to produce that disturbingly affectless delivery – it's not enough. In her own private world – the only one that counts – she is queen of all she surveys.

It's safe to say that the Trusster is completely unrepentant. She believes the only thing that went wrong is that we didn't get enough of her. *Elle ne regrette rien.* Her confusion is total. She was brought down by the establishment, unaware that she was once at the centre of that establishment as prime minister. Others were to blame for her ignorance. Britain was in the clutches of a socialist cabal led by the Tory and Labour establishment. Wokery was bringing down the West. She could have done a better job at the last election than Rishi Sunak.

Just make it stop. Just make it stop. I feel as if I'm colluding in someone's personal breakdown. That I'm a participant in something unpleasant. Please tell Liz she wasn't just a useless prime minister; she was also a useless constituency MP. Her Norfolk voters had had enough of her. She is now an irrelevance. Just that strange person whom no one will recognise at the Cenotaph in years to come. The session was billed to last an hour, but her interviewer, the *Telegraph* columnist Tim Stanley, wrapped things up after 45 minutes. It was the greatest kindness he could bestow upon her.

Elsewhere, the Tory conference trundled on in its own meaningless way. Jeremy Hunt opened proceedings in the hall. No one quite knew why. Who cares what a bloke who isn't going to be shadow chancellor in a month's time thinks? Jezza didn't seem to notice. He declared the economy to be in tip-top shape. You can't buy that kind of razor-sharp analysis.

Otherwise, it was the Fearless Four competing to say the same things to the same people over and over again in different meetings. Without anyone appearing to get bored. They must be on autopilot. We are in an echo chamber par excellence. Where supporters follow their man or woman around and laugh at the same jokes to give themselves a sense of purpose.

In the main hall, it was the turn of Tom Tugendhat and Kemi Badenoch to be interviewed for an hour each. Tom was so desperate not to remind people that he had been in the army and had killed people that he kept talking about his time in the army. Still, he kept his supporters happy. Kemi merely tried not to get into a fight with GB News's political editor Chris Hope, who was asking the questions. She gives the impression she doesn't really like anyone. Even herself. Not exactly the quality most people are looking for in a leader. But then the Tories are a law unto themselves.

Maybe after his book launch Boris Johnson will leave us all alone

8 OCTOBER 2024

Crack dens are going up in the world. Time was when you knew where you stood with a crack den. Assorted pipes and other paraphernalia. Blood on the walls. Tatty curtains blocking out the light from the windows.

Now we are asked to believe that while Theresa May was prime minister, the flat at No. 10 doubled up as a crack den. An upmarket concern, decorated throughout by John Lewis, for the more discerning drug addict. The sort of den to which Michael Gove could only aspire. You should see the state of his kitchen on a Saturday night.

I have to admit, I hadn't previously had the Maybot down as a crack addict. True, she rarely spoke, and when she did she sounded barely human. 'Brexit means Brexit' always came out as a deathly croak. But there was always something rather wholesome about her. How wrong can you be? First thing every morning – before she had even got dressed – she had her face buried in some rocks.

How do we know this? Because this is what Boris Johnson told LBC's Nick Ferrari on Tuesday morning, during an interview about his unreliable memoir, *Unleashed*. He had had to have the flat in No. 10 redecorated when he became prime minister because the previous incumbent had left it looking like a crack den. Though this didn't explain why he felt the need to turn it into a migraine-inducing boudoir. But never mind. Boris had told us it was a crack den. So a crack den it must be. Because Boris is not the sort of person to tell a lie.

It's been less than a week since Johnson began the publicity round of interviews for *Unleashed,* but it feels so much longer. I am now suffering from *Weltschmerz.* A world weariness that seeps into my very bones. I doubt I am alone. Too tired to fight when he talks over yet another question. Almost too tired to count the lies that compete to escape his lips. And yet, something forces me to go on. Someone needs to keep saying that this is not normal.

There's something wrong when you can't trust a word a former prime minister says. To be silent is to be complicit. So I force myself to listen. Maybe after this he will finally go away for a while. At least shrink back to not writing the Shakespeare book. To rehashing the same speech for £250,000 a go, for people who should know better. But good luck to him. Just as long as he leaves the rest of us alone.

For now, just imagine what it takes to believe Johnson. The lapses in cognition and judgement you need to make to accommodate his reality. Starting with the rest of his LBC interview. His outrage at Keir Starmer taking freebies. This from a man who persuaded Lord Brownlow to stump up the cash to convert the crack den into something even more hideous. This turned out to only be a loan after the story got out, and Boris was forced to spend his own cash. Then there were the foreign holidays. And his wedding. What sort of sucker ever pays for those sorts of things? But Boris has told us he doesn't accept freebies. And Boris would never lie.

Moving on to Brexit. What marks out of 10 would Johnson give Brexit so far? A solid nine. This was just gaslighting. Even most Brexiters don't think Brexit is a success. Largely because they never got round to saying what their ideal Brexit was. They just happen to know that this isn't it. The perfect Brexit is always out of reach. Apart from for Boris, who is near enough living his best life. So why can't we all just be a little more happy for him? After all, he is the centre of all our universes. Without Johnson the rest of us would not exist. But Boris has said Brexit is a success, so it must be true. Because Boris would not lie.

Living inside Johnson's head must be exhausting. The constant need to fend off anything approaching reality. On the prorogation, he was adamant that Lady Hale was bonkers. Because he knew more about the law than a Supreme Court judge. He had no idea why he kept appointing people to work for him who would always go on to let him down. He had believed Dominic Cummings' Barnard Castle excuse because it sounded plausible. Why did all these things keep happening to Johnson? He must have been the unluckiest prime minister in history. Yet they must be true. Because Boris would not lie.

It was much the same when Johnson came to be interviewed later in the afternoon by Matt Chorley on BBC Radio 5 Live. Everything was someone else's fault. Never his own. It was the whips' fault that the Tories supported Owen Paterson. Not Boris's for instructing the whips. It was Dilyn the dog's fault that the No. 10 carpets got trashed. Here you could sense a cover-up for an original lie being developed in real time. It doesn't seem to have occurred to Boris that it was his job to let Dilyn out into the garden. But it must all be true. Because Boris would not lie.

By now we were into scattergun territory, with new realities and altered states being presented almost as quickly as Johnson could breathe. He had won a record majority in 2019. Something even a casual glance at Wikipedia would disprove. It had not been his responsibility to implement Brexit in 2016, even though he was the person who had done most to persuade people to vote for it. At one point he even contradicted something he had written in his own memoir about the £350 million on the side of the bus.

For Boris, *Unleashed* is already out of date, and it's not even officially published till Thursday. The truth is constantly shifting sand, always tantalisingly out of reach. No matter how hard reality comes after him, he's always scrambling to keep it at bay. Locked into his own narcissistic fantasy. The sociopath's sociopath. For him, it's the rest of us who are out of step. So maybe now he will leave us alone for a while. To our small, miserable little lives. We could do with a break.

* * *

It was widely agreed that of the four leadership candidates at the Tory party conference, James Cleverly had been the star performer. He isn't overly gifted in the brains department – hence Jimmy Dimly – but he could achieve something that was well beyond his two main rivals, Kimi Badenoch and Robert Jenrick: he was a politician who could sound vaguely normal. Unusual for a Tory politician.

Within a matter of days, however, he was out of the race, bizarrely losing two votes since the previous round, having been expected to pick up more than enough to make it to the final two. No one was quite sure whether this was cock-up or conspiracy. This being the current iteration of the Tory party, cock-up was most likely. Cleverly supporters trying to game the system by lending their votes to the less charismatic Jenrick, in the hope of squeezing Kemi out of the contest. If so, it backfired badly. The Tory members were now left to choose between Kemi and Honest Bob. Lucky them.

The law of averages has let everyone down in the Tory leadership race

29 OCTOBER 2024

First, the good news. In just a few days' time you won't be subjected to a constant stream of unconsciousness from Kemi Badenoch and Robert Jenrick. Now, the bad news. In just a few days' time either KemiKaze or Honest Bob will become the new Tory leader, and you will get yet more white noise from one of them. Most likely Kemi. It's enough to turn anyone to drugs.

There again, maybe you're the type of person who can easily zone out the moment certain annoying sound frequencies kick in. Clearly, you're not alone. The more KemiKaze and Honest Bob battle for headlines, the greater the indifference. There are very few people who actually care who becomes leader of the opposition. Not even the Tories are that bothered. Partly because the choice is so dismal, but mainly because they suspect it's merely a temporary appointment. Give it a couple of years, and they'll be going through the whole process again.

The only two people who don't seem to be aware of their own existential futility are Badenoch and Jenrick. No one has informed them of their pointlessness. Or, if they have, neither has been listening. In an act of sadism towards their listeners, radio and TV stations have been giving blanket coverage to whatever drifts across KemiKaze's and Honest Bob's synapses. To general disappointment, the law of averages has been letting everyone down. Rather than proving that one of them might eventually say something vaguely coherent, there's been a race to the bottom. To appeal to the worst instincts of the Tory members by sounding clinically insane.

To Kemi's credit, she has kept her silence through much of the interminable campaign. Better to be thought a liability than to prove it. But, in the past week, she just hasn't been able to restrain herself. Appearing on any outlet that is dumb enough to have her. Her explanation for the change of heart was that she felt she needed to put herself out there a bit more, as only about half of the Tory members had bothered to vote.

Not for the first time – and certainly not for the last – KemiKaze had managed to get the wrong end of the stick. Her big takeaway had been that if only people got to see more of her, then they would fall under her spell. Such lack of self-awareness should have immediately disqualified her from the contest. Because surely by now she would have realised that the more people see of her, the more there is to dislike. But, like so many politicians, she suffers from a narcissistic personality disorder. She is oblivious to reality.

Tuesday morning saw Kemi making an appearance on Times Radio. Kate McCann tried to interview Kemi but found herself being constantly interrupted. Making unwanted corrections is the way Badenoch relates to people. There was just enough airspace to condemn herself. 'I like to make friends,' she insisted. Only she doesn't. Why bother, when it's so much easier to make enemies? She also claimed to welcome criticism and rudely denied that she's rude. You couldn't make this stuff up.

Though KemiKaze can't help herself. She was asked about her comment that Honest Bob had 'the whiff of impropriety' about him. Not exactly controversial stuff, as Honest Bob has form for handing out planning favours to wealthy Tory pornographers. But Kemi proceeded to round on McCann for accurately quoting her own words back at her. It was the same when the interview moved on to maternity pay, Badenoch again claiming that there was an evil Kemi inside the good Kemi that kept saying words to trip her up. A therapist would have her work cut out with Badenoch.

Meanwhile, Honest Bob was not to be denied. Wading in to the reparations row, Jenrick managed to get an opinion piece into the *Daily Mail*, in which he wrote that the UK had basically done countries a favour by colonising them. So, if anything, it was them that ought to be paying us money. As a token of gratitude. The reason so many former colonies were struggling is that they had made the mistake of wanting independence.

It's not entirely clear who Honest Bob thinks he's going to win over with this critique of pure reason. Not even Kemi goes this far in her endless culture wars. As so often, there is something inescapably inauthentic about Jenrick. As if he's just trying on unpleasantness as a pose. KemiKaze is the real deal. There's a purity to her nastiness. A seam of contempt that will almost certainly win her the contest.

Elsewhere in Westminster, everyone else was just filling in time before the budget. First, a meaningless Treasury departmental questions, where time and again Rachel Reeves and her team had to point out that MPs would have to wait a day before finding out the government's tax and spending plans. All of which is a charade, as ministers have been busy briefing almost everything over the past week or so. You'd have to have spent the last week in a news blackout not to be able to make a decent stab at delivering the budget yourself.

Which prompted the urgent question brought by the not very bright shadow chief secretary to the Treasury, Laura Trott. After the outburst from the Speaker about budget leaks, she wondered whether the government might have been in breach of the ministerial code. It was all a lot of fuss about nothing. The only budget in recent years that hasn't been extensively pre-briefed was Kwasi Kwarteng's. And look what that one did to the markets and mortgages. Trott's less than convincing patter was that just because the Tories had leaked everything, it didn't follow that Labour should do the same. Reeves should try to do a bit better.

In reply, paymaster general Nick Thomas-Symonds couldn't disguise his lack of interest. 'This government has the utmost respect for parliament,' he oozed. As in, next to none. The Commons could whistle for it. Ministers would continue to do as they always had. As far as the ministerial code was concerned, this hardly registered when compared with lockdown parties and dodgy Covid contracts. He had a point.

* * *

It had felt a strange misstep for Labour to delay their first budget until late October. It merely left everyone in limbo, as if Keir Starmer were in no hurry to fix the country. Far better to have got it over and done with in a matter of weeks, when the government was still in its honeymoon period.

But October it was, and the best that could be said was that chancellor Rachel Reeves just about got away with it. There again, any chancellor might have struggled, given the state in which the Tories had left the economy. Amid dark warnings of a £22 billion black hole, Labour increased employers' national insurance contributions and cut the winter fuel allowance for many pensioners. Reeves tried to sell the budget as a 'once-in-a-parliament' event, but there wasn't much cheer to be had. Labour would probably have been better off reversing the Tories' unaffordable 2p cut in national insurance, which Jeremy

Hunt had conjured as a pre-election bribe. But with a majority of 170, there was never any danger of Labour being unable to pass its budget.

There was also some not altogether welcome – if hardly unsurprising – news from the other side of the Atlantic. Donald Trump had secured a second term. Fair to say that Starmer and The Donald were hardly political soulmates. Foreign secretary David Lammy had previously described the president-elect as a racist. There was some bridge-building to be done. Starmer was nothing if not pragmatic. He would go on to spend much of the next six months sucking up to Trump, never offering a hint of criticism.

As for the new Tory leader, Kemi Badenoch, she had to appoint a shadow cabinet. There wasn't a whole lot of choice, with old-timers James Cleverly and Jeremy Hunt saying they fancied a spell on the backbenches.

Badenoch plucks Patel, Jenrick and Stride from the Tories' tiny gene pool of talent

4 NOVEMBER 2024

Just do the maths. There are 120 other Tory MPs from whom Kemi Badenoch can select her ministerial team. Or, to put it another way, there's about a one-in-five chance of any MP making it into the shadow cabinet, and a near

100% chance of becoming a ministerial bag carrier. These are days of plenty for ambitious young Tory MPs with one eye on their own career. It just requires a different mindset.

There again, not every Tory MP will necessarily want a place in Kemi's team. James Cleverly very publicly snubbed his new boss at the weekend, saying he'd rather return to the backbenches than carry on as shadow home secretary. He was fed up with having to defend someone else's brainless policies.

What goes around, comes around. Jimmy Dimly might not be the sharpest pencil in the box but he's one step ahead of Kemi. He's worked out that KemiKaze might not be around by the time of the next election and his best chance of replacing her was by remaining on the sidelines. All he needs to do is make sure he doesn't do anything unintentionally helpful in the meantime, and she will crash and burn of her own accord.

The former shadow foreign secretary Andrew Mitchell had also made it clear he wasn't looking to sign up to the new regime. Though, in his case, it was more about jumping before he was pushed. He was never Team Kemi and didn't have a big enough profile that the new leader of the opposition had to try and find a place for him. To put it bluntly, he was expendable. So he chose to go with something approaching dignity.

These were the just the two we got to hear about. There might well have been several other prominent Tories out there who also decided they would rather do without the hassle of being shouted at or ignored by their new boss. Though not Chris Philp. Obviously. Politicians don't come needier than the Philpster. Only on Saturday he had rushed to tweet a photo of him next to Kemi. 'Please, please give me a job,' he had begged. 'I will do anything. ANYTHING.'

But here's the thing. Despite having a tiny gene pool of talent from which to choose and the best part of a month to make up her mind – she had been the odds-on favourite ever since it became a straight fight with Robert Jenrick – KemiKaze has struggled to fill her ministerial slots. Just three frontline announcements in the two days since her coronation. Hardly what you might call hitting the ground running.

First to get appointed was Laura Trott as shadow education secretary. Mainly because Kemi had to have a shadow minister to send out for education departmental questions on Monday afternoon. A disappointment for Trott, as she had been hoping for shadow chancellor. There again, maybe KemiKaze remembered her abject BBC interview with Evan Davis earlier in the year, when she had no idea that government debt was rising. Even though she was Treasury no. 2 at the time. Clearly, numbers are not her strong point. Though no one knows what is.

Mel Stride got the shadow chancellor brief. On the surface, an embrace of the left of the party and a thank-you for the hours spent defending the last government on TV and radio when no one else would. But Mel isn't quite as sweet as he looks. He had it in for maternity pay long before Badenoch got the idea.

Rather more disturbing was Priti Patel as shadow foreign secretary. Not just dim, but dangerous with it. Twice found to have broken the ministerial code and once sacked for freelancing her own foreign policy in the Middle East. What could possibly go wrong there? If that wasn't enough, she was the architect of the disastrous Rwanda policy. But somehow KemiKaze looks on all these failures as advantages. She sees Priti as a woman with a future. She must think the country has collective amnesia.

Late in the day, we learned that Honest Bob had been handed the shadow justice brief. You couldn't make this stuff up. KemiKaze had literally given a prime job to a man who, she said a week ago, had 'the whiff of impropriety'. The message to the country? Granting planning permission, against departmental advice, to a Tory donor and pornographer-in-chief is the way to get ahead. Not to mention a shadow justice minister who had trashed the European Court of Human Rights. So much for the rule of law.

Still, all this was good news for a Labour Party struggling to find its way. Far better to have an opposition that is focused on making its own mistakes rather than on your own. Over in the Commons it was the mild-mannered farming minister, Daniel Zeichner, who was left to answer an urgent question on inheritance tax for farmers. Presumably the environment secretary, Steve Reed, was otherwise engaged on farming business in his Streatham and Croydon constituency.

Danny has clearly learned well from Keir Starmer. Both model their public speaking style on a rather tetchy narrator of a meditation tape. 'Just clear your mind,' they insist. 'Lie down and close your eyes. Everything's going to be fine. Stop talking at the back.' They want to put you to sleep; they want to be reassuring. They just can't understand why you're not taking them at their word.

'Look,' said Zeichner, time and again. The farmers didn't understand the sums. The only people who would have to pay were the johnny-come-lately types like James Dyson and Jeremy Clarkson, who had only got into farming as a tax avoidance policy. Everyone else had just let their imaginations run away from them. He may be right. But the farmers were going to need a lot more sedatives before they were convinced.

Then came the tuition fees announcement from Bridget Phillipson. All of which went completely over the head of Trott, who used her reply to demonstrate that she had no idea of how student loans operated. So on brand, Laura. Start as you mean to go on.

Congratulations, your serene highness: Starmer, Farage and Lammy call Trump

7 NOVEMBER 2024

RORY STEWART: Ladies and gentlemen, I give you the 47th president of the United States of America, Kamala Harris.

KAMALA HARRIS: Er . . . Actually, I lost.

STEWART: You can't have done. I'm never wrong. I'm the political messiah.

ALASTAIR CAMPBELL: I'm sorry to break it to you, but Donald Trump won. I can't believe American voters didn't pay attention to our predictions.

STEWART: I'm a broken man. I'm so, so sorry. I've never been wrong before about anything . . .

CAMPBELL: Can you just keep quiet about it? You're bad for business. Just pretend you always thought Trump was going to win.

STEWART: The hubris. I'm so ashamed. I've lost my sense of self.

KEIR STARMER: Is that his serene highness, the president-elect Donald Trump?

DONALD TRUMP: That's me.

STARMER: Can I just say that it is the honour of my life to be allowed to speak to you on the telephone, at such a historic time for both our countries?

TRUMP: I wish I could say the same.

STARMER: May I begin by offering you my heartiest congratulations on your stunning victory. It's so wonderful to see that being a sexual abuser and convicted criminal is no barrier to the highest office in the land.

TRUMP: That's very nice of you to say so. A lot of people have said I'm going to be the best president ever. The very best. The best of the best. That's not me that's saying that. It's the voices in my head.

STARMER: You are going to be brilliant. I'm sure of that. Do you remember that night we spent together a month or so ago? I have such fond memories of that . . .

TRUMP: Remind me.

STARMER: It was at your typically understated apartment in Trump Tower, and we shared a meal of a Deliveroo Big Mac.

TRUMP: Of course I remember. I remember everything. People say that I have the best memory of anyone they've ever met. It's almost as if I've got perfect recall.

STARMER: While I've got you on the line, there's someone next to me who would like to have a word . . .

STEWART: I'm so, so sorry. I can't tell you how sorry I am . . .

STARMER: Not you . . .

DAVID LAMMY: I just wanted to say that when I called you a 'woman-hating neo-Nazi sympathiser' a few years back, I was really trying to find an adequate way of expressing my admiration for you. I mean, since the Second World War, Hitler has always had a bad rep, so people tend to forget the good stuff he did . . .

JD VANCE: I couldn't agree more. Some of his watercolours are rather charming.

STARMER: So that's all from me for now. I can't wait to start working with you formally in the new year. But if you did fancy coming over beforehand to do some Christmas shopping, then Victoria and I would love to have you to stay at Chequers. *Mi casa, su casa.* Much love.

TRUMP: Who was that?

MELANIA: The prime minister of the UK.

TRUMP: He's even needier than me. The UK is somewhere in Europe, right?

MELANIA: Still as sharp as ever. Oh, by the way, there's a man at the door. Says he knows you.

TRUMP: Who is it?

MELANIA: No idea.

TRUMP: Better let him in.

NIGEL FARAGE: Hello, Mr President. Very good to see you.

TRUMP: You look vaguely familiar.

FARAGE: It's Nigel. The man you engagingly call 'No-mark Nige'.

TRUMP: It's coming back to me.

FARAGE: Can I just point out that I was the only person in the entire world to predict you would win the election?

TRUMP: You said that last time, when I lost. Leave the bullshit to me. Now, what do you want?

FARAGE: Can I persuade you to come on my GB News show?

TRUMP: Why would I want to do that?

FARAGE: Point taken. Then how about you join me in Clacton when you're next in the UK?

TRUMP: Where's Clacton?

FARAGE: I've no idea. But why don't I introduce you to some of the team? First of all, Dicky Tice.

RICHARD TICE: I am not worthy to be in the same room as you. May I ask you where you get your fantastic orange colour from? I spend hours on the sunbed every day, and I go only a dull copper.

FARAGE: And Lee Anderson.

TRUMP: Who's he?

LEE ANDERSON: Fuck you. Everyone knows who I am. Now fuck off, because I've got a train to catch.

FARAGE: Be nice, Lee. You're not speaking to a security guard now.

STEWART: Please accept my apologies. I am a broken man.

TRUMP: It's that guy again.

VOLODYMYR ZELENSKYY: Greetings from Ukraine. You will still back us, won't you?

TRUMP: I'm going to bring peace to your country. So much peace that you won't know what to do with it. No one will ever have seen so much peace. And I tell you something, you will be seeing this peace in 24 hours.

ZELENSKYY: What are you talking about? Are you about to sell us out to Russia?

TRUMP: I've got to go now. I'm on the golf course. It's my turn to putt. Things are kinda boring here. I was rather hoping to claim the election had been stolen from me.

OLAF SCHOLZ: Greetings from Germany.

TRUMP: I was wondering when you might ring to blow smoke up my ass.

SCHOLZ: Think again, old man. I'm about to lose my job, so I can say what I want. You're a menace to the world.

TRUMP: Suck up the trade tariffs, loser. And fund NATO yourself. Gotta go. Putin on the other line.

STEWART: I can't go on. I need help.

Kemi Badenoch is her own worst enemy . . . and a gift for Keir Starmer and Labour

13 NOVEMBER 2024

On balance, Keir Starmer can probably live with this. The first four months of his time in office may not have been quite as straightforward as he would have liked – he must have been hoping for a six-month honeymoon period – but at least he can tick off prime minister's questions as something he doesn't have to worry much about.

Kemi Badenoch is turning out to be the gift that keeps on giving . . . to the Labour Party. Put simply, the more you get to see of her, the less there appears to be. Behind her rather patronising, condescending facade there's a largely empty interior. She is riddled with *levitas*. Her self-confidence is in inverse proportion to her abilities. She's not nearly as bright as she thinks she is, and quite where she got the idea that she is a brilliant performer in the Commons is anyone's guess. It's Liz Truss levels of delusion.

Kemi clearly thought that being leader of the opposition was going to be a doddle. That all she had to do was turn up, sneer a bit and ask her six questions, and Starmer would dissolve in front of her eyes. Cue thunderous cheers from the Conservative benches. It turns out that PMQs is a lot more difficult than it looks. It takes detailed preparation, pitch-perfect timing and a razor-sharp mind. None of which she has yet demonstrated.

To be kind, one could say these are early days. KemiKaze is only a couple of weeks into her new job. But to make the necessary improvements will require a level of humility. The grace to admit that she has been a disappointment. The grace to admit that she's looked out of her depth. But grace and Kemi are not natural companions. So you can see the concern on the Tory benches. Realising too late that they have been conned. It's not yet a catastrophe for them. But it might well be soon if it goes on for much longer.

Meanwhile, Keir is living his best life in the Commons. Maybe it's something about being in government. Or maybe it's just knowing that nothing his opponent may say can wrongfoot him. As leader of the opposition, there was something a bit wooden about his performances at the dispatch box. Those 'Lego man' jibes hurt because there was a kernel of truth. But now Starmer is a changed man. Full of energy, quick-witted and often surprisingly funny. Who knew?

It helps that Kemi is her own worst enemy. She began by making a snippy remark about Starmer's attendance at COP29 in Azerbaijan. This may play well with the right of her own party, but it doesn't impress most of the country. Floods and droughts in many parts of the world are a genuine concern. Just not to KemiKaze. The empathy bypass was on full view. Is this really the new, caring Tory party?

The rest of the exchanges were no better. Kemi thinking she was on to a winner, only to realise she had set herself a trap. She huffed and puffed about a council tax increase that was entirely her own invention, and then tried to pick holes in the budget, while admitting she was thoroughly in favour of all of Labour's spending priorities. Keir almost looked sorry for her. Almost. Instead, he pointed out the blindingly obvious: that she was financially illiterate. She wanted all of the benefits but none of the pain. Kemi sat down with a wide grin, seemingly oblivious to the self-inflicted disaster. Her shadow chancellor, Mel Stride, took her by the arm and whispered, 'You were fab.' A lie.

Thereafter there was a litany of planted questions from Labour backbenchers that turned the Commons into a pointless echo chamber, before we got to the unofficial leader of the opposition. Step forward, Nigel Farage. Looking even more orange than his sidekick,

Richard Tice. Clearly, there has been a battle over the sunbed. Or maybe it's just been unseasonably hot in America. After all, it's been months since Nige was last seen in Clacton.

'Would the prime minister congratulate Donald Trump on his landslide victory?' he harrumphed. Er . . . If he had bothered to be in the Commons last week, he'd have heard Starmer brown-nosing the president-elect effusively. But then reality dawned. Nige no longer really sees himself as a UK MP. Rather, he is the member for Trump Towers. A man whose principal job is to advocate for The Donald. He either doesn't realise or doesn't mind that he is of little consequence to Trump. A useful idiot at best. Any amount of ritual humiliation is worth it for a few minutes bathed in the Shadow of his Goldenness.

Starmer used to treat Nige with suspicion. As if fearful of what he might stir up. No longer. Now he went straight for ridicule. Mocking him for a rare appearance in the Commons. Joking that he expected to see Farage on the US's immigration statistics. Nige tried to laugh along. Like all narcissists, he would rather be the butt of the joke than totally ignored. To be ridiculed is to be valued.

Minutes later, Nige was back on his feet with an urgent question about the Chagos Islands. Now, obviously he doesn't give a toss about the Chagossians, but he'd been speaking to his mate at Fox News, who will be The

Donald's new defence secretary, and had a few concerns. So could Britain please go back on the deal to hand the islands over to Mauritius?

Then up spake Brave Dicky Tice. America must have what America wants, he said. Britain's entire foreign and defence policy must be reconfigured to suit The Donald. He's got no idea how dim he really is. If there's one thing even sadder than Nige being Donald's Unloved Mini-Me, it's Dicky being Nige's Unloved Mini-Me.

* * *

Even with their majority, the Labour top brass soon realised they wouldn't get it all their own way. Many Labour backbenchers were still unhappy that the winter fuel allowance had been stopped for a significant number of pensioners and that more benefits cuts were in the pipeline. The farmers were also organising protests in central London over the proposed cuts to inheritance tax allowances on agricultural property. It had seemed a strange battle for Labour to pick, over a comparatively small return to the exchequer. Antagonising the farmers usually ends in tears.

No hiding place for Labour's farming minister as Whitehall teems with tweed and gumboots

19 NOVEMBER 2024

It was a very civilised protest. The sort of protest you might expect from roughly 10,000 asset-rich, cash-poor millionaire farmers from all over the country. The police officers there just to redirect the traffic. Only the occasional shouted slogan to punctuate proceedings. Most people were just happy to be there. 'What do we want?' 'To not pay inheritance tax on our farms.' It had a ring.

Whitehall has probably never seen so much tweed. Nigel Farage was out there looking like Mr Toad. Flat cap, pristine Barbour jacket, mustard trousers and green wellies. He can never resist a chance to cosplay. Someone might have told him that the streets had been tarmacked a while back. There again, Nige is always willing to piggyback on other people's grievances. Perhaps he might first like to explain why Brexit has hit farmers so hard.

Also on the march were Kemi Badenoch and Victoria Atkins, the shadow environment secretary, in a migraine-inducing Union Jack jacket. Kemi stood up to address the crowd. This is your new Defra team, she said, and I commit to repealing the end to agricultural property relief in five years' time. She may have got a little ahead of herself here. Most farmers don't have fond

266

memories of the past 14 years. Part of the problem is that the changes to inheritance tax are merely the final straw. Farmers tend to believe that they have been screwed over by both the Tories and Labour.

The guest of honour was newfound celebrity farmer Jeremy Clarkson. 'This is the end of farming,' he declared. Though first he wanted to backtrack a little. He hadn't – as he had previously told *The Times* in 2021 – bought his Cotswold farm as a tax avoidance measure after all. He had only said that because he was too embarrassed to say he wanted to have his own pheasant shoot. Mmm. Not entirely sure if I believe you on that one, Jezza.

But, like him or not, Clarkson knows how to get a crowd going. This was about farmers' survival, he said. Next up, a swipe at possible trade deals with the US. No one wanted chlorinated chicken – this was a knee in the nuts for farmers. Finally, after an ill-judged attack on the BBC, an appeal to the government for reason. To back down and accept that the budget measures had been rushed through with unforeseen consequences. He left the platform to warm applause.

All of which amounted to what Steve Reed, the environment, farming and rural affairs secretary, will look back on as one of his less successful days. Central London blocked for a protest, on your watch, is never a good look. And his afternoon was about to get a whole lot worse, as he was due to make his first appearance before the Defra select committee.

His first mistake was to arrive early and allow himself to become engaged in conversation with David Barton, a livestock farmer from Gloucestershire. Fair to say that Barton is one of many who think the government has got its maths wrong and that far more farmers will be caught under the new rules than had been predicted. Including Barton himself.

'Are you sure?' said Reed. 'You could always give it to your son.' This would prove to be a consistent theme throughout the afternoon. Reed would start by saying why the new tax measures had been necessary, only to then give suggestions on how the tax could be avoided. It was as if Steve had a split personality. Part cabinet minister, part moonlighting independent financial adviser. Even so, this cut no ice with Barton. Where was he supposed to live if he gave the farm to his son? Who knows? There must be an outbuilding somewhere. Steve was on a roll. Sensing an opportunity to close the deal and make a sale. Do you want to buy some life insurance? he asked. No pressure.

At which point, things took a surreal turn with the arrival of the Labour MP Barry Gardiner in the corridor. What he was doing there was anyone's guess. He's an inner London MP with no farming connections. Not that this stopped Bazza. He went for Barton. 'I don't believe you only earn up to £50,000 on a £5 million farm,' he said. Bazza clearly reckoned he knew more about Barton's business than Barton did.

Barton assured him that he did. Now Gardiner got huffy. 'Well, that's a very inefficient return on your capital,' he replied. Not wrong, but hardly the point. As Barton went on to observe: 'That's farming for you.'

Luckily for Steve, he got bailed out by an usher telling him the committee was about to start. He dashed in, flanked by two entirely mute Defra officials. Out of the frying pan. The thing is, Reed's heart just isn't in the job. He never wanted to be Defra secretary. He represents Streatham and Croydon and has almost no interest in the countryside. He really fancied the justice brief. So he merely goes through the motions. Never really saying anything that suggests engagement. Or deep knowledge. There's no malice here. He means well. But he's nobody's champion.

The committee chair, Alistair Carmichael, got the ball rolling. There had been no plans to limit agricultural property relief in Labour's manifesto. So what had changed? As night follows day, Steve said: 'A £22 billion black hole.'

Bingo. We were on to a pre-recorded script. The government still wanted farmers to pass on their farms to their children. It just wanted to make it a bit more difficult. People in the countryside cared more about a functioning NHS than farmers. It was just bad luck. In any case, farmers were making a lot of fuss about nothing. The Treasury's figures were more accurate than his own. In reality, very few people would be affected. And the farmers could afford it. They had the cash. Even if they didn't know it.

Round about now, you could see Steve's head beginning to go down. Whatever the truth, the government had lost control of the narrative. None of this had been his idea. It had all been dumped on him by the Treasury at the last minute. All over a measly £500 million. It would be better if Rachel Reeves could just back down a bit. Show a bit of flexibility and raise the threshold to £5 million. Get the farmers off his back. He was sick of telling the farmers they didn't know what they were doing. Sick of being a loyal apparatchik.

Back in his office, hope was at hand. Reed switched on the TV to catch Keir Starmer's press conference at the G20 in Rio. 'Should we prepare for nuclear war?' To Reed's amazement, Keir didn't say no. Bring it on. A first strike from Moscow would give the farmers pause for thought.

Is it time for another general election? I mean, it's been four months

25 NOVEMBER 2024

It's the logical conclusion to the disposable society. Don't like the result of the last general election? Then just have another one. Who cares if the new government has been in office for only four months? If you're not feeling markedly better off already, then the new prime minister is clearly a dud. No matter that it actually might take years to turn around an economy that has been on its knees for more than a decade. Just never give Labour an even break. Keir Starmer is like a Premier League manager after a run of bad results. On borrowed time.

At least that's what the likes of Nigel Farage and Elon Musk would have you believe. So thoughtful of the world's weirdest man to take such an interest in us poor Brits. You'd have thought he had enough on his plate running the new Department of Government Efficiency for Donald Trump. He could start by sacking himself. That would save several hundred thousand dollars.

The petition calling for a new general election has now got more than two million signatures. Which is probably no great surprise. Far more than that voted for parties other than Labour back in July, so they are probably not great fans of the government. What's more remarkable is that anyone is taking this stuff remotely seriously. In this new world, anything you don't like can be reversed within minutes. Apart from Brexit. That must never be tampered with under any circumstances.

We have arrived at the point where the wokest people are those who rail loudest against the wokerati. Poor Nige. Can't manage another second under a Labour government. Of course, like most things Farage, he tries to pass it off as just a joke. A bit of populist mischief-making. But you just know that beneath the surface, he's deadly serious. Because if there was any chance of blagging a general election through the petition, he'd take it.

To cap the sense of the surreal, Starmer was even asked about the petition when he turned up on the *This Morning* sofa on Monday. He was ostensibly there to talk about making the spiking of drinks illegal. I know it's already illegal, he said. But I am determined to make it even more illegal. That should do it. Still, he treated the petition with the contempt it deserved. As far as he knew, the UK still had a constitutional limit of a five-year parliament, and we were just four months in. Elon is going to be devastated.

But the idea that anything you don't like can be cancelled is gaining ground everywhere. Later in the afternoon, Priti Patel used an urgent question to try to get the government to ignore an arrest warrant from the international criminal court alleging that Benjamin Netanyahu has committed war crimes. In Priti's multiverse, we should be able to pick and choose which verdicts we like and which we don't. So, obviously, when the ICC issues arrest warrants against Vladimir Putin, we applaud its findings. But when the court finds grounds to believe that Netanyahu may have used starvation as an instrument of war, then Priti throws her toys out of the pram. The ICC was nothing but a pariah court. Understandably, Labour was reluctant to agree with Priti. And to think she's normally the first to complain about two-tier policing.

Still, no one is ever going to die wondering what Patel thinks. Most of us already know before she even speaks. It's always the nastiest take imaginable. She is someone of whom it's almost impossible to think the worst because she's already one step ahead of you. On the other hand, Kemi Badenoch has taken to speaking in riddles. You know that what she's saying is almost certainly unpleasant, but there's no way of verifying it. Her sentences begin somewhere in the middle and end in a different paragraph. There is no logic. No obvious signs of intelligence. She's going to bore or confuse us to death.

There was no CBI conference last year – the organisation was still in deep shame over sexual misconduct allegations – so all it managed was a 'winter moment'. But now it is back. Sort of. The numbers were down and the main hall was half the size of previous years. But it is still a force that politicians feel the need to keep onside. So KemiKaze was given the lunchtime slot for her keynote speech. It was just a shame she did not bring her A-game with her.

What she said was anyone's guess. Delegates were turning to one another in mystification. Looking for answers that were not forthcoming. But let's see if you can make more sense of it. Kemi wanted to deregulate because that was good for business. Er . . . Brexit, Kemi? Governments couldn't do everything, but she couldn't say what they could do. She wanted growth. Not just any growth, but a special kind of growth that you would recognise by looking outside. Some jobs needed to go. Some people needed social skills. Pots and kettles. There would be knobs and levers. The system was broken, but she couldn't mend it. Restaurants should forget about having menus. We needed an alternative strategy, but she didn't know what that was. She didn't even know if she would keep Labour's national insurance changes. Perhaps yes, perhaps no. Thank you and good night. She's either a genius or a halfwit. You decide.

Later on, Rachel Reeves joined us for a fireside chat. Or *je ne regrette rien*. There was no alternative to her tax rises. Have a go if you think you're hard enough, CBI. Tell us what you would have done differently. No one said a word. The Ministering Angel of Death was heard in near silence. As was Kemi. The applause was several claps short of polite. Fair to say most delegates don't seem to have a lot of faith in the government's ability to fix the economy. We are in a state of unstable stability. They will believe in growth when they see it. That way they can avoid further disappointment.

Another reset? Has Labour lost its marbles like the Tories?

3 DECEMBER 2024

There must be something in the water. It's normally in early January that people start to think of giving themselves a makeover. New year! New you! That kind of nonsense. But this year, everyone appears to be getting ahead of the game and relaunching themselves in December. Even Gregg Wallace, who is going out of his way to portray himself as a creepy misogynist. Just to eliminate any room for doubt.

Maybe it's just that everyone has already had enough of 2024. It has gone on far too long and has all been a bit underwhelming. Few things have quite worked out as anyone had hoped. Westminster itself is limping on to Christmas. While Jess Phillips was introducing a stalking bill, all the Tories really wanted to talk about was Labour giving back the Parthenon sculptures. Which they haven't even said they are going to do.

But no matter. Every time the Greek prime minister comes to visit the UK, the Tories can't help losing their . . . marbles. Boom, tish! This time, it was shadow junior culture minister Saqib Bhatti, accusing the government of giving in to the 'radical left' by even thinking of loaning the sculptures back to Greece. It's a matter of principle for the Tories. Taking the moral high ground. Because any country that allowed us Britons to ransack their heritage a couple of hundred years ago clearly couldn't be trusted to look after its own treasures.

Obviously, what would happen if we returned the sculptures to the Greeks is that, in next to no time, some other country would casually come along and help themselves to them. And this new country wouldn't look after them as well as us, so the only solution was to keep the marbles here at the British Museum. Just as well no one came to Britain and helped themselves to Stonehenge. Because the Conservatives would then be leading the campaign for it to stay in its new home.

Amid all this confected nonsense, Labour is planning its own reset on Thursday. Now forgive me for being a bit dim, but I could have sworn Labour had already had one or two resets already. Even though we're only five months into the new government. There was the one where Keir Starmer called everyone back early from their summer holidays to tell them that everything was even more shit than he had imagined and everyone was going to die. Then there was the reset after the freebies row. That time Keir had promised to stick to wearing cheap suits and to pay for his own footie tickets. After that, we got the reset where Labour ousted Sue Gray and promised to look less chaotic.

Now we have the big one. A reset so big that it was briefed to the papers a week before its launch. Presumably to allow the government a chance to rework anything that didn't land well. To reset the big reset. Here, we were promised some 'measurable milestones'. Hmm. Most of us would just settle for some basic signs of competence. At the moment, it feels like every cabinet minister is lying low, terrified of the sky falling in.

Labour aren't the only ones planning a reset. So is Boris Johnson. Sort of. Obviously, there's an ontological problem here. Because a sociopathic liar is always going to lie. It's what they do. So it's hard to know whether Boris is having a reset or just lying. Or, more confusingly, is lying about having a reset.

Whatever. Earlier this week, Johnson gave an interview to Spectator TV, prior to flying Down Under to inflict his dreary – and largely fictitious – memoir on Australia and New Zealand. Lucky them. Still, it gives us a break, I suppose. But in between talking about 'juddering climaxes' – truly, Boris is the Gregg Wallace of the political sphere; no opportunity to make inappropriate sexual innuendo gets missed – Johnson tried to position himself as a long-term Eurosceptic.

He had been campaigning for Britain to leave the EU for the past 30 years, he insisted. A claim that went totally unchallenged. He hadn't, of course. There are plenty of TV interviews with him this century in which he says that he would vote to remain in the EU and that the single market and customs union were things of beauty. Boris's long-term struggle to rewrite his life into a version with which he can live goes on. It will be a work in progress until he pops his clogs.

Jacob Rees-Mogg's reset is rather more prosaic: a reality show on Discovery+ called *Meet the Rees-Moggs*, in which Jacob comes across rather better than expected, largely thanks to the appearance of his wife, Helena, and his six children. That's not to say they won't need therapy by the time the last episode has aired, but so far, so good. Jakey has a lot to thank his family for. They have a lot to put up with.

As part of his promotion for the show, on Tuesday Rees-Mogg appeared on a Popular Conservatism webinar with Mark Littlewood, the former head of the Institute of Economic Affairs. A chance to remind everyone that he is still very much around and that reports of his political demise have been exaggerated. We have been warned.

Jacob began with the show. He'd wanted to be more like Nigel Farage. A man of the people in an oversized suit. We waltzed through the Tories' recent back stories. Amazingly, despite having been a minister under two prime ministers, Rees-Mogg didn't hold himself to blame for anything. It had all been someone else's fault. He was the last living true Conservative. The party had been overtaken by socialists. The Bank of England was full of commies. As was the civil service. It was time to forget about net zero. He has no idea how energy price tariffs work. If we were to frack the entire country, then we would have cheap energy for generations to come. Brexit was the one true religion. The importance of the nation state. Standing alone. Bowing to no international body. NATO. The UN. The ECHR. The ICC. They were all dead to him.

This was the Jakey that he had kept hidden in *Meet the Rees-Moggs*. There, he had been effortfully charming. Happy to be seen as an English eccentric. Here, he was altogether more disturbing. A fanatic who believed the country was in the hands of the hard left. For which the only solution was to tack ever further to the right. It's not a country many of us would recognise. Perhaps he needs yet another reset.

New year, new Keir: if only politicians would resolve to keep quiet in January

6 JANUARY 2025

Don't you just hate this time of year? The promise of Christmas giving way to the bleak reality of January. Cold mornings fading to grey by mid-afternoon. Nothing to look forward to except filling in your tax return. Hunkering down and praying to wake up some time in April.

And then there's the resolutions. Those empty, mindless promises you feel obliged to make. Frankly, no one cares whether you stay off the booze for a few months.

Or go cold turkey on the chocs. It's no big deal. Do what you like. Just don't bother the rest of us with your neuroses. The time for giving is well and truly over. We might have been interested at Christmas, but come the first week of January it's every person for themselves.

No one makes more of a song and dance about their resolutions than politicians. At least most ordinary people annoy only their close friends and family. Politicians feel obliged to make life miserable for the whole country. Going on and on about all the things they are going to do. Never stopping to think that they were saying much the same thing this time last year and nothing much has changed in between.

The first politician who promised that they were going to keep quiet for a few months while they got on with the job would be a blessing for us all. A guaranteed vote-winner. But no. They just can't resist a TV camera and news channels with space to fill. Out they come in the belief that the reason so many people are disappointed in them is because they just haven't managed to properly explain how wonderful they are. The search for the perfect sentence is their sole ambition.

New year, new Keir. So it was no surprise to find that the prime minister was out and about at Epsom hospital in Surrey on the first day of the new parliamentary session to let the country know of his new plans for the NHS. Though by the time he had finished speaking almost no one was any the wiser. That's Keir Starmer's cross to bear.

He's such a dull public speaker that his words curl up and die on his lips. Even when he's the bearer of good news, your first instinct is to kill yourself.

We have to assume that what Starmer had to say was important, because Wes Streeting stood behind him, nodding furiously. Much like one of those toy dogs that used to sit on the top of a Ford Granada's parcel shelf. The health secretary was flanked by more than 20 doctors and nurses, who began to look twitchy when they heard that part of the plan was to reduce waiting times. They had better things to do than be a backdrop for Keir. They had patients who were waiting.

Kemi Badenoch refrained from giving a new year speech. Instead, she chose social media for her new year messages. This is very on brand for KemiKaze. She actually believes that what happens on X is real life. She exists in a world in which the UK is reimagined as Great Twittain. Where people live in a state of suspended animation, waiting for the next deranged nutjob to say something toxic.

And in this new Great Twittain, we have a new leader – Elon Musk. The richest man in the world, who apparently has nothing better to do with his time than to take ketamine – billionaires can get anything on prescription these days – while sounding off about people and places of which he knows nothing whatsoever. Just to provoke a reaction. To prove that his life has meaning. What's the point of owning X, if not to turn it into a toxic hellhole?

To KemiKaze's great excitement, Musk has turned his attention to the UK. In particular, the child-grooming gangs that operated out of many towns and cities. For the Muskster, no real evidence is required for a few barely intelligible tweets.

But weirdly, Badenoch reacts as if she has been handed the Ten Commandments. Rather than just ignoring him, she regards Elon as the Second Coming. So she doubles down on everything Musk has said. All British Pakistani men should be treated as potential paedophiles. Keir Starmer and Jess Phillips are paedophile enablers. It's time for the US to invade in order to get rid of a tyrannical government.

All normal discourse is dead. As is rational thought. She has forgotten that just a few months ago, the Conservatives themselves were in power and had 14 years in which they could have held any number of public inquiries. Or even gone to the trouble of implementing the findings of the Alexis Jay inquiry. But this is Twittain, folks. The idiots are in charge of the Tory party.

Even stranger, KemiKaze – aided and abetted by the likes of Chris Philp and Robert Jenrick – has managed to position the Tories to the right of Reform. Nigel Farage has made it clear that Tommy Robinson is not welcome in his party. To Kemi and the Muskster, he is a much-misunderstood freedom fighter. Not someone banged up for contempt of court. Elon is even thinking of naming a new Tesla in his honour. The Tesla TR. Elegantly detailed, with a white hood.

All of which suited Starmer just fine. Far better to be dealing with this white noise than being questioned about his own new year resolution, which everyone had already forgotten. So once he had finished speaking in Epsom, nearly all the questions were on the space cadet's bizarre rants. Was Starmer worried about the impending invasion? Did he think Musk ought to be in prison?

No and no. He wasn't going to grace the Muskster's fantasies with any credibility. Nor was he going to get personal. Other than to call out Kemi for following Elon. Britain expected more of its party leaders than this. This was a rage confected entirely on X. No one other than a few cranks believed that Starmer and Phillips protected the abusers. It was time for the Tories to grow up a bit. Take time out from their own echo chamber. He was going to concentrate on the serious business of politics.

Here's hoping. Happy new Keir.

* * *

Only it wasn't a particularly happy new year for either Keir or Labour. His first six months in office hadn't exactly been a triumph, and there was no real good news on the horizon. A week after his first January reboot, Starmer tried another. When Rishi Sunak had done a big AI number to boost his falling poll ratings while in office, Keir had been extremely dismissive. Now it was his turn to big up AI. Except no one was really listening. Most people were more worried about the state of the economy.

Just about the only positive for Starmer was that Kemi Badenoch was still struggling to achieve any cut-through. The Tories were tanking, and so was she. Her performances at prime minister's questions had many of her own backbenchers covering their eyes in horror.

Meanwhile, over on the other side of the Atlantic, The Donald was about to return.

Donald Trump assumes office with promise to be the very bestest best

20 JANUARY 2025

They came in dribs and drabs, the unwanted, the uninvited and the unloved. First to arrive in Washington was Liz Truss, wearing a red MAGA hat and a bright blue coat and looking like an extra in a Paddington Bear film. Lizzie could be found standing on a street corner in downtown DC, screaming: 'I used to be prime minister of the United Kingdom.'

'Of course you did,' said a kindly passerby, giving her a wide berth.

'I did. I did. I really did,' she sobbed.

'Do you need help?'

'I'm fine. I'm fine. Anyone who says I crashed the economy will be getting a letter from my lawyers.'

'It's OK, ma'am,' said a police officer. 'Time to move on. Do you have anywhere to go?'

Lizzie didn't. She wasn't quite sure why she had come to America now. When even Donald Trump doesn't want to know you, then your sense of futility is complete. Maybe she could find an electrical goods store and watch the inauguration on a TV there.

The same went for Suella Braverman and Priti Patel. No place to go, no place to be. They had come only because they had hoped they were marginally more popular in the US than they were back at home. Priti had been sure that being found to have broken the ministerial code twice would guarantee her a front-row seat. Turns out The Donald has some standards after all. Suella had even turned up on the same flight as the freelance halfwit Laurence Fox. Hard to tell who was the most embarrassed.

Back in the UK, the sucking up started early on Monday morning. David Lammy on the *Today* programme, trying to be cool about not getting an invitation. He was sure it had just been a clash of diaries. And he hadn't wanted to upstage the president-elect anyway. He went into rhapsodies about the brilliance of The Donald, the extended dinner that had been the best dinner ever, the incredible grace and generosity of the Trumpster. Words no one had ever previously said. Least of all the foreign secretary, who, last we heard, had called him a fascist. Pass the sick bag.

It was a bitterly cold morning in DC. Something every reporter remarked on. Minus 11, said the Sky man on the White House lawn. He sounded as if he felt he had drawn the short straw. How come he wasn't anchoring the show from a warm studio? Or doing the commentary from the Rotunda?

The first real action was a sighting of Trump going to a prayer service at St John's Episcopal Church. Donald didn't look exactly thrilled to be there. But then he seldom does when he's with Melania. Joining him in the congregation was Javier Milei, Argentina's answer to Liam Gallagher, Elon Musk and Boris Johnson. This was a real moment of hubris for Bozza. The Donald was born again, while he couldn't even give away copies of his memoir. The service lasted 45 minutes. There were a lot of collective sins to be forgiven.

Cut to JD Vance and his wife Usha being greeted at the White House by Kamala Harris and her husband Doug. Awkward smiles. No love lost there. Moments later, the Beeb screened a ticker: 'Rump family arriving at Capitol Hill'. Start as you mean to go on, BBC. Cue Donald and Melania meeting the Bidens. Perhaps they chatted about why Trump had chosen to post a video about Joe having spent the night in the seniors' wing. That legendary generosity again. Still no smile from The Donald.

An hour before the ceremony began, the Rotunda started to fill with guests. There was Musk. As weird as only he can be. Friends, politicians, judges and ambassadors. But no Nigel Farage. Maybe not on quite such good terms with the president as he would like us to believe. George Bush and Bill Clinton were there with their wives. Barack Obama without his. The extended Trump family looking surprised to have been given day release. The ceremonials didn't come close to a British state occasion. More like the political Oscars, complete with cheesy announcer.

After a long procession of entrances, we finally got to Trump himself. The first flicker of a smile. He and Melania went to air-kiss. Their lips didn't get within six inches of each other. Then the opening addresses. A reminder that 'Equal Justice Under Law' was written on the Supreme Court building. Just not for presidents. Or the very rich.

Franklin Graham declared that God had spared Trump to save the country. At least we will know who to blame. The Donald swore the oath on his own bible. The one that says 'May all felons be spared' and 'Grab women by the pussy'. America had its 47th president. Chants of 'U–S–A' could be heard in the overspill hall. Trump began to join in the clapping for himself. He hasn't quite got the hang of this.

The gloves came off as he started his inaugural address. You couldn't escape the threat in his voice. Donald is still a man who feels that Donald has been wronged. All he had was a narrative of betrayal. He laid into Biden for the decline of America. But he was on hand to bring about the golden age of America. This was the moment the US had been awaiting for nearly 250 years. So modest.

He, too, believed God had spared him to save America. Everything was going to change. There would be a national emergency on the southern border. Immigrants, watch out. There would also be tariffs, though he wasn't sure how they would work. And bring on the climate-change deniers. Drill, baby, drill. He couldn't make the connection to the disasters in North Carolina and LA.

Try to look on him as the messiah. A peacemaker. A unifier. The best. The very bestest best. The Gulf of Mexico would be renamed the Gulf of America. The Panama Canal would be seized. Mars, here we come. By now, most of the audience were bouncing up and down in their chairs.

'The impossible is what we do best,' he ended. 'We're going to win like never before.' There was a minute's unscheduled pause before Carrie Underwood sang 'America the Beautiful'. It turned out it had been impossible to tee up the music on the laptop. Making America great again.

'It's been nice talking to you, Ken': imagining Starmer's first call with Trump

27 JANUARY 2025

KEIR STARMER: Good afternoon, your Most Serene Excellency.

DONALD TRUMP: Who is this?

STARMER: It's Keir Starmer. Prime minister of the United Kingdom.

TRUMP: Where's that?

STARMER: It's . . .

TRUMP: Just kidding. I know exactly where you are. You're that island near Europe. Good to speak to you, Ken. Thanks for calling.

STARMER: It's nice to have a chance to speak to you, Mr President. First, may I congratulate you on your inauguration? I was very sorry I could not be there in person.

TRUMP: That's because you weren't invited.

STARMER: But I'm sure I was busy anyway. And I was thrilled to see that Nigel Farage, Liz Truss, Suella Braverman and Priti Patel were also off the guest list . . .

TRUMP: I'm so over those guys. It was an amazing occasion. People have said it was the best inauguration we have ever had in America. In the world, even. My speech got the longest applause of any speech a president has ever made.

STARMER: The whole world was listening. Especially the Panamanians. They will be thrilled to hear you are going to seize the canal. Can I also add my thanks to you for your efforts in securing a ceasefire in the Middle East?

TRUMP: Thank you, Kevin. I'm going to bring so much peace to the world as you wouldn't believe. Even if it means killing a lot of people to get this peace. So much peace that people will say: 'I didn't know there was this much peace out there.'

STARMER: That's fantastic, Mr President. Maybe now would be a good time to discuss Ukraine. It's vital that the West continues to offer its wholehearted support for President Zelenskyy in his fight against Vladimir Putin.

TRUMP: I'm going to suggest they call it quits. Russia gets to keep all the territory it's gained, and the rest of Ukraine stays an independent nation.

STARMER: I'm not sure that's going to work . . .

TRUMP: Why not? No one really wants the bits of Ukraine that Russia has annexed . . .

STARMER: I think the Ukrainians do . . .

TRUMP: It's just a load of wasteland in the middle of nowhere. Who wants muddy fields and forests and some bombed-out villages? Ukraine should be happy to give it up. And America isn't going to bankroll NATO indefinitely. In fact, I might declare war on NATO if you, the French and the Germans don't start spending more on defence.

STARMER: Please don't do that, Mr President. We're all doing the best we can. But maybe we should just pretend we didn't discuss Ukraine and NATO when we give the press a read-out of this call.

TRUMP: Suit yourself, Kris. Is there anything else you want to talk about?

STARMER: The Chagos Islands deal. It would be very helpful if you were able to agree to the settlement we have made with Mauritius . . .

TRUMP: That's not going to happen any time soon. I'd rather obliterate Chagos off the face of the Pacific Ocean than hand the islands over to Mauritius.

STARMER: Chagos is in the Indian Ocean . . .

TRUMP: It won't be by the time I've finished with it. And don't call it the Indian Ocean. I'm planning on renaming all the oceans. American Ocean One. American Ocean Two. And so on . . . It's going to catch on, I'm telling you.

STARMER: Right. Then let's also knock the Chagos Islands off the read-out. This conversation never happened. Now, is there anything I can help you with?

TRUMP: There is. I'm sure you've heard that the Greenlanders have been begging me to make their country the 51st state of the USA. But it seems that the Danelanders aren't happy about this because they think it belongs to them. So if you could talk some sense into them, that would be much appreciated. I mean, what can Daneland do for Greenland? A new Ikea . . .

STARMER: Ikea is from Swedeland . . .

TRUMP: We can give the Greenlanders a McDonald's, a

KFC and a Taco Bell. Obviously, I will nuke Nuuk if necessary, but I'd rather not . . . Drill, baby, drill.

STARMER: My thoughts entirely. The way forward is growth. Now, there is one thing you can do for me, Mr President. Is it possible for you to ask Elon Musk to keep out of British politics? His interventions haven't been helpful . . .

TRUMP: That guy drinks more Diet Coke than me . . . Elon is a law unto himself. I told him the other day – 'Elon,' I said, 'you're going to have to rebrand your automobiles.' Tesla is so last year. What he should call it is the Swasti Car. That's just so catchy. Giorgia Meloni and Viktor Orbán loved the idea. The Germanlanders will go wild for it, too.

STARMER: Er . . . that's excellent. Before we don't talk about trade tariffs and anything else remotely difficult, can I just say that the royal family have asked me to pass on their best wishes and let you know how much they enjoyed seeing you in 2019? With a bit of luck, I might be able to swing another state visit for you.

TRUMP: That would be much appreciated, Karl. Though no more than I deserve. Me and the Queen became the very best of friends when we met. She looked up to me a lot and always rang to ask my opinion.

STARMER: Well, let's try to pencil in some dates for you to visit, Mr President. Let me look at my diary. Yes . . . it seems that I am free any time in February, March, April, May, June, July, August, September, October, November and December.

TRUMP: I'll get back to you. Gotta go. It's been nice talking to you, Ken. For a commie, you're not all bad . . .

STARMER: And may I say what an honour it has been for you to take my call? Our countries will always have a special relationship and have more . . .

Trump hangs up.

TRUMP: Jeez. What a total loser!

STARMER: How am I going to survive another four years of this halfwit?

Starmer leaves Brussels with a tariff-free Trump sycophancy surplus

3 FEBRUARY 2025

Don't mention the trade war. Don't mention anything much, come to think of it. Stick to generalised soundbites. Careless talk costs lives.

Keir Starmer's trip to Brussels to meet the EU leaders was fraught with danger. Don't say anything too complimentary about the EU as all the Brexiters will go mad and shout, 'Betrayal'. Don't sound too hostile about the EU as remainers will also be up in arms. Try to find the tricky balance of somewhere in between. A politeness that lands the right side of indifference.

Then there's the US to worry about. How to cope with

the orange manchild. Too much independence of thought, and you might feel the full weight of trade tariffs. Time to bury your self-worth and go into full fawning mode. Few people have ever come unstuck by telling Donald Trump that he is an undiscovered genius. No one said that being prime minister was going to be easy. Or dignified.

It was a tough act to pull off, but Starmer just about managed it in a very brisk press conference with the NATO secretary general, Mark Rutte, on Monday afternoon. Just the barest minimum. Opening statements that were so dull they died on the lips – precious little sign of Starmer's delivery being improved by a voice coach here – followed by three questions from the broadcasters. Then out of there.

Rutte got things under way. NATO was amazing. The UK was amazing. The West had never been more united. That's not quite how the rest of the world might see it, with the US imposing tariffs on Canada – the ones on Mexico have been deferred for a month – and Trump talking about making Greenland another US state. But hey. If the NATO secretary general says he's relaxed about all this, then who are we to argue? Situation Normal All Fucked Up.

Next up was Starmer. He, too, was thrilled about the NATO project. It was good to be in Brussels. Though not too good. No one should think the UK might be about to enter negotiations to rejoin the EU. We just wanted the best proper relations, while taking advantage of all the Brexit benefits. There was a 10-second pause while he tried to remember what they were. No. Me neither.

Moving on. Britain was standing up to Russia. NATO was standing up to Russia. We were all behind Ukraine. President Trump had rattled Vladimir Putin. A quick bit of fanboying the president never did any harm. We were spending 2.3% of GDP on defence. Tank production had reached a record high. Or something.

Mysteriously, the three broadcasters had little interest in what Rutte and Starmer had just said. They wanted to talk about The Donald. Was he bad news for Europe and international trade? asked Sky's Beth Rigby.

'There are always issues between allies,' said Rutte. The current difficulties were much ado about nothing. Trade war? What trade war? He was sure Trump would see sense about imposing tariffs on the EU. Hmm. This showed a touching faith in the president's proximity to rational thought.

Starmer wasted no time in praising The Donald. There was nothing remotely weird about a president who was so obviously an unreconstructed narcissist. If only more leaders were that shade of orange. The world would be a far safer place. Trump had been right to think about tariffs, because so many people now took free trade for granted. Only someone as brilliant as Trump could possibly have reintroduced them.

And Starmer was delighted to report that though the Office for National Statistics (ONS) had said that the UK had a trade surplus with the US, he was more than happy to accept the American figures, which showed it was the US in surplus. So tariffs were strictly an EU problem. Far be it from him to interfere in a dispute with two such dear friends. But just to wipe the slate clean, he was now going to sack everyone at the ONS for even suggesting the UK was in surplus. There. Was that brown-nosing enough? I rather think it was.

The second question came from the BBC. Could we return to reality? A trade war was not normal. Nor was the US threatening to annex Greenland. This wasn't how politics worked. Once again, Rutte went out of his way to point out that Trump was the only sane one in the room. It was the rest of the world that was out of whack. Above all, he was enormously grateful for Trump alerting the West to the geo-strategic nature of Greenland. Before The Donald's intervention, he had never really given Greenland another thought. It was just an empty white space on the map. And all the Mercator projections showed Greenland to be thousands of miles away from Russia. But now that he had had time to look at a globe, he had come to appreciate just how important the country was.

And guess what? Under all that snow and ice, Trump had discovered loads of rare minerals. So could we all have three cheers for the president? If I was a Greenlander, that little exchange wouldn't have been entirely reassuring.

Yes, said Starmer. Hooray for this Brilliant Orangeness. He just wanted to remind everyone that Trump had said he might not impose tariffs on the UK. So that was tremendously good news. There again, he had also said that 'the UK was well out of line' – but maybe that was a joke. Or maybe he wasn't entirely clear about the difference between the UK and the EU. But never mind. He was just Little Keir. And Little Keir wanted to get on with everyone. He loved the EU and the US. Couldn't we just all be friends?

Before Rutte and Starmer could declare their undying faith in the Supreme Intellect again, a NATO official intervened to declare that the press conference had been done and dusted in under 15 minutes. Mark and Keir needed no second invitation. Anything to get away from their cloying bath of enforced sycophancy. Let's hope they had a couple's therapy session straight afterwards to cleanse themselves of the shame.

On the way out, a *Sun* journalist shouted out a question. Had Starmer broken lockdown rules by employing a voice coach? Er . . . no, he hadn't. The rules on key workers were surprisingly loose in Westminster. Even I was a key worker. The bar doesn't get much lower than that. Still, nice of the Tories to keep reminding us that they were the ones who consistently broke the lockdown rules.

Trump trumps himself with his latest delusional fantasies

19 FEBRUARY 2025

Even by his recent standards, Tuesday night's stream of unconsciousness from Donald Trump took some beating. Hot on the tail of excluding Ukraine from the first round of peace talks with Russia, and in effect threatening to withdraw the US from NATO, The Donald has now suggested it was Kyiv who started the war with Moscow.

More than that, he declared that President Zelenskyy's approval rating in his own country had slid to just 4% and that he had assumed the role of dictator by not holding elections. Trump ended by claiming that the US had given more than three times as much aid to Ukraine than the rest of Europe combined. You could almost hear Vladimir Putin cheering from the sidelines. He couldn't have written the script any better. It was perfection.

It goes without saying that everything the US president had said was complete doggy bollox. Russia first invaded Ukraine in 2014 and seized Crimea. There was then a pause in hostilities, before Putin invaded a second time, almost exactly three years ago. Claiming Ukraine started the war was like believing that Poland invaded Germany to trigger the Second World War. Or maybe the Poles were just suffering from false consciousness and were yet to understand that they wanted to be sub-jugated by the Germans. Hell, maybe Trump thinks 'No means no' is just some politically correct wokery, and that when the Ukrainians said they would rather not become Russian, what they were really saying was: 'Yes, please. Do what you like.' Much like the Americans were gag-ging for the Japanese to bomb Pearl Harbor in 1941.

That was just the start. Trump's claim that Zelenskyy's approval rating was 4% was just one of his delusional, senescent fantasies. The real figure is 57% – about 10% higher than The Donald's own rating. And no one in their right mind is suggesting that Ukraine hold elections while the war is ongoing. There again, Trump is clearly not in his right mind. His aid figures were also way off. Collectively, Europe has given Ukraine £132bn since the start of the war. America has given £114bn.

While a shrink would have a field day trying to untan-gle the workings of the Trump psyche – Is he a narcissist or a solipsist? Does he actually believe what he says, or do his words exist independently of his brain? – it's left to the rest of us to pick up the pieces. Much as they might prefer not to, other world leaders have to find a way of engaging with him. The Donald is the most powerful man on the planet, and whatever he says counts for something.

So spare a thought for junior minister Diana Johnson, who found herself scheduled to do the morning media round for the government. She had hoped she would be called on to talk about the latest knife crime initiative, but found herself asked about Trump's latest dangerous ramblings. You could almost hear the panic in her voice. Whatever you do, don't criticise the president. Just say it's all very interesting, but Ukraine must be involved in its own peace negotiations. She just about got away with it, as the presenters took pity on her. They appreciated her dilemma.

The strangest response came from Boris Johnson. With Kemi Badenoch and other senior Tories strangely silent, the disgraced former prime minister popped up on X to offer his analysis. Trump was just doing his best to end the war. No one cared more about peace than The Donald. The US president had never meant for anyone to take him seriously about Ukraine starting the war or Zelenskyy's popularity ratings. It was just his way of trying to get everyone round the table. His funny little ways. As with Boris, Trump could be trusted to tell the truth only half the time. The trick was trying to work out which half was which.

Boris ended his tweet by suggesting that Russia was desperate to have its assets unfrozen so that it could hand them over to rebuild Ukraine. To think, Johnson used to consider himself Ukraine's biggest ally. Right now, he sounded suspiciously as if he had morphed into another Kremlin sycophant. He will certainly be off Zelenskyy's Christmas card list.

You might have half expected Johnson to have pitched up at the third, and last, day of the Alliance for

Responsible Citizenship (ARC) conference at the ExCeL centre in London. He would have fitted right in. A deeply unserious man for deeply serious times. The ARC seems to exist in its own ecosphere, cocooned from the real world. So much so that its members seem to be a year behind the rest of us. None of them has realised that their man is now calling the shots on wokery from the White House. They prefer to be the victim. On the outside looking in.

Any discussion on the most important issues of the day, like the war in Ukraine, appeared to have been kept off the schedule. Just speaker after speaker congratulating themselves on saying the unsayable, apparently unaware that no one was stopping them saying anything. If you want to understand the importance of free speech, ask Alexei Navalny. Except you can't.

But even all the endless complaints about political correctness came with a heavily sanitised air. No one was allowed to raise a voice in disagreement. Just endless self-congratulation. There weren't many female speakers, but those who were invited seemed happy to accept that their role in the new world order was simply to produce more children. A man got a standing ovation for fathering 10 children. And how did Dougie Murray, a gay man, feel about ARC's co-founder Jordan Peterson describing homosexuality as a deviation?

This felt very much like a day for the B-list speakers. First up was the deeply unpleasant Konstantin Kisin, who this week had suggested on his TRIGGERnometry podcast that Rishi Sunak was not English. Er . . . he was born in Southampton. Presumably Kisin thinks Kemi is also not English. But KK wasn't here to repeat that line; he was just there to make a couple of mildly racist jokes and wallow in his own imagined brilliance. Onanism par excellence.

Then we had Toby Young. Or, as we should now call him, the anti-establishment Lord Young. I'm surprised some peers haven't given up their titles in protest. He was there to wang on about free speech and how hard done by he has been. You can say what you like, Toby. Just don't expect congratulations for it. He rather undermined his whole point by admitting there was a law protecting free speech after all.

Others came and went. Eric Weinstein suggested we should defy physics and live on the stars. Nice work, if you can get it. The closest we had to a big name was Vivek Ramaswamy. Though he managed to get through the entire interview without being asked why he had accepted Trump's invitation to jointly head up Doge, and why he had subsequently fallen out with Elon Musk. At which point the last remaining particle of credibility ARC may have had left the conference centre. It had been that sort of day.

* * *

The Donald Trump whirlwind left everyone breathless. Unsure of whether when they woke up in the morning, the world would be the same as it was when they went to bed. Not even The Donald seemed to know what he was going to do next, be it turn Gaza into a riviera full of golf resorts or arbitrarily impose tariffs. Regarding the latter, no one was entirely certain if he understood that it was American businesses and consumers who would be paying for the increased tariffs. That was to say nothing about the matter of Ukraine, with the US president not seeming to be wholly on board with the idea that Vladimir Putin was the bad guy.

Understandably then, Keir Starmer found himself devoting a lot of time to playing geopolitics – and he turned out to be a great deal better at handling the US president than many other world leaders. While they took a more combative approach to The Donald's often confused ramblings, Keir played the softly, softly card. Not rocking the boat, resorting to almost sincere flattery and indulging Trump's narcissism to secure the odd small win.

On the domestic stage, though, Labour was still struggling. First, Keir annoyed his backbenchers by cutting the international aid budget in order to increase the UK's NATO spending in line with The Donald's demands. Then he alienated them further by announcing huge cuts to disability benefits in order to stick to the fiscal rules. Many Labour MPs threatened to rebel, saying they hadn't gone into politics to make the most vulnerable worse off. Rachel Reeves's spring statement did nothing to improve relations between the cabinet and backbenchers, nor to give the rest of the country much hope that things would get better soon.

Still, at least Starmer could rely on the Tories to not provide any real opposition. Kemi Badenoch was looking and sounding so desperate that she and her shadow chancellor, Mel Stride, had taken to calling press conferences at which they had nothing to say. They just wanted a tiny bit of attention. Even if it was all negative. For the real opposition, we had to look to Nigel Farage and Reform. God help us.

Nigel doubling up, Dicky in No. 11 and 30p Lee at foreign? Run for the hills!

12 APRIL 2025

With two opinion polls giving the Reform Party a clear lead over Labour and the Conservatives, it may be time to start thinking about some practicalities. Like, just who will be doing what job in a Reform-led government?

It can probably be taken as read that Nigel Farage will be prime minister, but that leaves three MPs – make that two, as James McMurdock isn't trusted enough by his colleagues to be allowed out in public – to fill the remaining

20-plus cabinet posts. Unless we take it that two dozen or so newly elected MPs with no experience of anything will be drafted in by Nige after the 2029 election. Run for the hills, everyone.

It's probably fair to assume that Richard Tice has his eyes on becoming chancellor. Dicky likes to think that a spell on the graveyard shift of the shopping channel flogging sunbeds makes him the ideal man to be in charge of the national finances. He has the misplaced confidence of a man in possession of a small fortune. Mainly because he started out with a large one. No one will ever love Dicky quite the way Dicky loves Dicky. A man who gets an erotic thrill from his own reflection. The embodiment of *levitas*. One budget from Dicky, and the country will be pleading for the return of Kwasi Kwarteng. Reform's collision with economic reality will make us all poorer.

As for Lee Anderson, the Ashfield MP who has crashed and burned his way through Labour and the Tories, before – for now – aligning himself with Nige, that probably leaves the Foreign Office. 30p Lee, masquerading as the UK's senior diplomat. A man who can always be trusted to handle delicate situations with tact and sensitivity. A new era in legitimised, plain-speaking Islamophobia. There's just the one problem: Anderson has no understanding of and no interest in foreign affairs. His world ends at the White Cliffs.

There was certainly no sign of Lee during Thursday's urgent question in the Commons on the ongoing peace talks to end the war in Ukraine. There again, probably easier for Reform to stay away. No point in pointing out that Nige is sometimes reluctant to criticise Trump and Putin. Put it this way: unlike many of the MPs on both sides of the chamber, Nige, Dicky and Lee are never going to find themselves on a Russian sanctions list.

The session itself was a looking-glass affair. One where you had to pinch yourself to make sure you hadn't slid into an alternative universe. One where Tory after Tory – including James Cleverly – stood up to condemn Agent Orange for trash-talking Volodymyr Zelenskyy and unilaterally conceding Ukrainian territory, while the Foreign Office minister Stephen Doughty repeatedly insisted that the US had nothing but Ukrainian interests at heart and that the talks were going swimmingly, despite the Americans having walked out. 'The talks had been productive because they were productive,' he said. Thank you and good night, Steve.

Nige himself was also missing from the Commons. That was because he was out and about in Dover, giving yet another press conference at which he had nothing new to say. Farage is convinced he will shrivel up and die if he isn't standing in front of a camera at least once or twice a day. His narcissism is ravenous, never satisfied. So it no longer matters what he says. All that counts is that he is saying something, and that someone is there to record it. One day we will discover that tucked away in an attic there is a portrait of him ageing by the day.

Still, one mystery was solved on the Kent coast. Because it emerged that Nige thinks Nige is best placed to be home secretary. After all, being prime minister is very much a part-time occupation. So Farage has volunteered himself to double up. He might even go for the hat-trick and take on the Department for Work and Pensions as well. Why deprive himself of the fun of cutting people's benefits? The highlight of any politician's career.

First, though, Nige wanted to have a serious talk about immigration. And to everyone's astonishment, he had come to the conclusion there are far too many foreigners in this country. Not that he didn't like foreigners. Some of his best friends were foreigners. Though these were all foreigners who had done the decent thing and stayed in their own foreign country.

Here was the thing about foreigners who had landed up in the UK: they were all pathologically lazy. Just here for the freebies and to make real Brits poorer. To steal social housing from white people. White people were not to be confused with Albanian white people. Albanian white people were all criminals. They come over here, steal our phones, sell us drugs and take up all the spare places in our jails.

But if there was one thing worse than foreigners, it was remainers. What you had to remember about remainers was that they were all closet traitors. The only true patriots were the Brexiters. Because nothing shouts 'I love Britain the most' than voting to make the country poorer.

Nige got slower and slower as he ran through his greatest hits, until his batteries ran out. He ground to a halt mid-crocodile smile. His minders hastily plugged in the charger as some questions from the media came in. He wanted to reindustrialise the whole of the UK to kick-start a rise in employment. It was as if the AI revolution had escaped him. He would get rid of all diversity, equality and inclusion criteria. May the best white Brit win. A man, preferably.

Kent council should close all its migrant hotels. Who cared whether that was legal or not? He went out on a high. Children were being over-diagnosed with special educational needs. Kids with autism should just pull themselves together. They should learn to do a proper day's work rather than sponging off the state. No one could say Nige wasn't all heart. Could they?

Sound the alarm for a Kemikaze breakfast, then hit snooze for the Starmer roadshow

28 APRIL 2025

Even Kemi Badenoch's closest friends know to give her a wide berth in the mornings. Especially her closest friends. They know what's good for them. Sometimes absence is an act of friendship. Intimacy by proxy.

Mornings are when Kemi is at her worst. Up at 6.30 a.m., checking her phone for the latest culture war.

Six double espressos. Then she's ready to get out of bed. Anyone who crosses her path gets swatted away. Don't even think of offering her a granola bar. An hour of bog-standard policing to follow. Making sure the right people go to the right toilet. Ready to pick an argument with anyone.

So it was a shock to find KemiKaze on the 8.15 a.m. sofa slot on *Good Morning Britain*. Which of her minders had let her loose at that time of day? It was even more of a shock to discover that she was almost charming. Non-combative, even. You wouldn't go so far as to say Kemi was friendly. She hasn't had a personality transplant. Her private hell is other people. But she didn't hit anyone. Didn't start a fight. Was more or less human.

She had taken the job of leader of the Conservative Party in the belief that she could make a difference. That she was the one who could halt the party's decline. Nearly six months on, and Kemi was almost out of ideas. Nothing she had tried had worked. Turned out that voters weren't prepared to forgive the Tories quite so quickly. Their eyes didn't light up at the sound of toxic arguments. They actually just wanted to feel as if things were getting better. When they weren't.

Now she could sense her time was running out. Robert Jenrick was positioning himself in the wings. Openly campaigning to replace her. Not even polite enough to be subtle about it. You know what? Let him try. Let's see if he can come up with any ideas that the country will reject. She had had a go. No one could take 'Leader of the Opposition' off her CV. And in truth, she had never really been up for it. You'd need to be a madwoman to take on a job for which you had been set up to fail.

GMB presenter Susanna Reid started off by talking about potential coalitions between the Tories and Reform. How nervous are you about notching up hundreds of losses? Given that Kemi appeared to be nodding off already, it was no surprise that she wasn't that bothered at all. When everything bad already appears to have happened, you get a bit blasé about local election results. She had already priced in the certainty that the Tories were going to have a disastrous Thursday. Bring it on. It wasn't personal. The voters didn't hate her. Well, not much. They just hated the Conservatives a whole lot more.

Kemi shrugged as Susanna tried to tease something – anything – out of her. Please, just say something, her eyes begged. It's how interviews work. She asks the questions, and then Kemi gives an answer. Anything would do. Just the structure of a conversation would be a start.

'We are fighting every seat,' said KemiKaze, eventually. Technically, this is true. She just didn't specify how strongly the Tories would be fighting. Then came the expectation management. Four years ago, the Conservatives had been riding high in the polls. Now, they were tanking hideously. She tried to correct herself. This wasn't about the opinion polls; it had just been a coincidence that the Tories had done so well in 2021. And it certainly wasn't about immigration. It was all about who you trusted to run local services. Dream on. If that was the case, no one would be voting Reform.

Now it was Ed Balls's turn. He, too, wanted to know how Kemi was feeling. Are you OK? Are you enjoying yourself? It was all going a bit Amol Rajan on *University Challenge*. For a moment, Kemi almost rallied. How do you think I'm feeling? I'm feeling like shit. People told me not to take the job, and they were right. The only crumb of comfort was the counterfactual notion that the Tories might have been doing even worse without her.

Kemi did spark vaguely into life when asked about the Supreme Court ruling on biological sex. 'I was right all along,' she yelled, punching the air. As far as she was concerned, trans people could use a disabled toilet. And if there wasn't one anywhere near, they could just hang on till they got home.

The interview ended with Ed mentioning the J-word. Why was she putting up with Jenrick when he was so obviously campaigning against her? Because she didn't care. He would fail. Just like she had. Good luck to him. Honest Bob was a loyal member of her team. Inasmuch as anyone in her team was loyal. Never mind. It would all be over soon.

Meanwhile, Keir Starmer was campaigning in the north-west. Though not in Runcorn, where a by-election will be held. Nothing could better show just how desperate the prime minister is to hold on to Runcorn than his absence from it. He knows how unpopular he is. Were he to campaign in the constituency, he would be in danger of his party losing votes. Best leave the hard graft to people on the ground who can keep their distance from the Labour centre.

It's election week. Though not as we know it.

Alone on centre stage, for Nige this was his triumph and no one else's

2 MAY 2025

Nigel Farage is one of this century's survivors. A man who walked away from not just a plane crash, but any number of iterations of parties carved in his image. Rising from near-death experiences time and again. The last cockroach standing after a nuclear holocaust.

In Reform, Nige has found his most successful reinvention yet. You've got a grievance? Then Farage is there to verbalise it and sell it back to you. Always on hand to spot division and feed on it. The politics of the far right may be his preferred habitat – he's yet to come across an asylum seeker he didn't want to deport – but he's nothing if not the consummate opportunist. Sensing he might have maxed out his fanbase among the right, he's happily dipped his toes into the politics of the left, championing the nationalisation cause. He will be whatever you want him to be. He's not fussy. Anything to ramp up Brand Nige.

And now it feels as if his time may have come. Previous triumphs have always felt transitory – ships in the night – but the results of Thursday's local elections have a patina of permanence. The possibility at least of an end to a politics dominated by Labour and the Conservatives. A new multiverse, where Reform – for now – has the most public support.

The danger for Farage is that with success come obligations. An expectation to deliver. A problem Nige has never encountered before. He's only ever carped from the sidelines. Trash-talked the governing parties, while offering no real solutions himself. Someone you wouldn't trust with his own debit card, let alone to run the finances of the entire country. His only real tangible achievement in the past 25 years was to front one half of the campaign to reduce the UK's GDP by 4% by leaving the EU. And then to disown his part in it by claiming Brexit hadn't been done in the way he had imagined. Shape-shifting avoidance of responsibility.

But all that could wait for another day. Friday was Nige's personal triumph. His new MP, Sarah Pochin, and the Lincolnshire mayor, Andrea Jenkyns, may have been the winners on the night, but everyone knew they were only there out of an act of kindness granted by Farage. Decoration. Largesse. Nothing more.

This is the fault line that runs through Nige's entire career. Nige is only ever about Nige. He can't do collaboration. His team are primarily followers – devotees – rather than MPs or mayors. Satellites to his lodestar. Anyone showing any sign of independence of thought is crushed. There can be no challenge. Nige is the centre of his own universe. A little man with grandiose narcissistic ambition. Dicky Tice and Lee Anderson are tolerated only because they understand the rules. Their ambition is to collect the crumbs that Nige drops.

So it was no surprise that for Reform's victory lap in Durham, it was Farage alone who took centre stage. You might have thought that with the hint of power would come some kind of leadership. A willingness to reach out to those who hadn't voted for him. Reassurance, even. But Nige has no personal charm. His smile is only ever a veneer. Behind it there is an anger born of the fragility of a man who believes he has been hard done by. He is the establishment man who feels he has been ignored by the establishment. The millionaire masquerading as the little people.

You might have thought Nige would want to thank his proxies. As an unheartfelt courtesy, if nothing else. But no. He was rushing on his run. This was his triumph, and no one else's. He owed nothing to anyone.

'We are the agents of change,' he said. The royal 'we'. Then he moved on to his familiar bugbears. Diversity. There was too much of it. Time for middle-aged white men like him to be given a chance. Too many foreigners. He'd make sure there were no asylum seekers in any council Reform controlled. They would be eradicated. Not just put in tents like Andrea had promised. As for net zero? Forget it. Let the planet burn. Drill, baby, drill.

Elsewhere, Starmer was out and about at a drone factory in Luton. For him, the biggest story of the day was defence manufacturing. It took a while, but eventually a journalist got a word in edgeways. What about the elections? Keir looked baffled. Elections? What elections? Oh, those elections. He had completely forgotten about them. They were mere nothings, really. A meaningless distraction. But the message Keir wanted to take away was that what the country really wanted was for him to keep doing exactly what he had been doing. Only doing it a bit faster.

That might spell bad news for pensioners and farmers, but Starmer was adamant he knew what he was doing. His victorious mayor, Ros Jones, and several MPs from the left of the Labour Party saw it differently. They reckoned their traditional voters were sick of a party that was Reform-lite. Why would anyone vote for that when they could have the real thing?

If it was a bad day for Labour, it was a crushing one for the Tories. Near annihilation. No wonder then that most of their MPs took a vow of silence. Nigel Huddleston popped up on the radio to say that the message he was hearing from voters was that people really liked Badenoch. You dread to think how badly the Tories would have done if they hated her. The only people who visibly loved Kemi were the Reform candidates. As for Kemi, she contented herself with a brief note on social media. Sorry, not sorry. I'm going nowhere. Other views are available.

The last word went to Nigel. 'I will be the next prime minister,' he said. It's a depressing possibility. A UK that has lost hope. Lost its moral compass. A country that no longer believes in itself. 'Take me or leave me,' Nige snapped. 'I just don't care.'

And he doesn't care. He never has done. About anything but himself. We have been warned.

* * *

Not even the near obliteration of the Tories could conceal the fact that the local election results had also been disastrous for Labour. Keir Starmer needed to make a response, and fast. It's just that no one expected that he would lean further into Reform and channel his inner Enoch Powell.

The race to the bottom is on, as Starmer delivers his great immigration reset

12 MAY 2025

You know how it is. You get on the 87 at the Vauxhall depot, and you suddenly realise you know no one on the bus. Time was when everyone in the queue would have been best mates. Off for pie, mash and jellied eels together, before a knees-up down the Old Bull and Bush. Worse still, some people may not even be talking English. We didn't beat the Hun in two world wars to hear German spoken on public transport.

Then there are all those Polish supermarkets. Who asked them to come over here, pay their taxes and business rates and set up on the high street? They don't even have the grace to relabel their produce in English. And why can't they sell something quintessentially British? Like Lurpak. What do you mean, that's Danish? Butter was invented by the Brits.

Truly, we have become an 'island of strangers'. There are days when I walk out of my front door and have no idea where I am. Everything has become foreign. Must be the palm trees I planted in my front garden. It can be only days before the thought police come round to have them removed. The same people that were happy to let Keir Starmer echo Enoch Powell's 'strangers in their own country' line from his 'rivers of blood' speech at his Monday press conference. Or maybe No. 10 is just a bit clueless and hadn't made the link.

This was the great immigration reset. Labour's chance to channel the national mood: that we are all fed up with foreigners. Hell, even foreigners have got fed up with foreigners these days. Here in the UK there are definitely hierarchies of foreigners. There are good foreigners and bad foreigners. But if in doubt, just assume the foreigners are bad. It saves time.

Keir wanted you to know that Keir has also had his fill of foreigners. Enough is enough. His patience has been tested to the limit. Time to call a halt to the 'squalid experiment in open borders'. A charming way of referring to people who had come to this country to work in the NHS and the care sector. But hey, it was time for Keir to deliver some home truths. He could be silent no more.

Some might have thought it quite the coincidence that Labour was choosing this moment to target immigration, little more than a week after Reform had cleaned up at the local elections. But Keir wanted you to know that Keir had always had it in for foreigners. He wasn't the sort of prime minister who would play politics with other people's lives. No. He had always believed this stuff. At least, he had believed it for the past three years or so. There was nothing more Labour than targeting immigrants.

'It's time to take back control,' he began. Something he went on to frequently repeat. A phrase that had also been borrowed from the Conservatives and Reform. The difference was that Keir insisted he meant it. The Tories had lied through their teeth. Promising to reduce immigration while letting it quadruple in the four years between 2019 and 2023. Keir was going to cut immigration by . . . a lot. He couldn't say how much exactly. Setting targets was to play into the foreigners' hands. By the end of the parliament, you would notice the difference. More white faces everywhere. Even if they were strangers.

Not that this was about prejudice. Heaven forbid. It was about fairness. Keir liked diversity, he stressed. It was just that you could have too much of a good thing. The thing with foreigners was, if you did them a favour, then sooner or later they would start taking the piss. It's about time migrants started talking English. That way anyone hearing a foreigner moaning about life in Britain could be reported to the authorities.

Then on to the details. The great Treasury experiment of using mass immigration to fuel economic growth had been disproved, Starmer insisted. The Tories had tried that, and the economy had flatlined. It didn't seem to have occurred to Keir that the economy might have been in an even worse state without the immigrants. But there is no place for those kinds of awkward counterfactuals in Labour's brave new world. That was one of the benefits of having fewer foreigners. We could go back to having good old British truths. Truths that Brits liked to tell themselves. Truths that weren't contaminated by awkward foreigner facts.

Time, too, for a major shake-up of the care sector. Keir had also had enough of foreigners coming over here to do the job of looking after our elderly men and women, which no Brits were prepared to do. Far better to close the care homes and let the old people die in the street. Because that's what the aged and those with dementia would have wanted. Pure Brits to the very last. Same with our hospitals. Better understaffed than fully staffed with the wrong people.

And if all this didn't have the desired effect? 'If we need to do more, then mark my words, we will,' Starmer said. That was more like it. Here was an immigration policy to get behind. A prime minister who really meant business.

None of this was enough to satisfy Kemi Badenoch. She immediately tweeted that she would have been a lot nastier to immigrants. Conveniently forgetting that she never got round to it while she had the chance in government. But give her another opportunity, and just watch her go. No foreigner would be able to sleep easy. Give her a chance, and she might even deport herself.

As for Nigel Farage, he was just a bit blasé. This was all the stuff he had been saying for years. Finally, the Tories and Labour were coming round to his thinking. But, ever the opportunist, he used the occasion to muddy the waters. Most Reform voters think illegal immigration makes up half of the official figure. Nige wasn't about to disabuse them. The small boats were full of Iranian terrorists, he said. The race to the bottom is on.

* * *

You could have been forgiven for thinking that the left hand didn't know what the right hand was doing in government. Having used up what political capital they had in cutting the winter fuel allowance for pensioners, Labour now decided to do a U-turn. Only no one was allowed to call it a U-turn. It was all perfectly planned. Confused? You will be.

Reeves struggles to explain the genius of Labour's winter fuel U-turn

9 JUNE 2025

Hmm. That went well, didn't it? One of the first things Labour did after winning the election was to cut the winter fuel allowance (WFA) for most pensioners. To show that they were strong. A signal to the bond markets that they would take the tough decisions to balance the Treasury books.

And it was just one of those things if a handful of old people decided to die of hypothermia. They were dying in a good cause. *Pour encourager les autres.* Let no one take being warm for granted again. Time for some proper pensioner gratitude.

After that, things started to unravel. MPs on all sides of the house – not least the Labour benches – began to ask whether this was the sort of policy a Labour government, any government come to think of it, ought to be introducing. Hell, the Tories had tried starving old people with a cost-of-living crisis, and now this? Rachel Reeves unconvincingly said the real aim was to make sure all those eligible for pension credit had claimed it, but there would be no U-turn.

Then came the U-turn. Two and a half weeks ago at prime minister's questions, Keir Starmer announced the reverse ferret. Something that everyone other than Kemi Badenoch heard clearly. Kemi isn't the quickest on the uptake. Now, on Monday morning – a couple of days before the spending review – came the details from the Treasury. Any pensioner with an income of under £35,000 would now be entitled to the WFA, starting this winter.

Genius. It would be hard to create a bigger cock-up if you tried. Not just the denials of the U-turn, followed by the inevitable U-turn. But the logistics. With the extra 100,000 people claiming pensioner credit, Labour has ended up with a bigger spending bill than if it had left the WFA as it was. Plus, it has managed to dent its own economic credibility by not being able to explain how the £1.3bn extra cost will be paid for. Wait until the budget, we are told. Only, just a few weeks ago, Reeves had said she would live or die by balancing the books.

The chancellor was out and about in north London trying to smooth things over on Monday lunchtime. When is a U-turn not a U-turn? When it's a Rachel U-turn. It was like this. She had originally made the spending cut to partially fill the black hole in the country's finances. Just one of those things. But then she had miraculously found that the economy was doing far better than expected, so she was able to reverse her decision. She couldn't say how the country was doing better – she has yet to find anyone to back up this suggestion – but we should take her word for it. Any connection to the withdrawal of the WFA being unpopular was a coincidence. She was sorry but not sorry. Yeahbutnobutyeahbutno. Everywhere she went lay the telltale sounds of burnt rubber.

You could tell that Rachel wasn't having one of her best days. She looked confused. Embarrassed even. As if she couldn't quite believe some of the nonsense coming out of her mouth. A feeling confirmed by the fact that when it was time for her to make a statement to the Commons, she was nowhere to be seen. She had just checked her diary and had found that there was a flurry of subsequent engagements.

Nor was anyone else senior in the Treasury to be found, willing to take her place. They, too, had found themselves unavoidably detained elsewhere. Appointments at the doctor. Unexpected open heart surgery. Anything. Any excuse will do. 'I've got a very important lunch. I can't cancel.' 'But the statement isn't until 4.15.' 'Ah, but it's a very long lunch. And then I have a coffee.'

What goes around, comes around. In his time as head of the Resolution Foundation, Torsten Bell would have had a thing or two to say about the cuts to the WFA. None of them good. There was a Torsten once who didn't think killing pensioners was a good idea. But that Torsten was very much last year's Torsten. He has moved on since then. Wised up. But when he became a fresh-faced MP last year – Torsten looks about 12 – he was immediately promoted to the most junior role in the Treasury. One step up from the receptionist. So there was an air of inevitability when he was forced to take Rachel's place.

Luckily, Torsten is hopelessly naive. Thinks there is an air of nobility in being made to look like a halfwit. It's as if he is yet another ego straight out of Oxford who believes that he was born to rule. That the union was just a stepping stone to a life that will probably end up in the House of Lords. Monday was just a staging post.

It's a brilliance that is almost entirely self-imagined. He managed to turn what was always going to be an embarrassment into a humiliation. All ersatz macho posturing as he tried to pretend the U-turn was a clever piece of government time management. Hell, he even managed to make the shadow secretary of state for work and pensions, Helen Whately, look good. Something that never happens. She was prone to her own delusions – namely, that it was the Tories that had forced the U-turn – but her main point was unarguable: why no apology? Just say sorry. You've fucked things up, you're trying to fix it, let's move on. The story might then go away. But Torsten didn't apologise, choosing instead to bluster for more than an hour. The kindest thing to do was to look away.

Down in Port Talbot, Nigel Farage, too, was trying to take the credit for the U-turn. Though he was also trying to make it sound completely normal for someone to walk out of their job one day and walk back in the next. Zia Yusuf must be thrilled to be talked of as a temperamental teenager who had got cross with Daddy. Nige also observed that Yusuf had suffered loads of racist abuse. He forgot to mention that almost all of it had come from Reform UK supporters.

Mostly, though, Farage was keen to reopen the steelworks that can't be opened to make a type of steel we don't use and to reopen the coalmines so that all those former miners who swore blind that they wanted their kids never to go down the pits could tell their kids to do just that. The regeneration of Wales starts in the 1950s. Vote Reform. Back to the future.

Reeves, the Archangel of Hope, fails miserably at making us all feel better off

11 JUNE 2025

When Rachel Reeves took over the Treasury last year, she went out of her way to portray herself as the Ministering Angel of Death. Her stock answer to any question was that 'Everything is terrible'. The Tories had bankrupted the country. There was no money for anything. Pensioners were going to have to die to save the rest of the country. Everywhere she looked there was only a world of pain.

And more pain was all she had to offer. But hers would be a Labour pain. A fiscally responsible Labour pain. A pain for which the country had voted in the last election. A pain which everyone would stoically bear in the national interest. The sunlit uplands would have to wait a while.

Only less than a year on, and it turns out that people aren't all that thrilled with being offered a diet of yet more pain. They had enough of that under the Tories. They had voted for Labour because they hoped they would offer an alternative.

A morally superior, fiscally responsible pain might sound good in theory, but people have had enough of everything being a bit shit. Even if they can logically understand that it might take a while for Reeves to turn things round, they don't want to hear about it. They would rather hear lies about quick fixes being available. Just text Nigel Farage, and he will offer you any number of them.

Rachel had promised us only one major financial event a year. After the budget and the spring statement, we now had a third: the spending review – a budget without the tax rises. For this review, the Ministering Angel of Death had tried to reincarnate herself as the Archangel of Hope. A beacon of light and joy who was here to tell us that things were going to be great after all. More than that, they were great now. A lesson to all of us in cognitive dissonance.

After a prime minister's questions in which Kemi Badenoch had reminded everyone that she really wasn't that good at her job by saying how much she hoped to improve, the Archangel of Hope got to her feet. She did her best to sound upbeat, but it didn't come naturally. Still, fake it to make it.

Her purpose in life was to make everyone feel better off. And she had more or less done that. Tick for Rachel's life goal. If you didn't feel better, then the problem was with you. She had done her bit. This was a contract with the people, and the people had to pull their weight. It was all going to be an uphill struggle. Yes, she knew that most of the money she was going to promise was for capital projects that wouldn't see the light of day for years, but she wanted everyone to look on the bright side. Day-to-day spending might be down, and you might still be waiting too long for a life-saving operation, but it was a good moment to go and look at a field and imagine how it would look in 15 years' time with an affordable housing development on it. Labour MPs nodded along and cheered. They could do this. Keir Starmer looked slightly preoccupied. Maybe he knew something they didn't.

Next, the Archangel of Hope switched her attention to the opposition parties. Here she was on much stronger ground. You might think that she wasn't entirely in command of all the numbers, but just spare a moment to think of the alternatives. Then you will come running back to Labour. The Tories she dismissed in a sentence:

14 years and Liz Truss. She and the country no longer take them seriously. The real opposition is Nigel Farage. Much of her speech was aimed at Reform. Nige had loved the Trusster's budget and was now making even bigger fantasy tax and spending commitments than she had. If you wanted to be broke, then Farage was your man.

We then went into a 20-minute lacuna of suspended animation. Rachel might have been talking about her excitement in terms of renewal – a time of plenty for housing, defence and health – but it didn't come across in her delivery. Rather, the words died in her mouth. She isn't a fluent communicator. There had been a month-long build-up of leaks and speculation to this speech, and now we were in danger of nodding off.

Even so, it didn't really feel as if we were missing that much. Sure, there was a promise to end the use of hotels for immigrants – something Labour should have done much earlier – and there were some large sums mentioned elsewhere, but the devil would be in the detail. The areas of public spending that the Archangel of Hope said she valued but which came with no money attached. Presumably these were just honourable mentions in dispatches. Areas that were actually in line for real-terms cuts.

But today was not a day for bad news. This was a day when the money tree was turned on. Especially for Labour MPs in areas that are threatened by Reform. Of the 20 Trailblazing English towns in line for a £20 million handout, 19 are Labour seats. Even better, Reeves had identified £14 billion of efficiency savings. The UK was going to get its very own Doge. Only this time the money would be passed back for public spending elsewhere. These were Labour choices. The choices of the British people. Everything was for the best in the best of all possible worlds.

It's becoming increasingly hard not to feel just a little bit sorry for Mel Stride. OK, we know he's out of his depth and has the air of a Home Counties bank manager whose branch has been scheduled for closure, but it's a thankless task being shadow chancellor. He mumbled something about tax rises that may or may not come in the autumn, but mostly he was made to betray the fact that he had no clue what the Tories would do if they were in power. Not that anyone is about to make the mistake of handing them power any time soon. But the Melster smiled gamely. He is content with his own mediocrity.

That just left the Archangel of Hope to wind things up. It was time for everyone to cheer up. The era of miserabilism was over. Labour had turned the corner. Everything was going to be great, whether you liked it or not. Happy days were here again.

* * *

Over in the Middle East, an already delicate situation became worse as Israel decided to bomb Iran. The world

wondered how Iran and the US would respond. There
was little Keir Starmer could do but call for calm heads,
certain in the knowledge that no one was listening to
him – Israel, Iran and the US would do as they pleased
without any help from us. Thankfully, a global crisis was
avoided, despite the US bombing Iranian nuclear sites.

Back at home, the welfare bill was due to have its sec-
ond reading. The Labour rebels were growing in number
and showed no sign of backing down. It was shaping up
to be another self-inflicted disaster for Starmer's govern-
ment. Happy days . . .

Liz Kendall is a listening kind of woman but can't seem to hear Labour discontent on welfare bill

30 JUNE 2025

It was clear from the start that this was largely a domestic dispute. The Labour benches were as tightly rammed as they are for prime minister's questions, and everyone had come determined to have their say. No longer willing to be sidelined by ministers as 'noises off'. No one had just turned up because they had nowhere better to be.

On the other side of the Commons, only a handful of Tory backbenchers had made the effort to show up. Fair enough. Disabled and vulnerable people have never really been their priority. To be charitable, maybe they just found it a bit awkward intruding on the government's private grief.

If Liz Kendall had any nerves about facing down her own party over the concessions – or measures, as she preferred to call them – that had been forced out of the government, then she kept them well hidden. It's counterintuitive to imagine that some Labour MPs came into politics to make life harder for disabled people, but Liz might just be that person. She knows – as we all do – that the welfare system isn't working properly. That we have a far higher proportion of people on benefits than almost every other European country. But she is prepared to make life worse for people with disabilities and see it as collateral damage. For the greater good and all that.

For the first five minutes of Kendall's statement, you would have been hard pushed to know that for much of the last week, she and Keir Starmer had been scrabbling around to prevent a rebellion that could have killed off her welfare changes at Tuesday's second reading. Liz spoke of her commitment to equality and social justice, how she was creating real opportunities and support. Just not necessarily for everyone. 'The system we inherited doesn't work,' she said. No one was going to disagree with that.

Then we got to the concessions. Sorry, measures. I will try to keep up. Liz had come to this conclusion entirely on her own. Had no idea so many of her own MPs were not just unhappy, but furious with it. First, she wanted everyone to live entirely in the present. Well, between now and November next year. It seemed to work for her. Here was the deal. Everything would continue as is till November 2026. After that, anyone who became disabled would have to look after themselves. It would teach people to be more responsible. To think harder before they went down with life-changing illnesses or injuries.

I can't say fairer than that, said Liz. People get stuck on legacy benefits the whole time. A two-tier benefits system was the norm. Nothing to see here. You win some, you lose some. It was time to treat personal independence payments (PIPs) on a first come, first served basis. But look, Liz continued, I'm a listening kind of woman. And I'm listening now. Only she didn't appear to be hearing the murmurs of discontent coming from the benches behind her. She was in a world of her own. She will go to her grave swearing she has always been one of the good guys.

Listening also involved announcing a review of PIPs, in consultation with various disability charities. Only this review was going to have a novel twist: it wasn't actually going to listen to anyone or accept any recommendations because the changes to PIPs were going to come into force regardless, well ahead of any report that nice Mr Timms, a junior minister in the department, might publish. Sorry, but not sorry. Liz knew she was right, and that was all there was to it. But people with disabilities would feel they had been included. Which was nice.

Liz took off her glasses as she neared the end. To show she meant business. There would be an extra

£300 million of real money for employment support. Not pretend money. Money that had already been announced. It would all cost £2.5 billion, and she hadn't a clue how it was going to be funded. But that was the chancellor's problem, not hers. It was she that had made her do this. It wasn't easy, she said. Something of an understatement. Her own MPs were twitching, desperate to have their say.

First, we had to sit through the reply of Helen Whately, the shadow work and pensions secretary. She had plenty to say about how she thought the welfare bill might be cut – stop paying out for less serious mental health disorders – but nothing on why previous Tory governments had failed to make any of the necessary reforms. You could almost feel Helen dying a little as she sank into her own irrelevance. Kendall merely observed it was all the Tories' fault and that they had caused the two-tier system. The very two-tier system that she had just defended. Liz does need to stop living entirely in the present. It's playing havoc with her memory.

During the next 90 minutes or so, the only person defending the reforms was Liz. Not one Labour MP came to her rescue. The closest we got was the odd damning with faint praise. Thank you for making some concessions, but do you think you could go away and come back with something a little better? We're all for reform. Just not at the expense of the most vulnerable.

Debbie Abrahams expressed concerns that the review would be pointless as the reforms were going ahead

333

anyway. Liz praised her insight. That was precisely the point of the review. Never start a review before you know what the conclusions are going to be. Rachael Maskell said she hadn't come into politics to push 150,000 into poverty. Liz shrugged. You win some, you lose some.

The chorus of disapproval got even louder. Vicky Foxcroft was also dismissive of the review. Andy McDonald asked for the bill to be pulled. Florence Eshalomi wanted to make sure carers would be protected. They would, said Liz. But only up till November next year. After that, carers should stop enabling newly disabled people by refusing to look after them.

Come the end, Kendall looked out on her feet. Even her righteous certainty seemed to have taken a small dent. But we'd all be back again on Tuesday for the second reading. Liz would have to suck it all up once more. And hope that the whips had done their job in keeping the number of rebels as low as possible. This hadn't quite been a humiliation. But losing the vote would be.

* * *

It was déjà vu all over again. Another day, another U-turn. But at what cost?

Survival-mode Starmer throws tearful chancellor to wolves at PMQs

2 JULY 2025

It was painful to watch. An intrusion into something deeply private. A grief observed. Rachel Reeves breaking down in tears. Her face lined with misery as Keir Starmer failed to guarantee that she would still be in her job at the next election. A reminder that politicians are humans, too. If you prick us, do we not bleed?

Rachel, a woman alone in the uncaring public gaze of prime minister's questions. A mere punchbag for the leader of the opposition. Undefended by Starmer. Keir couldn't even bring himself to make sure she was OK. Too wrapped up in his own world. Maybe he didn't even notice. Too busy trying to protect his own reputation.

In the brutal world of Westminster, it's now every person for themselves. Perhaps it was always that way. Politicians just like to kid themselves otherwise. Only at the end did Reeves's sister, Ellie, get the chance to comfort her.

It wasn't meant to be this way. For the past few years, Labour has been the Keir and Rachel show, the rest of the party there to make up the numbers. Keir to be the frontman, Rachel to be the economic brains behind the operation. The woman to reassure the country and the markets that Labour was credible. In opposition, they were the perfect couple, the antidote to Tory incompetence. Now, their joint project is in chaos.

On Tuesday night, the Commons was reduced to something like the farce of the Brexit years as last-minute concessions were made. The welfare bill reduced to the status of WINO – Welfare In Name Only. The legislation gutted and £5 billion lost in planned government savings. Money that Rachel didn't have and for which she was being asked to carry the can. Welcome to Labour's first 2024 election anniversary. Just the success story they had in mind on election night. This was never going to be an easy PMQs for Starmer. Or for any of the cabinet, for that matter. Most of them looked as if they had been up for days. Several sleepless, long, dark nights of the soul. Few caught one another's eyes.

Liz Kendall never made it to the frontbench. She preferred to stay hidden behind the Speaker's chair. Presumably on the advice of her therapist. She had spent enough time getting humiliated the day before. Enough was enough.

Keir himself looked pasty grey. Attempting a grin as the ironic Tory cheers outdid those from his own benches as he took his place at the dispatch box. Trying to normalise things. As if everything that had happened to his government in the past few days was par for the course. And he settled in nicely with a friendly question from Labour's Paul Waugh. The kind of question that will get you a long way with the whips. Would he agree that Labour had done brilliantly on free school meals? Unsurprisingly, he would.

Over to Kemi Badenoch. Surely even she couldn't mess this one up. An open goal. All she needed to do was tap the ball over the line. For a while, it looked as if she might not manage even that. But somehow the ball rolled slowly into the net for her first-ever win against Starmer. Though Keir could probably thank his lucky stars that he wasn't facing someone else. Then it could have been an annihilation.

The thing with Kemi is that her manner is so off-putting. That weird sense of superiority, when she has so little to be superior about. The arrogance and the condescension. The perpetual sneer. The feeling she is permanently doing the rest of us a favour. All of which makes it hard to like her. Your sympathies are naturally drawn to whoever her opponent happens to be.

Kemi began with a gratuitous swipe at Waugh. Everyone knew he was trying to limit the damage to his party, and every MP has been used as toady fodder at some time. The gracious thing to do would have been to ignore it. But Kemi just can't help herself. She's never yet passed up the opportunity to kick a man when he's down. Any backbencher is fair game to her. Then on to the main question. How much money would the welfare bill save?

This prompted a bit of euphoric recall from Keir. Memories of the welfare bill he had wanted it to be. It would be the best bill ever. It was like the day before had never happened. The Tories had broken the system, and Labour was mending it. There were millions of people back in work, and everyone couldn't be happier with the way things had gone during the government's first year.

Now it was Kemi's turn to indulge her own fantasies. The Tory attacks always look better on paper than they are in reality. Because the Conservatives have got their own record of failure to defend. You can't go around blaming someone else for not yet fixing what you broke. Except you can if you are Kemi. She must be the only person who thinks the Tories left government having improved the welfare system.

Then we came to the tears. Kemi observed that the chancellor was toast. How long would she be around? This was too much for Rachel. Labour would later try to claim she had something else on her mind, but it didn't look that way at the time. Rachel does care. She has wanted to be chancellor for years. She might yet even turn out to be a good one. But will she be asked to lay down her life to save Keir's? Not everyone in Westminster gets to have a second chance. Not even Kemi. The chances of her still being leader of the opposition come the next election are even worse than Rachel's chances of still being chancellor.

There was time for a hostile question from Keir's own benches. This from Kim Johnson, asking where his much-promised Hillsborough law had got to. Starmer insisted it was on its way. Other Labour MPs chose to keep things constituency related. Desperate not to rock the boat. Wanting to forget WINO. At least for 30 minutes. Keir tried to sound appreciative. Anxious to prove he was a listening man. He could start by hearing Rachel.

SMILE! It's just a normal day for Labour's happy family of Keir, Rachel and Wes

3 JULY 2025

The show must go on. Less than 48 hours after the government's welfare bill was left in tatters, and a day after Rachel Reeves breaking down in tears at prime minister's questions had caused falls in the financial markets, Keir Starmer, his chancellor and the health secretary were keen to present a clean slate.

Everything was totally normal. Couldn't be more normal. This had been just another ordinary week in Westminster. Everyone cries during PMQs at some stage in their career. The kind of thing that happens all the time. So it was normal that Keir, Rachel and Wes Streeting had come mob-handed to make the same announcement. What could be more normal than that? Denial will get you a long way in politics.

First, though, Keir had popped up on the Chris Evans show on Virgin Radio to tell listeners how much he admired Rachel and how central she was to the Labour project. He and the chancellor were in lockstep. He couldn't manage without her. She would be around long after he had shrugged off the Downing Street mortal coil. She was irreplaceable. He walked in her shadow.

Was that enough hyperbole? Keir had more, if more were needed. Simply the best. Better than all the rest. It just made you wonder why he couldn't have said a simple 'yes' when Kemi Badenoch had asked him if Reeves would still be in a job come the next election. That could have saved him, the chancellor and the government a whole world of pain. Not to mention the financial markets. Just a thought.

Then to the main event: the launch of the government's 10-year plan for the NHS. Old lags will need no reminding that previous governments have had countless 10-year plans to save the NHS of their own. All of which have ended with the NHS even further down on its knees. These days, it often feels as if it is on life support. But hope springs eternal and all that. Today marked the day when the NHS would start its rise from the ashes. This 10-year plan would be different. Provided Labour won the next two elections and got to see it through. What could possibly go wrong?

Wes is the ideal warm-up man. Invariably chipper and upbeat. Everything is always great in WesWorld. Wes is lucky enough to be one of those who always knows he's loved by everyone. By himself more than anyone.

Change is happening around us, he declared. Maybe we wouldn't even need 10 years. Maybe he could achieve miracles sooner. It just needed people to believe.

Now, said Wes, I want to introduce you to the woman without whom none of this is possible. The woman who has single-handedly saved not just the whole NHS, but the entire UK economy. Please say a huge thank you to . . . Rachel Reeves.

This was, of course, just another perfectly normal speech to show just how normal everything was. No matter that when the media invitation had been sent out, there had been no mention that the chancellor would also be showing up at the community health centre in Stratford, east London. The note had promised us only the health secretary and the prime minister. But sometime between sundown and sunrise, Rachel had been told she was needed onboard. To show just what a normal, tight-knit family everyone was.

You had to feel for Rachel. Here she was as Exhibit A in the battle to keep the Labour roadshow going. Politics as performance. Under the spotlight. Damned if she did, damned if she didn't. A barrage of questions if she didn't show her face sometime soon, a barrage of questions if she did. All we had been told was that she had very personal reasons for crying at PMQs, and she was planning to keep them private. As if having one of the most stressful jobs in the country and not getting publicly backed by your boss was not personal enough.

Reeves had just one job. To look relaxed and smile a lot. She managed half of that. The autocue had constant reminders. SMILE. SMILE AGAIN. SMILE BETTER. The relaxed bit was not such a success. Happy was hard. Her eyes gave her away. A bit like Gordon Brown trying to be chilled out. She would clearly rather have been anywhere but here. But she said a few dull, instantly forgettable words, and it was job done. Her first ordeal after her tears over and done with. There would be questions, which she wouldn't answer, but then she would try to move on. The next time wouldn't be so bad.

Then came Keir. No mention of WINO – Welfare In Name Only. No mention of Wednesday's unusual Keir and Rachel show. In this new hyper-normal reality, it was time to focus on all the things Labour had done brilliantly in its first year. Four million more hospital appointments. More houses. Trade deals. And now the 10-year NHS plan. He hated to say this, but he was spoiling us.

Lives were about to be transformed. Disease prevention. Fat jabs for everyone. Here, Westminster was well ahead of the curve. You're hard pushed to find an MP of any party who hasn't managed to secure themselves access to a doctor who will prescribe them a course of weight-loss injections. Not forgetting the NHS app. That was going to transform everything. Here, I started getting euphoric recall of Matt Hancock. He had also believed in the power of his NHS app. Maybe this new NHS app will be different from Matt's. Pray for Matt. Last heard of giving evidence to the Covid inquiry.

Most of the media's questions focused on the chancellor. What had made her cry? Was she really OK now? Not just putting on an act? Would she still be in a job in four years' time? Keir tried to channel his most caring, protective self. Rachel was fine. It had been personal, and would remain so. Could we just focus on the Labour success story? After the press conference, Reeves gave a short interview off camera. She was fine. Really fine. SMILE. Things had never been so normal.